Class Interruptions

Class Interruptions

*Inequality and Division in
African Diasporic Women's Fiction*

Robin Brooks

The University of North Carolina Press CHAPEL HILL

This book was published with the assistance of the Authors Fund of the University of North Carolina Press.

© 2022 Robin Brooks
Set in Merope Basic by Westchester Publishing Services
Manufactured in the United States of America

The University of North Carolina Press has been a member of the
Green Press Initiative since 2003.

Library of Congress Cataloging-in-Publication Data for this
title is available at https://lccn.loc.gov/2021030587.

ISBN 978-1-4696-6646-4 (cloth: alk. paper)
ISBN 978-1-4696-6647-1 (pbk.: alk. paper)
ISBN 978-1-4696-6648-8 (ebook)

Cover illustration © Nechayka/shutterstock.com

Chapter 4 was previously published in a different form as "The Haves and the Have-Nots:
Globalization and Human Rights in McCaulay's *Dog-Heart*," *Journal of West Indian Literature* 26,
no. 1 (2018): 70–91.

For my mother and brother
May they rest well eternally

Contents

Figures

Class Interruptions

Introduction

Class Lines: Look Both Ways before Crossing

> Nowadays it is fashionable to talk about race or gender;
> the uncool subject is class.
>
> —BELL HOOKS, *Where We Stand: Class Matters*

News headlines such as "Florida Emerges as World's New Epicenter for COVID-19" and "Miami Now 'Epicenter' of Coronavirus Pandemic" sounded the alarm in July 2020 that Miami, Florida, was officially a hot spot for the novel coronavirus (COVID-19) pandemic that first emerged on the shores of the United States roughly six months earlier. Born and raised in the county of Miami-Dade, I was downright frightened to see it become an epicenter for this outrageously contagious and deadly virus (see figures I.1 and I.2). The maternal and paternal sides of my family, both descendants of African Americans who were legally enslaved in the United States, have called Miami home for nearly a century. While many know Miami for its famous beaches, those who live there are aware that all parts of Miami are not a vacation paradise. It has a population of nearly three million people from multiple ethnicities and racial backgrounds with 16 percent living below the federal poverty line.[1] "Nearly a quarter of Miami's Black population is impoverished," and Black workers are overrepresented in front-line industry work or what we now commonly call "essential jobs," which made them more susceptible to exposure to the virus.[2] Before COVID-19 began ravaging Miami, data already existed about the disproportionate impact of the virus on Black people in the United States, and Black communities in Miami, which include thousands of people of Afro-Caribbean descent, were twice as likely to be infected with COVID-19.[3] None of these realities are mere coincidence; rather, a variety of factors, such as the continued history of systemic racism, racial capitalism, and neoliberalism, have helped lay the groundwork for the disproportionate impact of the global pandemic on the lived experiences of Black people.[4]

The disparities, inequalities, and inequities in matters associated with people's class position, including housing, education, and employment—which this pandemic has highlighted—are focal points in *Class Interruptions:*

1

Inequality and Division in African Diasporic Women's Fiction. During the COVID-19 moment, and especially since the "Great Recession" (2007–9), scholars in fields such as public policy, economics, sociology, and history have been increasingly attentive to matters of class in their publications.[5] While my book addresses similar issues, *Class Interruptions* stands apart in that, at its core, it is an analysis focused on Black cultural production, and it does not present a narrative of white working-class populations. *Class Interruptions* enters this discussion by offering perspectives on Black working classes via portrayals of class consciousness and class conflict within contemporary African Diaspora literary studies. Though some recent publications in literary studies do include some discussion of class, an emerging body of scholarship that foregrounds class matters is rapidly expanding because a need still exists for more detailed analyses of its role among contemporary discourses. Taking up the challenge of voicing how such matters circulate among Black working-class populations, *Class Interruptions* examines how modern-day writers confront issues of class in their fiction.

The role of class, particularly working-class portrayals, in African American and Anglophone Caribbean women's novels in the post–civil rights and post-independence era (1970–2010s), or the Black women's "second renaissance," is the focus of this book.[6] I argue that contemporary African American and Caribbean women writers advocate for a reassessment of economic, social, and political practices within U.S. and Caribbean societies while leading readers to greater class consciousness. Specifically, the creative artists use what I call a "cross-class relationship trope" in their literary portrayals as a central way to critique class inequalities of their respective nations and class division within African American and Caribbean communities. Authors under study in this book, including Toni Morrison, Olive Senior, Gloria Naylor, Diana McCaulay, Dawn Turner, Merle Hodge, and Oonya Kempadoo, clearly evince this trope in the representative novels examined. Fundamental to the unfolding of this central claim is an examination of the pendulum swings between setbacks and progress, failed hopes and aspirations in this era. *Class Interruptions* demonstrates that failure to focus on or include critical examinations of class in the readings of canonical works means that the analyses of such works are incomplete.[7] Aside from reinforcing the fact that class is not static among Black populations, the literary portrayals in the post–civil rights/post-independence era illustrate how the meaning of class has been changing and complicated by contemporary developments, including modern-day globalization, neoliberal practices, and worldwide economic change.

FIGURE I.1 The Hard Rock Stadium, in 2021, still operates as a COVID-19 testing site in Miami Gardens, Florida—a majority Black city in Miami-Dade County (AP Photo/Wilfredo Lee).

The cross-class relationship trope is a literary technique that pairs two characters from different class backgrounds—generally, working-class characters and middle-class characters—in order to critique these existing realities and their impacts on various segments of the portrayed or imagined communities. Connections appear between the cross-class relationship trope and a foil. By foil, I mean a character who contrasts with the main character in a literary work. To be sure, some of the characters forming the cross-class relationship may be considered foils, particularly in cases where the relationships are antagonistic. In the fiction, the protagonist can be working-class, middle-class, male or female. The authors pair the protagonist with another character who is usually close in age and/or the same gender (but from a different class background). In each case, the authors connect the cross-class pair to a concern or issue that unites the two characters. The common concern or issue is a key theme or it is associated with a key theme that the authors are emphasizing in the cultural production (for example, housing discrimination or access to education), and the contrasts expose the wide span of inequality and its grave influence on the fictional characters. Although some scholars examining working-class portrayals in literature and/or

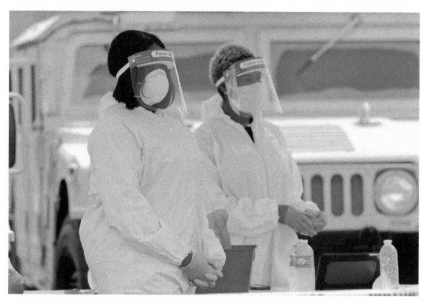

FIGURE I.2 Healthcare workers assist people at the Hard Rock Stadium COVID-19 testing site in 2020 (AP Photo/Lynne Sladky).

working-class literature note that the workplace and struggles associated with it are commonly primary concerns, other scholars note that work is not continually a focus.[8] Interestingly, the literary artists in *Class Interruptions* do not always concentrate directly on workplaces or job sites, settings where there are obvious power imbalances between an employer and employee. This is noteworthy because it reveals that the authors are not solely or simply dealing with wages; their depictions and discussions of class expand beyond income brackets. The writers construct class in their novels as a descriptive and analytical category in order to account for a range of class indicators—instead of primarily the income and wealth parameters favored in political contexts.

But why are writers documenting and highlighting these conditions? What does having a particular class status mean for Black people in the contemporary moment? What do the authors suggest impedes or facilitates upward class mobility? Why is it significant to think about what Black cultural production adds to conversations on class inequality (which are often dominated by the social sciences)? Why does the imagination matter as we think about novel ways to address long-standing and simultaneously evolving issues? More pointedly, the overarching question undergirding this book is: How does the field of African Diaspora literary studies participate in contemporary discourses on class relations? *Class Interruptions* is motivated by such questions because an analysis of writing that deploys this trope demonstrates that the methods by which these writers examine class are more critical than scholars have previously recognized. My interpretation of African American and Caribbean writers' pronounced focus on class broadens discussions of the ways people have been experiencing class change over the past fifty years, adds to the literary history on inequality, and asserts the writers' role in the larger context of the modern historiography of class—illustrating how class status has been tied to key historical events in U.S. and Caribbean societies. As scholars in various disciplines within the United States and Caribbean become increasingly critical of economic, social, and political reverberations that stem from volatile national economies, analysis of the role that writers play in calling for positive change is crucial. If we want comprehensive understanding of how U.S. and Caribbean societies are addressing egregious class gaps and their impacts, the answer must include the influences of a wider range of fields—including African Diaspora literary studies.

The Trauma of (Racial) Capitalism and Neoliberalism

In a book on literary cross-class relationships within Black communities, considering the wider relationship between people of African descent and racial capitalism is significant. By *racial capitalism*, this book does not mean some type or kind of capitalism. Rather, my use of *racial capitalism* instead of the more familiar term *capitalism* accounts for the historical interconnections of capitalism with racial difference and, specifically, the transatlantic trade in enslaved Africans, which is often left out of our "conventional understanding of capitalism's origins."[9] *Class Interruptions* is situated within this broader analytical framework of racial capitalism because it allows this book to center and take as a starting point both the historical and present experiences of people of African descent—the very ones who were simultaneously capital and labor (and remain so, in some contexts), and thus laid the foundation for what we know as *capitalism*. Experiencing a surge in interest over the past two decades in the discipline of Africana Studies and other fields with the reprinting of Cedric Robinson's *Black Marxism* in 2000, this framework is essential to my reading of Black women's cultural production because it also resists the continued denigration, marginalization, and/or elision of the priceless "value" of Blacks in discourses on class inequality. Robinson, who receives credit for applying racial capitalism more universally to the Americas after his exposure to its use in a South African context, explains that "the development, organization, and expansion of capitalist society pursued essentially racial directions."[10] As Robinson also critiques Karl Marx's "universalist" approach and lack of attention to the significance of slavery to capitalism, an important point of departure for Robinson's study is the work of W. E. B. Du Bois—a pioneer on studies of people of African descent and the racist exploitation that they endured and that led to the enrichment of white Europeans and their descendants. *Class Interruptions* builds on this Black intellectual tradition, which includes dedicated scholars both from the past and present who engage the racial dimensions of capitalism, among them Eric Williams, C. L. R. James, Oliver Cromwell Cox, Walter Rodney, Angela Davis, Ruth Wilson Gilmore, Carole Boyce-Davies, Robin D. G. Kelley, Peter J. Hudson, Stephanie Smallwood, Donna Murch, Nathan D. B. Connolly, Jennifer L. Morgan, Daina Ramey Berry, Charisse Burden-Stelly, Walter Rucker, Nell Irvin Painter, and Barbara Ransby.

Extending from capitalist greed, contemporary neoliberalism, which gathered force in the 1970s, offers an important lens through which we can understand the changes in class inequality in the post–civil rights/post-independence era. *Class Interruptions* illuminates and explains literary depictions of how neoliberalism affects people's living conditions whether they are cognizant of it or not. Underscoring the sovereignty of neoliberalism, literary and Africana Studies scholar Jodi Melamed describes it as "a world-historical configuration of governance and biological and social life, premised on the belief that the market is better than the state at distributing resources and managing human life."[11] While the term carries multiple meanings, Melamed's delineation of neoliberalism is useful to this book because of its deliberate emphasis on matters beyond the economic realm. In fact, neoliberalism is an ideological, political, and economic project that spans from deregulated markets to virtually every aspect of people's daily lives, and it emerged as a response to post–World War II legislation and civil rights achievements.[12] It presents a misleading narrative that ignores the role of capital and power and purports that the market is unbiased and color blind; accordingly, individuals who are not thriving are personally at fault for supposedly lacking responsibility and not working hard enough.[13] In reality, the "private sector, and market alone, has never been adequate to deal with reinforcing inequalities, worker vulnerabilities, and obstacles to social mobility."[14] *Class Interruptions* insists that neoliberalism contributes to a narrow set of opportunities—whether economic, social, or political—that have adversely and disproportionately impacted Black people across the Diaspora since the 1970s. Neoliberalism participates in the expansion of class inequality and its masked ubiquity makes it that much more dangerous. A part of the neoliberal project, modern-day globalization facilitates the obfuscation of the ways that inequality has manifested itself since the late twentieth century. In addition to noting the changing or reconstituting of class standards, historian and Africana Studies scholar Robin D. G. Kelley explains that "not only has globalization continued to transform black culture, but it has also dramatically changed the nature of work, employment opportunities, class structure, public space, the cultural marketplace, the criminal justice system, political strategies, even intellectual work."[15] The late twentieth- and early twenty-first-century novels in *Class Interruptions* engage with these shifts through a wide range of characterizations, plots, settings, and other elements to illustrate that we are all implicated in class politics.

My methodological approach entails or is made visible by close readings of Black women's cultural production, particularly novels, oral interviews (that I or others conducted with the authors), and a literary diagramming of the anatomy of the cross-class relationship trope. The historical frame offered by Deborah E. McDowell is useful for its articulation of three critical periods, or what Thomas Kuhn calls "paradigm shifts," in African American women's literary history: the "Woman's Era" of the 1890s, the Harlem Renaissance of the 1920s and 1930s, and the second renaissance of the 1970s and 1980s.[16] *Class Interruptions* includes the upsurge in Caribbean women's writing as part of this latter renaissance. This "rebirth" marks a change in the aesthetic and ideological approaches between the civil rights/pre-independence period and the post–civil rights/post-independence period, as this time witnessed an increase in African American and Caribbean women's literary output as well as critical attention to these writers.[17] While literary history categorizes this broad timespan as "contemporary," a better description for *Class Interruptions* is "the long contemporary," in that it covers the impact of significant historical events on people's class positions across generations in this time period. Novels, in particular, are the primary focus of my study because a large portion of the fiction produced in this period is in novel form. During the literary and cultural arts period known as the Black Arts Movement (BAM) and the Caribbean Artists Movement (CAM), which began in the 1960s, women writers were not the most popular voices, and the majority of writing appeared in the genres of poetry and drama.[18] Male writers such as Amiri Baraka, Ishmael Reed, Calvin Hernton, Edward Kamau

Brathwaite, John LaRose, and Andrew Salkey dominated these movements, though some women writers, including Sonia Sanchez, Nikki Giovanni, and June Jordan, did rise to prominence.[19] Since the 1970s and 1980s, Black women's creative writing genius, as well as the public recognition and celebration of it, has flourished. This book asserts the importance of keeping and bringing more women writers to the fore, as a way of performing historical reconstruction and intervening in present-day reality.

Class Interruptions reveals that, since the beginning of the second renaissance of the 1970s and 1980s, the cross-class relationship has remained a significant trope in African American and Caribbean women's novels. The outlined framework allows me to examine how African Diasporic women writers unfold and advance a specific approach for underscoring seemingly ever-present inequalities; in fact, this book demonstrates how they have shifted the paradigm for analyzing class in this contemporary period by identifying and chronicling their use of the cross-class relationship trope. This is of notable consequence because the writing portrays not only a shift in the sociopolitical moments of the time but also a shift in the literary landscape — by which is meant their chronicling of class representations via this trope. This book conveys how as well as why these writers incorporate the trope in their writing and uses interviews to illustrate further how the authors address these representations in their fiction. For sure, they offer this trope in their novels so readers can be not merely enlightened but motivated to act as well. In response to my interview question about her desires for her readers, McCaulay unabashedly revealed that she aims to raise thought-provoking questions so that readers see that our future and potential are dangerously at risk.[20] As Morrison states in her Nobel lecture, "The vitality of language lies in its ability to limn the actual, *imagined and possible lives* of its speakers, readers, [and] writers."[21] The writers, in essence, highlight what does not yet exist but what can exist in the future, and they desire the reading to be engaging and challenging for readers.

This book builds on scholarship by academics such as Candice M. Jenkins, Lisa B. Thompson, Aneeka A. Henderson, and most notably Andreá N. Williams, who highlights nineteenth-century antecedents of novels exhibiting cross-class relationships.[22] Even within some of the earliest Black writing, including slave narratives like that of Harriet Jacobs, intraracial class tension is present. Focusing on Black middle classes in the United States and intraracial class antagonism during the late nineteenth century, Williams examines how writers themselves and the middle-class Black characters they portrayed negotiated their class positions. She argues that the authors, though bold in their emphasis on middle-class achievements and assertions against a monolithic Black community, expressed anxiety in their work about highlighting these differences for fear that they would impede racial solidarity and civil rights gains.[23] Like Williams, my book reinforces the idea that Black writers still turn "to literature to theorize class differences" even as they did in the nineteenth century "when sociology was still developing as a professionalized field."[24] However, *Class Interruptions* moves beyond the fraught times of the postbellum era.

My research reveals that contemporary writers and their fictive personas have shifted from mere demonstrations of anxiety, as Williams skillfully demonstrates, to portrayals of urgency concerning the state of class affairs among Blacks. The more recent fiction reveals severe repercussions of intraracial class antagonism and worsening ramifications for Blacks, in general, from the growing class gaps in global society. Death, by avenues such as suicide, murder, drug abuse, and/or imprisonment, is featured in many of the narratives. The writers exhibit a critical understanding of the effects of systemic inequalities. What accounts for the historical disjuncture represented in the narratives in large part are neoliberal policies, which operate under a racial capitalist system that is, in many respects, the rule of law affecting national and international relations. Africana Studies scholar Clarence Lang, among others, notes the ways in which neoliberal practices, which are common within the modern-day phase of globalization and particularly since the 1970s, have devastated Black communities globally.[25] Discussions of gender injustices in relation to globalization are also prevalent; often, women in these populations fare worse than their male counterparts and whites of both sexes.[26] This book extends the discussion of class relations that Williams addresses in her work to contemporary authors to underscore the serious historical changes and predicaments that literary artists, specifically women literary artists, choose to delineate.

The literature in this book is a demonstration of the shifted focus of writers during a contemporary period with a fluctuating economic and sociopolitical climate—fluctuating in the sense that, aside from novel coronavirus–generated recessions, this period has witnessed punitive structural adjustment policies and growing national debt crises in the Caribbean, Reaganomics (neoliberal economic policies of former U.S. president Ronald Reagan that negatively impacted people of African descent in the United States and the Caribbean), the 1994 Violent Crime Control and Law Enforcement Act (which accelerated growth of the prison-industrial complex), the Great Recession, and Trumpism.[27] People were experiencing class differently in, for instance, 1985 than in 2005 because class is not static and is linked to societal changes. Gone are the days when homeownership, for example, signified a stable middle-class existence as portrayed in Dorothy West's *The Living Is Easy* (1948), Paule Marshall's *Brown Girl, Brownstones* (1959), and Lorraine Hansberry's *A Raisin in the Sun* (1959).[28] While homeownership was tenuous then because of racism and a myriad of other factors, home foreclosures and being house poor are realities of our present, and the settings of some contemporary novels display this reality. The texts examined in *Class Interruptions* urge and help us to learn more about, for example, the continuum of class among Black communities and about specific ways the writers have engaged decisive moments of U.S. and Caribbean sociopolitical history.

On Definitions: Class, Intersectionality, and Politics

Emphatically, *Class Interruptions* rejects stereotypes and the misinformation that all Black people are working class. Furthermore, in her thorough discussion of the "misspecification of class," sociologist Karyn Lacy observes that some people misidentify themselves, as categorizing people in class positions is more so an art than a science.[29] The parameters or measures people use to determine class position vary and can include traditional indicators such as income, wealth, occupation, and education.[30] For instance, Lacy separates middle-class Blacks in the U.S. context into three income categories: lower middle class (below $50,000), middle class ($50,000–$100,000), and elite middle class (above $100,000). While her study is unquestionably enlightening for its attention to underscoring gradations within the Black middle class, Lacy's delineation, as she notes, is not the same as that of other social scientists, and this in itself reinforces the fact that class is not a cut and dried affair.[31] *Class Interruptions* emphasizes that a major point of agreement among scholars across fields who study class is that concepts such as *working class* and *middle class* do not fit into neat categories; instead, they are often controversial, with some scholars identifying four to seven classes in U.S. and Caribbean contexts.[32] Indeed, such terms are difficult to define because people are not fixed in classes. Various contexts, including cultural ones, influence ideas about class and who fits into different classes. Notions of class also vary within different nations and geographical regions. This book addresses issues of class according to each society's descriptions or hierarchy. Class systems in the United States and Caribbean nations differ for a number of reasons, including government type and population size.[33] While defining terms such as *class* is a complex and debatable matter, scholarship in other disciplines helps illuminate the structure of the cross-class relationship trope.

Class shifts and is shaped by historic events; therefore, it is necessary to analyze classes in relation to one another. Paul Lauter and Ann Fitzgerald provide a useful definition in asserting that class is an economic and social phenomenon and is "a set of relationships that change over time and in different historical circumstances."[34] They clarify that class entails "how you look at the world, what you see there, how you experience what you perceive—and how all of that differs from what other groups of people look at, see, and experience."[35] Their definition highlights an interconnected relationship among classes. Taking into account this definition as well as specific markers of class that social scientists identify in their class analyses, such as income, occupation, and education, *Class Interruptions* offers a composite definition of class that highlights specific areas of comparison among people, asserting that class is a dynamic set of relationships between groups of people with similar economic, social, and political standing. This definition of class bridges and agrees with many definitions or explanations of class by both social science and humanities scholars. Whereas class is often over-determined in political contexts by income and wealth, this book's expanded definition includes personal and cultural preferences or tastes—invoking Pierre Bourdieu's work—which are important because they widen the unyielding, confining strictures that foreclose the reality of blurred boundaries.[36]

People use various titles to classify the group I identify as working-class people, including poor, working poor, inner-city, low-income, lower class, and poverty class; further, some working-class people, unfortunately, do not always have work, which is significant in my discussion on defining *working class*. To outline class groupings, *Class Interruptions* applies economics and working-class studies scholar Michael Zweig's categorization of three classes: the capitalist, middle, and working class.[37] Notably, this categorization does not separate *working class* and *poor*, as do some scholars who debate whether poor people should be studied as being a part of working classes.[38] To explain the nuances and complexity of my decision not to separate *working-class* and *poor* in *Class Interruptions*, history is important. In the United States, Black people, aside from those with fame, are often assumed to be in poverty no matter their financial circumstances because assumptions about Black poverty continue to be cemented in American discourses about class. The root of these assumptions exists in the institution of slavery and the various forms of anti-Black racism that followed (the sharecropping system, Jim Crow, and so on). In Jamaica as well as the twin-island nation Trinidad and Tobago—the two Caribbean nations that this book focuses on—disconcerting assumptions about certain groups of African-descended (Afro-Caribbean) people continue to exist. The history of transatlantic slavery and indentured servitude in these nations color these assumptions. In this book, which is interested in cross-class relationships in literature, the very juxtaposition of middle- and working-class characters allows the examined texts to disrupt the naturalization of blackness as poor or working class, pushing readers to interrogate class in a broader way because intraracial class distinctions are laid bare.

Furthermore, this book does not draw a hard line between *working class* and *poor* because my focus is on dealing with systems of power fueled in the modern-day period by the deterioration of governments' provisioning of services, by deregulation, and by privatization.[39] What is to be gained in grouping *poor* and *working class* is a dedicated concentration on centering the most vulnerable in societies; it allows emphasis to be on combatting exclusionary and damaging neoliberal policies and practices without further stratifying those negatively impacted by them. This choice of grouping aims to see these groups as a potentially unified, coalition-building bloc that can work together to counter and challenge increasingly austere forms of regulating societies that benefit the wealthiest to the detriment of the rest. *Class Interruptions*, additionally, uses the plural (i.e., working classes) throughout to acknowledge diversity within this broader group.

Occupation or employment is critical to defining *working class*. Nicholas Coles and Janet Zandy highlight contradictions concerning working-class people, defining *working class* as a "class of people that works, producing the goods and services that build the economy and meet social needs . . . [and] because of [their] relative lack of economic and political power, [are] frequently out of work."[40] This definition is instructive because often what people use to differentiate between *poor* and *working class* is employment or the work that people do. In *Class Interruptions*, I do not subscribe to only the "most commonly imagined version of the working class" as blue- and pink-collar, construction, and factory workers, for example.[41] Contemporary neoliberalism has dramatically altered the landscape of work across the globe so that many skilled laborers and those desiring to hone a skill have found themselves jobless and for extended periods. Aside from this fact, employment conditions since the 1970s have hampered people's living conditions and upward mobility, as "workers' real wages have remained roughly flat . . . [and] despite the continued trend of increased productivity, the promised 'trickle-down' to all workers from neoliberal supply-side economics hasn't happened."[42] In *Class Interruptions*, my definition of *working class* is broad and refers to the group of people at the bottom of a society's hierarchy in terms of economic, social, and political matters. Moreover, working-class people of color (specifically those in African American and Caribbean communities) simultaneously experience multiple jeopardies (class, race, gender, location, and so on) that differentiate their circumstances from other working-class groups (or those who are not people of color) who do not have these experiences because other privileges are at play. This reality explains some of the inattention by some scholars to foregrounding class.

In addition to its focus on working classes, *Class Interruptions* aligns with Zweig, Lauter, and Fitzgerald in emphasizing multiple-class analysis or the necessity of studying other classes when trying to better understand the intricacies of working-class populations.[43] Such a premise aligns with the cross-class relationship trope, as the African American and Caribbean writers in this book deliver portrayals of other classes, mostly middle-class characters, in their analyses of working classes. My delineations of the cross-class relationship trope also coincide with sociologist Erik Olin Wright's observation that friendships across class boundaries are most likely to occur between middle-class and working-class people due to their close proximity; my analysis in chapter 2 on the cross-class friendships in African American novels expands on this research.[44]

Recognizing the centrality of intersectionality to Black feminist thinking, this book desires not to separate class from other significant elements but rather to highlight class. The Black feminist theory of intersectionality, in particular, has played a crucial role in developing and analyzing Black women's literary traditions, and, in many respects, it has become the dominant analytic rubric in Black women writers' literary and cultural studies. Although intersectionality can account for the confluence of class, gender, race, sexuality, and nationality, *Class Interruptions* usefully emphasizes class in order to better understand its multi-dimensionality. It desires to make an intervention in more prominently attending to class in ways that intersectionality does not always. In essence, this book centralizes intersectionality as well as emphasizes how focusing on class shifts its traditional uses or brings its significance to bear even further. The genealogies of Kimberlé Crenshaw's intersectionality, such as Frances Beale's theory of double jeopardy and Deborah King's multiple consciousness, also offer insight about the under-accentuated role class has had in these discussions. Patricia Hill Collins, in the pioneering *Black Feminist Thought*, observes that "despite its size and significance, the Black working class has been rendered mostly invisible within contemporary U.S. Black feminist thought";[45] just as bell hooks makes a similar point in her scholarship.[46] While things have substantively improved on this front over the past three decades, such assertions continue to be true. Caribbean scholars such as V. Eudine Barriteau and Patricia Mohammed have attended to class matters in Caribbean nations as well as the influences and connections between Black and Caribbean feminist thought.[47] More recent Black feminist scholarship, by writers such as Terrion Williamson, Saidiya Hartman, LaMonda Horton-Stallings, Tanya L. Shields, Angelique V. Nixon, and Lia T. Bascomb, also considers issues of class in this period and highlights working-class people in the United States and Caribbean.

Class Interruptions concentrates on women writers' interventions in the feminization of poverty—a phrase coined by Diana Pearce signifying that women represent the majority of the disenfranchised across the world.[48] The way in which such a widespread occurrence manifests in societies liberally infiltrates the pages of their novels. Given how these writers accentuate the closely intertwined roles of class, race, gender, and sexuality in defining identity and shaping people's experiences, some Black feminist scholars continue to move away from strictly race and/or gender approaches that were common in the 1980s and 1990s.[49] While much scholarship has considered the Black women's literary renaissance of the 1970s, this body of work remains a rich site for examination, and my analysis of class further illuminates neoliberalism's role in contributing to the feminization of poverty.[50] *Class Interruptions* ultimately participates in feminist traditions of resistance. Relentlessly, Black women have been accused of destroying Black family structures and blamed for unjust situations—situations that truly result from global racist, classist, and sexist structural systems. This book challenges myths that demonize and pathologize Black people and provides a much more nuanced vision of Black women via literary representations, especially Black working-class women and their families.

As class systems are interconnected with governmental systems, a book on class is always already engaged with politics. Unmasking this understudied approach, specifically the cross-class relationship trope, for analyzing class injustice in literature expands ways for us to consider how class permeates our everyday lives and confirms that it should not simply be relegated to obviously class-invoking subjects like labor unions or political parties. While most people are not actively involved in labor unions or extensively committed to political parties on the local, state, and federal levels, many people can say that they have read fiction. The writers in this book exemplify that post–civil rights/post-independence novels are a crucial site of inquiry in class studies and that fiction is critical in the fight for class justice similar to but different from these more traditional methods of involvement and activism. To be clear, my thinking here is informed by Gene A. Jarrett's and Richard Iton's articulations of formal (or real) and informal politics, or infrapolitics, where the latter "refers to the context of cultural media, representation, and subjectivity that has long intrigued literary experts," and the former denotes "electoral processes, policy-making" and the like.[51] As Kelley urges in his historical study of Black working-class people and culture, "We need to recognize that infrapolitics and organized resistance are not two distinct realms of opposition to be studied separately and then compared; they are two sides of the same coin that make up the history of working-class resistance."[52] Essentially, the two work in tandem or alongside one another. The authors examined in *Class Interruptions* do not simply create broad, abstract plots; they script realistic, relatable, and comprehensible storylines that can present tools for or work in the service of confronting the intricate nature of class in daily life. Their work can be seen as sites for exploring working-class conditions, life, and culture.[53] With characters that are representative of scores of people, African American and Caribbean writers are putting in fictive form the stories of many people's lives or real-life battles people are facing. Yet, as Philip B. Harper's formulation of *abstractionism* indicates, "even the most realistic representation is precisely a *representation*, and . . . as such it necessarily exists at a distance from the social reality it is conventionally understood to reflect."[54] Still, the authors craft a dialogic work of art, where they are mindful of racist seeds that were planted in our past and continue to blossom into debilitating policies in our present reality. At the same time that it allows us to interrogate the past, present, and possible future, cultural production works dialogically with issues of class and politics.[55]

Even as literary artists are cognizant of what lies behind us, they are forward-looking, engaging in solutions to the predicaments of neoliberalism and its tentacles. Their use of male and female protagonists and different types of relationships among them also indicate that their focus is not only Black women and girls but also Black men and boys. Being concerned about the whole family—and the group, community, and race—is characteristic of many Black feminist literary texts. They demonstrate what is at stake for the entire group of people in the absence of class justice.[56] Aware-ness is the first step in being able to make changes. As my book title sug-gests, the writers are interrupting the existing state of affairs concerning discussions of class, with the intention of reexamining class conditions and the broader frameworks in which they sit, including racial capitalism and neoliberalism. This interruption brings attention to inequalities in an at-tempt to undermine and destabilize an unjust status quo. More specifically, the writers are calling out how capitalism is insidious, how neoliberalism assumes a just functioning market, and how structural inequalities often get reframed as personal failures, thus obscuring how to actually amelio-rate inequality. Their attentiveness to these realities is a step toward facili-tating positive change in class dynamics, as they put forward or imagine potential solutions. Indeed, they both offer and elicit imaginative thinking in their cultural production. Instructive here is Robert J. Patterson's concept of *political imaginative possibility*, which "aims to capture how black cultural production identifies sociopolitical shortcomings, intraracial antagonisms, and/or philosophical and/or ideological blind spots *and* provides a *radical* solution that pushes conventional ways of thinking about the matter."[57] The texts in *Class Interruptions* encourage us to practice and nourish our class con-sciousness even if the impact is diffuse and does not directly or immediately end in policy overhauls.[58]

The specific inequalities the texts in this book underscore and consider solutions to involve matters of housing, education, sexual violence vulner-ability, and other state-sanctioned abuse—the key topics in the body chapters of this project. Concerning education, the contemporary neoliberal period has witnessed affirmative action court cases on school admission policies, funding battles in public versus charter school debates, and an overreliance on standardized testing, which has limited the career trajectories (and thus, paths to upward mobility) for some working-class students in the United States and Caribbean. My discussion in chapter 3 of fiction that concentrates on barriers and intricacies of educational attainment in Jamaica and Trini-dad and Tobago illustrates a range of steps working-class characters take (and do not take) that can improve their access to education, including by using the knowledge they gain to challenge the very school systems in which they are educated. Readers can extrapolate from the characters' jour-neys insight into how to maneuver biased educational systems. Also, the exacerbation of housing insecurity in the United States during this period is motivated by the history of de jure segregation, redlining practices, and the subprime mortgage crisis undergirding the housing bubble that targeted

African Americans. Issues with affordable as well as quality housing and the weakened foreign demand for real estate in the Caribbean, which is associated with the tourist industry and contributes to the nations' economic struggles, unsettle housing security in Jamaica and Trinidad and Tobago. With the fiction examined in chapter 1 on housing and communities, this book encourages thinking about how positive cross-class relations upend limitations that ideologies of class impose on disparate neighborhoods and how that upending in the interpersonal realm can provide a way to rethink the impact and construction of class. Moreover, growing within the neoliberal moment are challenges to inequalities around sexual violence, including the support for gender-neutral statutory rape laws beginning in the 1970s, campaigns against sex trafficking and sex tourism, age of consent laws, passage of the Sexual Offences Act in Trinidad and Tobago, and the #MeToo movement's spurring of both the passage of the Sexual Harassment Bill in Jamaica and the banning of nondisclosure agreements in sexual misconduct cases in the United States. The topic of sexual violence is foregrounded in African Diasporic cultural production of this period in works such as Toni Morrison's *The Bluest Eye*, Ntozake Shange's *For Colored Girls Who Have Considered Suicide/When the Rainbow Is Enuf*, Terry McMillan's *Mama*, Sapphire's *Push*, Edwidge Danticat's *Breath, Eyes, Memory*, Jamaica Kincaid's *The Autobiography of My Mother*, and Nalo Hopkinson's *Midnight Robber*. Chapter 2 of *Class Interruptions* looks at portrayals of characters fighting against historical legacies of sexual violence stemming particularly from transatlantic slavery, pressing the importance of and need for laws combatting present-day continuities. Lastly, international human rights have been under siege with neoliberal globalization fostering increased abuses, as my analysis in chapter 4 indicates. Characters reach across class boundaries to attempt to improve conditions for people who are less privileged; yet, their uneven success in doing so demonstrates for readers both the problem with the neoliberal paradigm that eschews structural explanations for unequal playing fields and the need for more equitable structural solutions—as opposed to solely individual-based solutions.[59]

Class Interruptions facilitates a conversation between the humanities and the social sciences, as the literary writers in this project are invested in the same inequality phenomena as social scientists. The literature contends with the exclusion or marginalization of Black people in some social science spaces that typically or traditionally think about these issues, and the literature builds upon other, important ways of knowing that are not normative. African Diaspora literary studies works in concert with and complements, rather than corrects, social scientific discourses about various forms of inequality. While it is common knowledge that fiction sometimes draws inspiration from real-life events and the subject matter of other disciplines, it is perhaps less acknowledged, yet equally important to know, that other fields draw on fiction and literary studies. Cultural anthropologist Faye V. Harrison, for instance, argues that fiction "can be read for its implications for and insights into ethnographic and ethnohistorical analysis and writing, particularly analytical writing on questions of race, gender, class, and the politics of knowledge and culture in the postcolonial and postmodern world."[60] She further suggests that ethnographic writers should explore fiction because "it represents a rich mode of *writing the cultures, cultural politics, and history* of our multicultural world structured in relations of dominance and colored by the contradictory dynamics of resistance."[61] Indeed, the choice to look at fiction by writers in the African Diaspora in order to theorize differences in class and other related factors is not new. Literary scholars note that certain topics illuminated within Black fiction actually prefigure some sociological and historiographical studies of Blacks and that there are genres of Black fiction that developed alongside certain academic fields of study. African American writers theorized class differences while sociology was still being developed as a professional field and before formal sociology departments were formed in some major universities.[62] Similarly, literary and cultural studies scholar Arlene Keizer notes that "in both the United States and the Caribbean, the historiography, sociology, and literature of slavery developed together and facilitated one another."[63] *Class Interruptions* does not "merely supplement census records, residential patterns, or case studies—archives from which sociologists, historians, or scholars in other disciplines might write about class."[64] Instead, it views the creative work as offering aesthetic value, various forms of commentary, and a spark to our imaginative natures to think beyond existing thought processes on Black freedom in order to imagine different models and possibilities. In fact, the writers are creative artists as well as informed critics of socioeconomic and political matters.[65] The use of literature to offer critical evaluations of contemporary injustices can work well to advance thinking around socioeconomic abuses. Again, though, *Class Interruptions* does not conflate fiction and reality, and it is not an exercise in essentialism. Much diversity exists among classes in African American and Caribbean communities, and individuals experience oppression in a variety of ways. The writers studied here are fashioning characters in ways that represent their visions of societies and the role of class within these imagined communities.

In this manner, this book also engages with a popular debate within working-class literary studies over whether political or social activism should be an objective of the literature. Forerunners in the field, such as Janet Zandy, Renny Christopher, and Carolyn Whitson, assert that it should.[66] They point out that working-class literature often rouses readers to take action concerning the depicted conditions in the literature. The literary history of African American people and Caribbean nations is closely tied to issues of justice in these societies, as the literature participates in their struggle for political, economic, and social freedom. The fiction examined in *Class Interruptions* advances the struggle for justice and redresses class inequalities through foregrounding literary representations of the lived experiences of working-class people and highlighting matters of agency. This book presents the cross-class relationship trope to explore the literary activism of women fiction writers, and it focuses on the reality that many in working classes face extreme and increasingly unjust circumstances. Ultimately, in this book, I highlight class representations in cultural production because of the fluctuating economic, social, and political conditions that continue to affect people's lived experiences.

An Anatomy of the Cross-Class Relationship Trope

Class Interruptions delivers a comparative analysis of African American and Afro-Caribbean people with shared transatlantic slavery experiences while acknowledging that the African Diaspora encompasses more than just these people.[67] Yet, studying the calculus of slavery in this context yields a direct analysis and critique of racial capitalism, wherein Black bodies have historically operated as labor and capital, as well as neoliberal policies that, in many ways, replicate conditions that allow for the continuation of Black bodies to operate as labor and capital. To examine the cross-class relationship trope among these groups within the second renaissance of Black women's writing, I created specific criteria for the selection of the literary works. Each novel identified in this study not only features a cross-class relationship but also has class tension or conflict as a substantial part of the plot, with the working class being one class level explored via setting, scene descriptions, characterization, and other literary elements. In essence, class tension is central to each of the novels under consideration. *Class Interruptions* deals with literary productions by a select group of African American writers and writers from (or who write about) Jamaica and Trinidad and Tobago because of deep commonalities, but the cross-class relationship is a significant trope within works by other writers as well.[68] Despite the diverse historical experiences of African American and Caribbean people, common ground exists among their literary and cultural history. Literature from these groups has long been a part of struggles against various forms of oppression, forwarding resistance agendas, clarifying objectives of resistance to those with power (and, in fact, capital), promoting community-building, and asserting authority over self-definition.[69] The creative writings in *Class Interruptions* share similarities in the depictions of working-class characters and often have similar commentary about class inequalities and divisions in the United States and Caribbean nations. Some writers and literary critics attribute the parallels (and particular distinctions) to the character and shared history of transatlantic slavery, in which Africans were violently transported to different geographical locations but subjected to similar forms of abuse and violence.[70] They use the trope to convey that class disparities are working in comparable and detrimental ways. In fact, they illustrate that class conflict impedes access to adequate resources for a healthy standard of living as well as the formation of cross-class alliances and that intraracial class division causes further strife within these already marginalized groups. Furthermore, the writers' utilization of the trope shatters a perspective or myth that all African American and Caribbean populations face the same barriers. The writers highlight the intersectional identities of characters who share the same geographic spaces and illuminate the different life experiences, trajectories, and outcomes among them. The writers depict working-class populations in general as rarely experiencing upward class mobility due to broader structural problems associated with neoliberal policies and practices.

The novels also use the trope to expose how some characters come to understand and resist dominant class ideologies.[71] Some earnestly emphasize counterhegemonic resistance or resistance to various forms of oppression on the parts of working-class characters, and they underscore that consciousness of ruling ideologies is the first step in resisting them. For example, the protagonist and other characters in Olive Senior's *Dancing Lessons* examined in chapter 3 not only recognize the injustice of unequal access to education and paths to upward mobility by the end of the novel, but they also make plans and take steps to change their immediate surroundings. The fiction specifies types or areas of inequality and fashions characters who come up against this inequality to heighten readers' class consciousness. Resistance in these literary works should not be a surprise, however. As Collins asserts, resistance is integral to Black women's lives, and "as long as Black women's oppression persists, so will the need for Black women's activism."[72] Still, while presenting potential models for readers, the novels also present countermodels, as the actions of characters at the endings of novels such as Kempadoo's *Tide Running* involve illegal activity or questionable morals.[73] The writers ultimately present an understanding that "class provides a fuller perspective on the economic, political, and psychological realities that frame all of our life experiences."[74] The authors' use of the trope to interrogate the damaging impact of inequalities and disparities among African American and Caribbean populations is a form of resistance in itself.

In addition, *Class Interruptions* chronicles how African American and Caribbean writers use a parallel repertoire of features to advance their stories. They use markers of class such as education, occupation, and housing, as well as behavior, speech, dress, attitudes, and value orientations. These elements are dispersed throughout the plots and settings and visible via narrative techniques, including outer and inner dialogues, flashbacks, backstories, and varied points of view. For instance, Dawn Turner offers descriptions of differing lifestyles and housing to aid in scene transitions from the middle-class to the working-class neighborhood in her novel *Only Twice I've Wished for Heaven*. When the protagonist leaves her middle-class home to visit the working-class neighborhood, the shift in environments is obvious. Turner transitions from mapping class solely onto physical landscapes to encoding class onto physical bodies. The protagonist Temmy describes her friend's neighborhood: "In front of me stood a twelve-story redbrick building, surrounded by a group of clapboard row houses—homes to children too numerous to count. They were sitting on front stoops, dancing in the parking lot, chasing one another in the street" (33). Turner's details of the protagonist's home contrast greatly with this latter depiction (such as homes with "Japanese gardens and marble swimming pools" [15]) so as to highlight the class differences in the environments in which the cross-class pair in the novel live and to draw attention to the inequitable distribution of resources among the two communities.

While some characters occasionally use basic class terminology such as "rich" or "poor" for self-identification purposes or to identify other characters, the authors' range of literary devices clearly marks the characters' standing. Some authors capture the class tension or conflicting perspectives between the characters through the narrative structure of their fiction as well. For example, McCaulay uses her two protagonists as alternating first-person narrators throughout the novel, presenting a cross-class narrative structure where the form of the novel mimics the content. This arrangement reinforces the juxtaposition between their worlds and facilitates the comparisons and contrasts of their material realities. Strategically, the writers craft their stories using various narrative techniques and class indicators.

Class Interruptions also identifies four types of relationships used to address the spectrum of concerns highlighted by the cross-class relationship trope in the novels studied. While not exhaustive, these include community-based relationships, family relationships, romantic relationships, and friendships. Community-based relationships develop through interaction in a common community space. The relationship between the protagonists in McCaulay's *Dog-Heart*, for example, fits this description, as the protagonists meet in a parking lot of a plaza. Additionally, cross-class relationships can exist within families. An individual may experience upward or downward mobility, which results in a separation from the family or discord within the family. In Hodge's *Crick Crack, Monkey*, the feuding family members are united by marriage rather than blood; the families agree that they are not of the same nature. While the cliché states that love is blind, the novels by Morrison and Kempadoo that are studied here demonstrate that is not always the case via portrayals of troubled cross-class romances. Eventually, the lovers' eyes come to be opened to the reality of differences in material possessions and personal values, underscoring that class structures interpersonal relationships in ways that may not be easily recognized or acknowledged at first.[75] Furthermore, some of the novels portray friendships that form among characters representing different classes. School settings tend to be a popular location where such relationships blossom, and so the characters forming the friendships overwhelmingly tend to be children or young adults. Given sociological studies on the close proximity of Black working- and middle-class neighborhoods and the subsequent contact in public spaces such as stores and schools, this is not a surprise.[76] Documenting these patterns of relationship types that the authors use with the cross-class relationship trope helps to better trace an overarching commonality among the authors.

Although the African American and Caribbean writers in this project use the cross-class relationship trope in nearly identical ways, points of difference exist among their portrayals. Among the African American novels, the most common type of cross-class relationship is a friendship between two characters, whereas in the Caribbean novels the cross-class characters tend to be antagonists. Also, more variety exists in the types of cross-class relationships in Caribbean novels. To be sure, the characters who comprise the relationships in the African American novels are largely African American, whereas the ethnic makeup of the protagonists varies in the Caribbean novels due to the history of intermarriage among various ethnic groups. The ethnic variety allows the novels to convey a strong correlation between class and phenotype; the lighter the characters are, the more likely they are a part of a higher class, as chapter 4 explores. In other words, favorable treatment toward those with a lighter skin tone is rather overt in these literary works. If one considers the phenomenon of passing depicted, for example, in early twentieth-century African American literature such as Nella Larsen's *Passing* (1929), it may be easier to understand how lighter skin allows for the possibility of increased economic privileges and mobility. Cultural theorist Stuart Hall examines the intricacies of race, class, and color in various societies in his large corpus of work. He, along with other scholars, emphasizes the important role of physical characteristics, including skin color, in Caribbean class systems. Portrayals of colorism or shadeism, which is prejudice or discrimination in which those with a lighter skin tone are treated more favorably, are much more pronounced in the Caribbean novels. Only in minor ways do the authors differ in their use of the trope concerning characterization.[77]

The authors' greatest differences involve choices of topic or thematic emphasis, as is expected, given the book's premise that a relationship exists between literary texts and the historical circumstances in which they are produced. Thus, for example, Caribbean writers from the 1970s onward have moved away from depicting the novelty of independence for nations. Many now probe the failure of Caribbean nations to realize full citizenship or equal opportunities for all in the decades following independence. A lack of access to adequate education is a specific concern. Also, an increased concentration on external influences (particularly from the United States) is present, underscoring the fragility or dependency, in some cases, of Caribbean nations.[78]

Alternately, during this same period and up to the present, African American writers focus on intraracial class antagonism, stressing its self-sabotaging nature and the dangers it poses for African American communities in a majority white nation. What differs across the period, however, is that the writers greatly intensify their scrutiny of intraracial stratification. Reflecting the increasing disparities between African Americans, all of the African American novels in this project include this antagonism as a significant part of the narrative, but those published later possess more blatant condemnation of the separations by featuring characters that boldly protest this particular state of affairs. Although intraracial antagonism exists in the Caribbean novels, extreme strife is more pronounced in the African American novels examined. African American writers also challenge the myth or elusiveness of the American Dream and the costs associated with chasing the dream in the later published novels, invoking the progression-regression paradox in the post–civil rights era.[79] Some African American writers, such as Morrison in *Tar Baby*, expand their purview beyond African Americans to include other members of the African Diaspora. African American and Caribbean fiction emphasizes that upward class mobility is not simple or easy and, in some cases, they deliver an alternative narrative in which tenacious working-class characters do not excel in mainstream society as a result of the workings of a neoliberal system. By comparing representative novels from the two bodies of literature, *Class Interruptions* reveals how these authors have carefully fashioned the trope to address key or specific issues affecting populations in their national communities.

A Critical Period in History

Class Interruptions emerges at a crucial time in world history, as downward mobility has increased in the past few decades. Besides being a timely enterprise, its intellectual contributions are needed in today's global climate—a climate in which national politicians and various other authority figures refuse to center concerns of working-class people. At the present juncture, approximately sixty years removed from significant sociopolitical gains of civil rights and independence movements, a number of scholars and creative writers are examining the status of African American and Caribbean people and evaluating whether progress has been made. Legislation enacted in the civil rights and independence period produced impacts in multiple arenas. In the United States, such legislation included *Brown v. Board of Education* in 1954, the Civil Rights Act of 1964, and the Voting Rights Act of 1965, which were aimed at opening access to previously disenfranchised communities or leveling the playing field for minority groups. In like manner, Caribbean nations began to achieve independence from European colonial powers during this time period, with Jamaica and Trinidad and Tobago being among the first English-speaking colonies to become independent in 1962, and formed governments to address the needs of the people.

Yet, the rise of neoliberalism in the 1970s forestalled continued progress in many respects. Despite some growth in the Black middle class, economic gaps have widened between Blacks and whites to the point that an uneducated white head of household has more wealth than an educated Black head of household.[80] A steady increase in unequal distribution of income and wealth as well as a decline in wages (regardless of race) has occurred since the early 1970s. Moreover, whites comprise the majority of the U.S. working-class population despite enduring stereotypes that the majority of Blacks are working class (or poor, as I discussed earlier in this chapter).[81] In the Caribbean, some people have been excluded from partaking in advancements, such as quality education, and some people have not gained acceptable standards of living because of bias in government agencies. Some scholars note that the Black populations in some Caribbean nations remain largely working class.[82] Furthermore, many Caribbean nations still suffer from exploitation similar to colonialism but in a different form, what Frantz Fanon and many postcolonial critics refer to as neocolonialism. As previously mentioned, the late twentieth- and early twenty-first-century novels in *Class Interruptions* engage with modern-day globalization—a part of the neoliberal enterprise—with its advancements in transnational communications and exchanges on economic, social, and political fronts. While benefits include large-scale technological developments, increased trade, and improved cultural information exchanges, the negative effects of globalization, including the elimination of job opportunities in the Northern Hemisphere and exploitative labor practices in the global South as a result of outsourcing labor, have been particularly acutely felt by African American and Caribbean peoples because of their positionality as marginalized subjects. In other words, the racial discrimination Black people face in the labor market makes them especially vulnerable, so that when economic downturns occur they find themselves disproportionately under/unemployed.

The texts examined in *Class Interruptions* are associated with key historical moments that have had class impacts. For example, novels such as Dawn Turner's *Only Twice I've Wished for Heaven*, Olive Senior's *Dancing Lessons*, Toni Morrison's *Tar Baby*, and Oonya Kempadoo's *Tide Running* connect with a critical moment or event that impacted class. Whether it was the 1990s ushering in the United Nations' Committee on the Rights of the Child and the third wave of feminism that brazenly denounced violence against women or the Iraq and Afghanistan wars of the 2000s that heightened global debates on U.S. imperialism, the novels in this book engage their impressions on people's lived experiences via their characters. Published in 1985, in the heyday of Reaganomics, Naylor's *Linden Hills* also evinces influences of the political milieu in which it appeared and interrogates class difference through its representative working- and middle-class protagonists. Reagan's policies impacted U.S. society tremendously, especially the working classes, via increased privatization, eliminating government safety nets, and placing blame for people's subpar living conditions on claims of deficient personal responsibility, for instance.

Hodge's *Crick Crack, Monkey*, published in 1970, focuses on connections between class and education and the difficult and precarious journey working-class people in an earlier period in Trinidad and Tobago underwent to achieve education and upward class mobility. Gaining independence from Great Britain in 1962, Trinidad and Tobago began to restructure itself as a nation under Prime Minister Eric Williams (its first prime minister), and this included expanding access to education for its citizens. In many instances, however, the educational system reinforced the class hierarchy within the society, leaving the most privileged to reap the social and economic benefits. Those who were fortunate secured employment with their education in fields where they could increase their wealth, improve their class standing, and gain access to a wider range of resources, whether material (e.g., food, quality housing) or immaterial (as in networking contacts), as my analysis in chapter 3 demonstrates. In both the Caribbean and African American texts, the political and social climates in some way or another ultimately operate not only as backdrops for the writers but also as spaces where the authors could potentially intervene or call further attention to unjust systems.

As academics have become increasingly interested in class, partly as a result of widening class disparities, the contemporary growth in scholarship on Black women and Black culture coincides with the growth of the multidisciplinary field of working-class studies, starting in the 1990s. This decade saw a proliferation in publications and the establishment of centers and programs in universities dedicated to examining working-class life. Both Africana Studies, during the 1960s, and working-class studies have had to demand acceptance into the academy or university settings.[83] Africana Studies shares with working-class studies an interest in objectives such as showing the agency/humanity (experiences, culture, lifestyles, and beliefs) of people, calling for economic, social, and political action, and understanding the (often oppressive) systems of a society. Still, the bourgeoning field of working-class studies can further benefit from substantial research on portrayals in African American and Caribbean literature. *Class Interruptions* seeks to fill such spaces in the research.

Notably, although some authors whose novels are discussed in this book were born into working-class families, their social milieus tend to be middle class. Hence, the middle-class authors in this project present working-class portrayals in their literature, although they are not working class.[84] This book acknowledges this reality, and it does not encourage or participate in the vilification of Black middle classes. Moreover, the novel itself is a middle-class form. Scholars in the field of working-class studies have long debated who is eligible to write working-class literature, which some define as "literature by, about, and in the interests of the working class."[85] Coles and Zandy explain that contemporary writers of American working-class literature tend to be college-educated and from working-class backgrounds. George Lamming, too, observes that many West Indian novelists have a middle-class education,[86] while Leah Rosenberg also notes that there is a history of middle-class authors writing about folk culture in the Anglophone Caribbean. This reality leads to some questions, including: What are some of the subjects, topics, and themes present in the work of those who currently identify as working class or who have recently emerged from an immediate working-class background? Are the ideas they explore in their writing different from canonical writers such as Morrison and Senior? In an attempt to answer such questions, I conducted literary fieldwork to find authors who describe themselves as working class and write novels, plays, short stories, or poetry.

While I am an African American "straddler," Alfred Lubrano's term for someone reared working class but who has entered another class, and I am still closely associated with African American working-class communities via family, friends, and activist causes, I was not familiar with working-class culture in Caribbean nations.[87] Therefore, to find Caribbean authors who identify as working class and gain a better perspective on Caribbean culture and class dynamics within a Caribbean setting, I spent a year living and researching in the Caribbean, specifically Jamaica, as well as shorter periods researching in Trinidad and Tobago and the Bahamas.[88] I am a literary analyst who took a cue from the field of anthropology and decided to immerse myself in a society to learn more about it. During my residence, I interviewed writers, participated in community-based cultural events, and volunteered in downtown (working-class) and uptown (middle-class) communities. My experiences allowed me to better understand the connection between texts and the "real world" in important ways, as I was able to obtain the perspectives of working-class residents and writers.[89]

In several cases, it was apparent that working-class people in the United States experience "better" standards of living than working-class populations in Jamaica in that the former have more access to basic necessities. Having gained this insight, I conducted more in depth, nuanced readings of the novels in this book. For example, my reading of McCaulay's *Dog-Heart* changed considerably. I recognized the narrative was not simply about an uptown woman's haphazard experience trying to help a young boy; rather, it was about exposing the serious hardships of life and human rights injustices in working-class areas in a fictional Jamaica. The fieldwork certainly underscored the importance of researching region-specific and nation-specific scholarship on class conditions. Ultimately, this book draws on a wide range of approaches and materials from different disciplines and fields of study, including literary theory and criticism, Africana Studies, working-class studies, sociology, anthropology, economics, Marxism, and postcolonialism to address how African Diasporic literature helps us think about structural inequality and how this thinking becomes an important piece of the broader examination of (informal) politics in efforts to redress class inequalities.

Class Interruptions is separated into two parts: the first part focuses on African American literature and the second part concentrates on Caribbean literature, specifically on Jamaica and Trinidad and Tobago. The epilogue examines more closely the convergences of the two bodies of literature specifically around one of the most prevalent types of cross-class relationships—romantic cross-class relationships. In the first and second parts, an entire chapter is dedicated to an individual author, Toni Morrison (in the first) and Diana McCaulay (in the second), because these authors have explicitly commented about their investment in notions of class and address issues of inequality outside of their fiction; but each chapter in this book highlights class inequality or division, and the cross-class relationship trope is a connective thread throughout.

Focusing on African American literature, the first chapter explores intraracial class antagonism by examining the portrayals of neighborhoods in Naylor's and Turner's novels, which serve as a backdrop for the relations between the African American characters. The chapter argues that the cross-class relationship trope exposes myths among the classes and engages the long history of discrimination in housing against African Americans. In the second chapter, I focus on Morrison's treatment of rape, consent, and vulnerability to sexual violence. Morrison's *Love* uses a cross-class relationship trope to illustrate and disrupt the continued silence around Black people's historical legacy of sexual violence and commodification. It also exposes how society villainizes African Americans who have a working-class status, whether they are survivors or perpetrators of sexual violence.

In the second part, chapter 3 examines connections between class and education and analyzes how Hodge and Senior portray the difficult, precarious journey working-class characters in their fictive Caribbean societies undergo to achieve higher education and upward class mobility. Their novels are in conversation with Caribbean social scientists and historians who explore interconnections between educational systems and class hierarchies. The novels use a cross-class relationship trope to examine ways people participate in reproducing hegemonic power relations that negatively affect their communities and to offer alternative modes that resist or take advantage of systems that perpetuate social and economic inequalities. The fourth chapter focuses on the middle-class (uptown) and working-class (downtown) inhabitants, or those who make up the so-called Two Jamaicas, in McCaulay's *Dog-Heart*. The chapter extends the discussion of class inequalities to the realm of human rights violations and demonstrates how McCaulay's novel, and particularly her use of the cross-class trope, acts as a cultural lens through which to view the intersections of class relations, globalization, and human rights.

The epilogue examines cross-class romances in Kempadoo's *Tide Running* and Morrison's *Tar Baby* and shows how the novels reveal the extent to which contemporary society is reproducing the asymmetry and disempowerment of traditional colonialism and slavery under neocolonial and neoliberal conditions. The epilogue also brings the study to a close with a consideration of the present moment, when the COVID-19 pandemic is heightening class anxieties and the need for studies of class in the African Diaspora remains urgent. Ultimately, *Class Interruptions* foregrounds the cross-class relationship trope and identifies it as a recurring feature in the literature that operates as a tool for these authors to challenge traditional or dominant narratives on class and comment on contemporary class ideologies.

PART I | African American Literature

CHAPTER ONE

The Wrong and Right Side of the Tracks

Mapping the Intraracial Class Dynamics in Gloria Naylor's Linden Hills *and Dawn Turner's* Only Twice I've Wished for Heaven

> It is not just white people who refuse to acknowledge different class status among blacks; many of us want to ignore class.
>
> —BELL HOOKS, *Killing Rage: Ending Racism*

> You don't want to have nothing to do with what's on the other side.
>
> —MISS LILY, in DAWN TURNER, *Only Twice I've Wished for Heaven*

In the contemporary neoliberal moment, discussions of the U.S. housing market, particularly as it relates to African Americans, have been colored by problematic and discriminatory practices. Even after the passage of legislation such as the Fair Housing Act of 1968, de facto segregation, redlining, predatory mortgage lending, gentrification, and bias among real estate actors (agents, brokers, realtors, and property managers) remain commonplace (see figure 1.1).[1] The subprime mortgage crisis especially represented a climax for greed in the housing market that had a negative ripple effect across numerous arenas. Gloria Naylor's *Linden Hills* (1985) and Dawn Turner's *Only Twice I've Wished for Heaven* (1996) engage with many of these practices.[2] These two novels evince striking similarities, most notably in the portrayals of their fictive neighborhoods, which interrogate the sensitive topic of intraracial class divisions, even as broader structural predicaments lay the groundwork for and reinforce these divisions. Both novels depict a strict physical barrier between the African American working- and middle-class neighborhoods. In Naylor's novel, a marble banister and a stream of water separate working-class Putney Wayne and suburban Linden Hills. A conspicuous ten-foot fence, in Turner's novel, separates the working-class community on Thirty-Fifth Street on one side of the fence and the elite residential area of Lakeland on the other.[3] In both novels, the friendship between a working-class character and a middle-class character, a cross-class relationship, breaches the separation between the classes. This chapter argues that the cross-class relationship trope in Naylor's and Turner's novels exposes

FIGURE 1.1 President Lyndon B. Johnson signs the Fair Housing Act of 1968 (AP Photo).

class myths to dismantle antagonism impelled by neighborhood structures as well as to confront the long history of discrimination in housing against African Americans.

By visualizing class division through space, both novelists convey how the neighborhood spaces are ideologically charged. Many of the main and minor characters in the novels grossly stereotype one another and create invisible barriers that complement the physical barriers of separation. These visible and invisible barriers fuel misinformation, prevent the characters from building relationships with one another, and lead to various forms of destruction in both communities. In fact, both novels conclude with the death of a key character, implying that intraracial class antagonism can lead only to a breakdown of community; there is never a happy ending. At the same time, both novels present the cross-class relationship as potentially representative of the broader working- and middle-class communities in the fictive urban cities they portray. Naylor's and Turner's novels demonstrate the importance and possibility of productive relationships that span class lines, and the pairing of a main character with another character of the same race but from a different class background ultimately offers readers a glimpse of hope that intraracial class antagonism can be quelled with mutual understanding. The novels can help us think about ways the productive relationships upset limitations imposed by class ideologies and can suggest ways to challenge unjust power relations.

A summary of both novels will facilitate the ensuing discussion. Naylor's *Linden Hills* has a double plot line, one concerning the Nedeed family, particularly the women in the family, and the other chronicling Willie and Lester's journey performing odd jobs throughout the Linden Hills community to earn money for the holiday season. My focus is on the friendship of Willie Mason and Lester Tilson, who first met in school and are now twenty years old. Naylor begins her novel with meticulous descriptions of the Linden Hills neighborhood layout and a historical view of its creation. She presents it as a structural hierarchy and the brainchild of Luther Nedeed, the African American patriarchal figure in the novel, who purchases the land during the 1800s.[4] Over the years, the Nedeed family saw "the outlines of his dream crystallize into a zoned district of eight circular drives that held some of the finest homes—and eventually the wealthiest black families—in the county" (13).[5] Lester is a resident in the affluent Linden Hills neighborhood, while Willie lives on the other side of the banister in Putney Wayne.

Focusing like *Linden Hills* on two contrasting neighborhoods, *Only Twice* chronicles the Saville family's journey toward upward social mobility. The novel begins with the Saville family preparing to move from their middle-class neighborhood to the upper middle-class Lakeland community to be "among the 'bourgeoisie'" after Mr. Saville assumes a new profession (16). The very plot of the novel enmeshes economic and geographic mobility.[6] Like Willie and Lester's friendship, which underscores a cross-class dynamic between Linden Hills and Putney Wayne, Turner's protagonists, Tempestt (Temmy) Saville and Valerie Nicholae, also develop a cross-class relationship. Temmy moves to the elite Lakeland, where she meets Valerie, who is from the working-class area of Thirty-Fifth Street but has been living in the basement of the Lakeland apartment complex for the past year with her older brother who is the residential janitor. While Temmy lacks Lester's mature level of class consciousness, she, too, forms a cross-class relationship that begins at school (a cross-class space in both novels).[7] This chapter focuses on the novels' chronicling of these relationships.

Class and Space in Literature

Several scholars have applied research from other fields to theorize and examine literary portrayals of the interrelations between space and class, including Katherine McKittrick, Adrienne R. Brown, Edward Said, and Raymond Williams.[8] Focusing on a form of mapping within African American literature, literary scholar Andreá N. Williams illuminates a narrative strategy that nineteenth-century writers employed in their fiction, which she refers to as "mapping class." In her discussion of Paul Laurence Dunbar's use of this strategy in his writing, she explains that this narrative strategy emphasizes "details of setting, including interior design, architecture, neighborhood divisions, and regional landscapes, to convey status."[9] Williams adds that "spatial metaphors not only shape Dunbar's literary representations of class but also provide a framework for theorizing how and why he addresses class divisions and black mobility in his writing."[10] Naylor and Turner similarly engage in "mapping class," though not for the same reasons as Dunbar, who was encumbered by nineteenth-century audiences that preferred to see Black immobility.[11] Rather, Naylor's *Linden Hills* and Turner's *Only Twice* map class to expose and critique the contemporary lived experiences of the narrative's marginalized African Americans.[12] The interconnection of the novels' geographies with social processes is manifest in a complex dynamism whereby physical barriers dictate relationships among those residing on either side. Focusing on this dynamic, this chapter explores the correlations between ideology and space in *Linden Hills* and *Only Twice*.

My analysis contributes to the body of research on these novels and the wider topic of space and place in African American literature by demonstrating the significance of the cross-class relationships in bridging the physically and ideologically opposed neighborhoods and underscoring the impact of housing discrimination on the communities.[13] The novels suggest that an understanding of the connection between the architecture and class antagonism can lead to a recognition of how the communities are not so drastically different after all in that both desire healthy living conditions but have different ideas on how to achieve this goal and thus also lead to a dismantling of hostility between them. Through inclusion of key characters who are not hostile, both novels suggest that unity or, at least amicable alliances, is a desire of some of the residents.

Because *Linden Hills* focuses primarily on the middle-class (and upper-middle-class) residents of the suburb, its portrayal of the working-class community has not received much critical attention. Nor have critics addressed the way that Naylor's novel makes use of a cross-class relationship to illuminate the detrimental social and psychological impact of class division. While critics recognize the blatant portrayal of class in Turner's novel, they do not examine the preadolescent protagonist's relationship with her peer, nor the influence of their distinct class status on their relationship. This chapter emphasizes that *Linden Hills* and *Only Twice* convey that enmity is present even in conversations or dialogues about the architecture and physical layout of neighborhood features; the novels demonstrate how housing structures exacerbate or are a part of the antagonism and thus suggest how the novels themselves can serve to bring awareness to inequalities.[14] Further, this chapter identifies three specific myths the narratives present and attempt to dismantle—namely, myths about the living conditions of other classes, myths about total uniformity in the mentality of class groups, and myths about individual behaviors alone rather than structural constraints dictating all of a person's circumstances. These myths are discussed later in the chapter.

Moving on Up? Housing Discrimination

The novels engage in a project that is similar to the one undertaken by social scientists, and this chapter draws from and builds on historical and sociological studies concerning Blacks and housing. Like sociologist and Africana Studies scholar Mary Pattillo, they are "concerned with the sphere of lifestyle distinctions not for the mere fact of describing how different people live and what they value, but rather because lifestyles both reflect and impact the lived realities of stratification," including those "lived class schisms" that "constantly challenge attempts at racial solidarity."[15] These matters are significant because they convey that housing and access to quality housing represent far more than places where people lay their heads to rest at night; rather, housing impacts various other aspects of people's lives, such as education and healthcare, for example.[16] These issues deserve critical consideration, especially as the United States continues to endure increasing wealth gaps and the ongoing concentration of wealth among the nation's top few, a factor that inevitably will lead to an increased strain on the lives of working-class people. Housing status is another marker of class, and the authors demonstrate wider structural constraints that limit the housing choices of the African American characters. While attending to some of these matters, the novels suggest that a part of the solution lies in increased unity among classes to combat the issues; yet, critical to this point is awareness that the possibilities for class allegiances in a racial/class-stratified society can be challenging.

Naylor's and Turner's novels join a longstanding body of scholarship that examines African Americans' access to quality housing and opportunities for upward mobility, and they expose the challenges to and possibilities for these gains. After the publication of several studies of African American working-class neighborhoods, scholars began to publish research beginning around the late 1980s and early 1990s on African American middle-class neighborhoods, and the segregation of middle-class African Americans away from working-class African Americans emerged as a notable topic.[17] The history of class divisions extends back to U.S. enslavement, when whites afforded distinct privileges to some of the formerly enslaved, and where some of these individuals attempted separation from other African Americans, especially in the wake of Emancipation.[18] Despite the reality that working-class and middle-class Blacks still lived (and currently do live) extremely close to one another, an increase in the number of African Americans in the academy resulted in an increase in the attention to Black middle classes in their scholarship.[19] Economic growth during the post–World War II period coupled with the civil rights movement contributed to the growth of Black middle classes who now had access to an expanded range of occupations and neighborhoods.[20] *Linden Hills* and *Only Twice*, which were published in the 1980s and 1990s time period, represent part of a dialogue about the relationship between housing and Black upward mobility, as well as the realities and repercussions of contemporary intraracial class divisions among African Americans. Conveying their awareness that a connection exists between physical spaces and the people who form relationships in those spaces, *Linden Hills* and *Only Twice* creatively infuse socioeconomic realities within their fictive urban environments. Representations of Black urban life in literature have served as a popular topic in fiction, as revealed in Asha Bandele's *Daughter*, Toni Morrison's *Jazz*, Sapphire's *Push*, Gloria Naylor's *The Women of Brewster Place*, and many others.[21]

Naylor's and Turner's novels begin with elaborate descriptions of the middle-class neighborhood not only to emphasize the power and significance of the neighborhood spatial arrangements, but also to reveal the discriminatory history behind their construction, which laid the foundation for intraracial class antagonism. The neighborhoods in both novels are based on a history of different forms of housing discrimination perpetrated by whites. When Nedeed begins making inquiries about purchasing the land for the area that would become Linden Hills, the white landowners are excited to sell it to him because the land was infertile and seemingly unprofitable. White stereotypes about Blacks play a role: "Had to be half-witted — who'd want to own land near a graveyard, especially a darky who is known to be scared pantless of haints and such?" (2). Relying on stereotypes that paint Blacks as superstitious, the previous landowners assume Nedeed eventually will try to sell the land back to them. Once Nedeed turns the land into a lucrative funeral business, many whites try, unsuccessfully, to steal the land from him (7). While Naylor's novel casts the 1820s as the setting for this early part of the narrative, Nedeed's experiences call to mind events in the 1920s, where the homes and businesses of thriving Blacks were subject to white racial violence, as in the case of the destruction of "Black Wall Street" in Tulsa, Oklahoma, in 1921—the Tulsa Race Massacre. A disconcerting trend in U.S. history is that racist and discriminatory behaviors have limited the options for where Blacks can choose to live and that there are long-term consequences for this structural discrimination and economic disparity; economic disparity is not just coincidental or because of Black people's lack of trying or effort, which is a major belief in neoliberal ideology.[22] Despite having more income and other assets than his average Black contemporaries, Nedeed, like most African Americans, still was limited by circumstances beyond his control concerning where he could make a home for himself.

While the genesis of the Lakeland neighborhood in Turner's novel does not extend as far back as Linden Hills, it, too, depicts the intersections of class and race, as racism was a part of its foundation. The narrator notes, "Lakeland had begun in the early 1960s as part of Chicago's Life Incentive Project," and it was "an apology to the rat-infested and blighted tenement houses blacks had to endure during the migration" (19). Turner's fictive representation of this Chicago community is based on the true history of the Chicago Housing Authority and federally funded housing for low-income people developed under Franklin D. Roosevelt's administration.[23] Instead of African Americans living along Chicago's lakefront in public housing, or "the projects," Turner's novel flips the actual occurrence to middle-class African Americans living in lakefront housing.[24] Although the focus is on intraracial class antagonism, *interracial* class antagonism plays a role and also serves as a backdrop for the current tension in the novel and in reality.[25]

Insecurity: The Foundation of the House and the Antagonism

Mimicking nonfictional circumstances, Naylor's *Linden Hills* and Turner's *Only Twice* illustrate that the standard of living for middle-class Black characters remains insecure, even when they were able to move past some barriers. Both novels offer detailed descriptions of their respective neighborhoods, the type of people who live there, and how the areas have thrived over the years. Regarding Linden Hills, "only 'certain' people got to live" there (15): "Applications from any future Baptist ministers, political activists, and Ivy

League graduates were now given first priority" (17). Linden Hills possesses "homes that had brought a photographer out from *Life* magazine for pictures of the Japanese gardens and marble swimming pools on Tupelo Drive" (15). In Turner's *Only Twice*, Lakeland is similarly elite. Its residents are "the world's wealth of top black professionals: surgeons, engineers, politicians" (19), whose children "were groomed and pointed, some said from the womb, in the direction of either Morehouse, Spelman, Harvard, or Yale" (19–20). It is an "urban utopia" and an "idyllic community" with "every amenity: a twenty-seven-hole golf course, an Olympic-size swimming pool, coffeehouses with the classics lining oak shelves" (19). In both novels, however, these features only mask underlying fears that the community members felt or experienced before reaching their current status. The behaviors of characters reveal how psychological impacts of racist, classist, and discriminatory behavior exert a lasting toll.

The Linden Hills and Lakeland communities may be prestigious, but the insecurity of residents plays a role in their mistreatment of Black working-class characters. Fear and insecurity are at the root of the strife between the distinct groups in the novels. After the growth of the Black middle class from the 1950s to the early 1970s, its expansion halted.[26] The novels, which are published after this time frame, illustrate the characters' awareness of their vulnerability in that while they have ascended the socioeconomic ladder, they recognize the threats to them as Blacks in America.[27] The interrelationship between race and class is apparent in this awareness. Their place in the greater American society is challenged by entrenched systems of discriminatory practices beyond their immediate control. Invoking the history of redlining and the role of neoliberalism in its modern-day manifestations, the middle-class Black characters are concerned with the financial investments in their homes and about their safety, while middle-class whites have been able to set great distance between themselves and areas of poverty; that has not been the case for middle-class Blacks, and this representation of Black middle-class characters' inability to fully separate themselves remains a concern for many of those who have not separated.[28] While these are serious concerns, Naylor's *Linden Hills* and Turner's *Only Twice* are advocating that middle-class Black characters find ways to help resolve these problems rather than being solely concerned with running as far away as possible from them; they are making a call to action to imagine generative possibilities that turn attention to needed structural solutions.

In Naylor's novel, Lester's middle-class family members are palpably insecure about their place in the class hierarchy. They live on the margins of the middle class, literally and figuratively, in a modest house in the part of Linden Hills that is closest to the working-class Putney Wayne area. Acutely cognizant of her precarious position in the Linden Hills suburb, Mrs. Tilson, Lester's mother, goes to extremes to protect her place on the lowest rung of the Linden Hills hierarchy. Their house is "the smallest house on a street of brick ranch houses with iron picket fences" (47) at the top of the hill on First Crescent, so Mrs. Tilson tries to compensate for their perceived austerity by showcasing other material possessions. Clearly, she feels her inferiority among her peers. In conversation with Willie, whom Lester invites to stay overnight one time, she mentions her newly upholstered furniture (49). Claiming that she "was never one for keeping up with the Joneses, but it's pretty embarrassing to have the worst house on the block and to just settle for that," she also notes that "there are homes across Wayne Avenue that are better than this one, and we live in Linden Hills" (51). In this scene, the novel demonstrates that Mrs. Tilson possesses a level of spatial consciousness, recognizing the relationship between her and her neighbors.[29] Because of her insecurities, Mrs. Tilson does not want Lester to be friends with the working-class Willie; she does not want her Linden Hills neighbors to shun her. The peer pressure that Mrs. Tilson feels demonstrates the type of pervasive condescension among the middle-class residents that the novel critiques.

While Lester possesses a degree of insecurity about his class status, he handles it differently and does not use it as justification to mistreat Willie or other working-class characters. Lester uses his family's marginal position to convince Willie that the two of them are not all that different, but various scenes with Lester and Willie demonstrate that the differences must be acknowledged and cannot simply be glossed over. In a scene where Lester and Willie get into an argument, the unaddressed contrasts in their backgrounds come to the surface. Willie interrupts Lester when Lester tells Willie he does not need to be cautious about being physically attacked because they are walking in Linden Hills and not in a back alley. Willie says, "Go ahead, finish it. Some back alley in Putney Wayne, huh, Shit?" (193). Red-faced, Lester denies Willie's suggestion that he considers Putney Wayne unsafe, but Willie refuses to acknowledge the defense. In return, Willie attacks the character of Linden Hills' people, saying, "I just want to tell you something though: I've seen things done to people down here that are a lot worse than anyone would have the heart to do up in Putney Wayne" (193). The two eventually make amends and continue to embrace one another. Such exchanges reveal examples of tense moments that exist in Willie's and Lester's friendship due to class differences, which offers evidence that cross-class relationships are not problem-free. In other words, the novel is forthcoming about intraracial conflict; the tense moments can and must be addressed so as not to develop into insurmountable barriers, which is what happens when problems are left unattended.

A level of insecurity also leads Temmy Saville, the middle-class half of the cross-class pair in *Only Twice*, to try to downplay the class differences between her and her friend Valerie. Valerie tells Temmy that despite her brother being the head janitor, they are still poor. She assumes that Temmy will have her maid's help in preparing for the annual Lakeland ball and says to Temmy, "You sure don't act like the other girls, to be rich enough to have a maid" (94). In her denial of the claim, Temmy displays a hint of anger and her response demonstrates how any class is capable of class shame: "We're not rich at all" (94).[30] Earlier, Temmy also claims that the working-class Thirty-Fifth Street area is better than Lakeland (80), but Valerie immediately rejects that statement. Having lived in both places, Valerie recognizes the stark contrasts in the two environments and feels that the area where she was reared—Thirty-Fifth Street—is lacking. Like Willie in Naylor's novel, Valerie calls attention to the class privilege her friend possesses, but the two still are able to continue their friendship. Being physically and socioeconomically liminal, Valerie is more class conscious than Temmy. As a result, she sometimes takes on the role of teacher in their exchanges. In these instances, the novel foregrounds the agency of working-class characters, pointing out the knowledge they have to share.

Alternately, the novel details how Temmy's father, Thomas Saville, in particular, longs to be a part of the Lakeland community because of his fears and insecurities about being successful and able to provide for his family. He is proud to live in Lakeland, as his aim is to leave behind a past that he believes is lacking in material possessions. Before they leave their old home, he reveals some of his insecurities and thoughts in conversation with Temmy, who had been reluctant to move. He says, "I wanted to give you somebody who does more than drive a cab, and write letters to newspapers and hand out pamphlets in his spare time. . . . I want you to be proud of where you come from and I want you to be proud of me. I'll be a teacher, honey" (16–17). A loving father, he reveals his change in employment that leads to financial increase and their subsequent move on up is because he wants Temmy to have more than what he had as a child, and his words reflect traces of shame about his parents and upbringing. Shortly after, Temmy's mother, Mrs. Saville, has a conversation with her aunt about Thomas's insecurities, and speculating about Thomas's fears, the aunt responds that his absentee mother and alcoholic father have negatively impacted him. This piece of background information about Temmy's father provides insight into why he desperately wants to flee all traces of his past as well as some of his behaviors. Later in the novel, when Lily, their Lakeland maid, speaks of the hidden imperfections of the Lakeland complex, he is rude to her and asserts his authority over her, stating, "And shouldn't you be swishing around in somebody's toilets instead of wasting time here?" (140). He does not want anyone or anything to hinder him from fully escaping his past, and he does not want any perceived threats to his enjoyment of the present.

Borders/Barriers: The Limits of Stereotypes and Myths

Both novels ultimately underscore the problematic thinking and behaviors underlying the aims of some middle-class characters to forget their pasts and deliberately separate themselves from Black working-class characters so as to forestall any potential interruptions to securing a better life. One thing at stake in remembering the past is being forced to acknowledge the structural constraints that have shaped it, even as the middle-class characters call attention to the working-class characters' supposed lack of personal responsibility. However, the desire to forget the past and enjoy social mobility is not the sole cause of intraracial class antagonism among the characters; the belief systems and behaviors that accompany these desires are what have influenced the antagonism. For instance, Turner's *Only Twice* highlights how the beliefs of middle-class characters evolved as they altered their geographical locations: "And they vowed to put their bodies and their beliefs into this great blender and leave it there until the whitewashed folk who came out no longer resembled the pageant of folk who had entered" (20). The use of the term blender invokes the melting pot of the United States where all people are theoretically equal. Along with a shift in their belief systems, the middle-class African American characters began to stereotype the less economically advantaged African American characters and create myths about them (discussed in detail in the latter half of this chapter). Based on their stereotypical and discriminatory beliefs, the myths that they possess help build invisible barriers that reinforce the physical barriers represented, for instance, by the fence and banister between the neighborhoods. The myths demonstrate their attitudes, values, and ideologies. While the myths, in essence, justify people's treatment of others, stereotypes do not function equally, as power imbalances make stereotypes' accessibility and reach different, with the working-class characters receiving the most harmful impacts.[31] Seduced by middle-class status, and notwithstanding their precarity within this class, the African American characters become increasingly invested in the ideologies of racial capitalism—even if subconsciously. This investment contributes to the intraracial antagonism. Rather, the novel highlights a desire to remove barriers to access and a recognition of the power of ideas about scarcity that undergirds class stratification.

Despite the reality that their predecessors were victims of racism and various other forms of discrimination, both the middle-class and working-class African Americans in the novels discriminate against one another due to myths they entertain about those who exist outside of their class group. Further expressing the desire to obliterate the past, in Naylor's *Linden Hills*, Nedeed is shrewd in identifying the vulnerabilities of those with working-class roots and seeks their help to build Linden Hills into its current state. They had circumscribed choices due to broader structures, thus the text underscores that all choices are not created equally. Turner's narrative highlights a similar vulnerability, yet the novel reveals that forgetting the past is hard when living near groups whose current conditions serve as daily reminders of those hardships. As a result of their proximity to each other, middle-class and working-class African Americans come in contact with one another, particularly in public spaces such as grocery stores and, for youth like the cross-class pairs in both novels, schools.[32] These are examples of cross-class spaces that should or could be used fruitfully to create united and mutually beneficial alliances, instead of being breeding grounds for prejudicial attitudes or beliefs and mythmaking. While the middle-class characters are aware of the degree to which racism, under-resourced school systems, and challenging labor markets impact the lived experiences of a number of characters, some of them still choose to stereotype and accept myths about the working-class characters, including their work ethic and values.[33]

The cross-class friendships in the novels destabilize the myths, however. The pairs in the novels reveal an awareness of class separations and engage in sometimes heated debates about the differences, but they still find common ground. In this sense, they clearly serve as models for how to wrestle with difference. Constructive or meaningful contact between individuals can undercut social-class stereotypes that reinforce inequality.[34] The narratives underscore that mutual respect is a necessity in the cross-class relationships (and any productive relationship), and this respect can disrupt myths. Like Betsy Leondar-Wright and other working-class studies scholars, Naylor and Turner identify impediments to alliance formations and stress the importance of cross-class alliances in aiding struggles against injustices. Leondar-Wright notes that "middle-class conditioning can make it hard for middle-class allies to build bridges," and "working-class activists can react to middle-class activists with deep-seated rage and mistrust."[35] These attitudes are present in both novels. Both parties ultimately have to be self-reflexive and recognize their biases so that they do not hinder the relationship.[36] My analysis demonstrates how the journeys of the cross-class pairs not only highlight roots of the strife in the neighborhoods but also indicate cures for it.

While myths help ensure the physical barriers at the borders of the neighborhoods will remain stationary, the physical barriers did not start out as symbols of class separation. In *Linden Hills*, the physical markers eventually came to represent divisions. People initially erected a marble banister on sides of the stream that separated Linden Hills and Wayne Avenue because "two white children drowned in the stream" (13), and the text does not intimate anything about the white children's social class. As time passed, class divisions became apparent, as various residents wanted to name the area where they lived Linden Hills. They all claimed to be a part of Linden Hills and separate from the working-class Putney Wayne, despite the fact that Putney Wayne residents wanted to name their area Linden Hills as well. Naylor notes in an interview that she intentionally used the concept of space in *Linden Hills*.[37] To be sure, by detailing the physical markers they erected to distinguish themselves, the text reveals that all of the Linden Hills residents have knowledge of their slightly different distinctions within the larger spectrum of the middle class:

> Because the cemetery stopped Linden Road at Fifth Crescent Drive,
> Tupelo Drive could only be entered through the center of Fifth
> Crescent, and the Tupelo residents built a private road with a
> flower-trimmed meridian headed by two twelve-foot brick pillars.
> They then put up a bronze plaque on the pillars and had the words
> LINDEN HILLS engraved in deep Roman type. This caused the resi-
> dents on First through Fifth Crescent drives immediately to erect
> a wooden sign—WELCOME TO LINDEN HILLS—behind the marble
> banister and the stream, separating them from [Wayne] avenue.
> They didn't know what those people down in Tupelo Drive were
> trying to pull; maybe their homes weren't as large and fancy as those
> down there, but they definitely knew that they also lived in Linden
> Hills. (14–15)

The narrative gives no indication that the class enmity was as strong before residents created the physical markers, yet the various barriers reaffirm that Linden Hills is not a homogenous class community. From this description, readers can infer a three-tier hierarchy among the African American middle-class residents in the novel, with Nedeed's house at the bottom of the hill representing the top tier. In essence, Nedeed is the foundation on which the class divisions rest. The neighboring middle-class residents fail to create a true sense of community, even among themselves.[38] There also exists an irony in the community's structure, given that the farther down the hill the people lived, the higher their class status. In other words, moving downward physically signifies moving upward socially. Throughout the novel, characters aim to climb the socioeconomic ladder and move farther away from the Wayne Avenue area toward the bottom of the hill near Nedeed. No matter where they are on the class spectrum, characters recognized the class separations within and around Linden Hills, and they fabricate myths that rationalized a need for separation. Within the broader African American literary tradition, Morrison's *Sula*, for instance, also exhibits the intersections of race and class in its depiction of the geographical space termed "the Bottom."

The architectural design of the Lakeland complex in Turner's *Only Twice* provides an environment for class myths to thrive. In fact, the architectural design of the Lakeland complex allows residents to pretend Thirty-Fifth Street does not exist. The west side of the Saville family's apartment that faces Thirty-Fifth Street has dummy windows, as "architects, forefathers, and the lot had toiled diligently to design a building where most of the views opened east, out to the lake" (25). Seemingly, the goal is to create an "illusion of material happiness,"[39] but the illusion comes at the expense of literally making others invisible—a devaluation of human worth. The history of the ten-foot fence that separates Lakeland and the Thirty-Fifth Street area is not as intricate as the physical markers in Naylor's narrative. Early on, the novel announces Lakeland residents' physical separation from working-class people on Thirty-Fifth Street by the ivy-lined fence that serves as a metaphor of separation between the classes throughout the novel.[40] Bored at the annual back-to-school carnival celebration at the Lakeland complex, Temmy crosses the fence after spotting an opening, and, in turn, allows readers access to the cross-class depictions throughout the narrative.[41] Lakeland residents have no concern for viewing what lies outside their perimeter. Residents on both sides of the fence eventually become aware of its ultimate symbolism, as Lakeland janitors deposit trash from Lakeland on the other side of the fence, the Thirty-Fifth Street side (81).

NAYLOR'S *LINDEN HILLS* AND TURNER'S *ONLY TWICE* demonstrate how various myths that the class groups have about one another are barriers to healthy relationship patterns among the neighborhoods. One myth the novels expose concerns people's problematic perceptions of the living conditions of those outside of their class. In fact, *Linden Hills* and *Only Twice* present a myth of perfection among those with a higher class status, which, in both novels, are the middle-class residents. This myth supports the idea that there is constant happiness in the lives of middle-class residents and that a high net worth and material assets equate to a problem-free life. In essence, only they are able to enjoy their lives fully, and as a result, they are envied by those not possessing this status. By dismantling this myth, the novels emphasize commonality over difference as a way to rein in the overemphasis on differences because both the working-class and middle-class communities possess strengths and weaknesses. Both friends in the cross-class pairs are present in the scenes my analysis highlights that portray this myth. Their presence is a constant reminder of the possibilities of common ground. Furthermore, this myth brings to the fore the conditions within working-class environs in the novels. Being able to thrive while staying in one's own neighborhood should be an option for all people; not all working-class people want to leave their neighborhoods. The novels suggest that some working-class characters want access to other resources that do not necessarily reside in their neighborhood. They desire a healthy standard of living where they are residing, and they should not have to leave in order to experience it. Hence, *Linden Hills* and *Only Twice* broach a discussion about what resources, for instance, are present and absent in working-class areas, as well as what can be done to make the neighborhoods satisfying for people to want to remain. This is critical to the larger conversation about discriminatory housing practices because working-class areas are outlined (or, rather, redlined) as being areas in which to exclude investments. Ultimately, the myth underscores that location on either side of the physical border does not guarantee happiness and calls attention to matters beyond physical landscapes.

Concerning this idea that perfection or constant happiness exists in the middle-class neighborhoods, Naylor's novel contains several scenes that contest this myth. The novel, for example, includes scenes depicting suicide, characters being forced to hide their sexuality, and violent domestic situations. These scenes do not exist merely to portray the middle-class residents in a negative light; rather, they are instructive in that they allow Willie and Lester—and by extension, readers—to experience enlightenment about common struggles among people despite class status. In Turner's novel, the myth of perfection among the middle-class residents is shattered particularly by scenes detailing domestic violence, gambling addictions, and adulterous activities, which the two young girls, Temmy and Valerie, discuss while attending school or playing. Similarly, these scenes function as a way of tearing down false assumptions, so that readers will imagine more open lines of communication between distinct classes; the scenes reiterate, in spite of class status, the reality of problems. *Only Twice* does not include these scenes merely to chronicle how preteens discuss adult subject matter; rather, it does so in order to deflate ideas that those with a higher net worth have a problem-free life.[42] While struggles may be shared in common, class still inflects the experiences, highlighting their differences in access to resources.

Perhaps one of the most shocking revelations in Naylor's novel that shatters the myth of perfection is the abuse that Nedeed inflicts upon his wife and son, keeping them locked in their basement. This depiction of domestic violence certainly reads like fiction, but daily revelations regarding the prevalence of domestic abuse and illegal captivity are reminders of how fiction and real life sometimes imitate one another. This scene in the final pages of the novel where Lester and Willie are at Nedeed's house to perform a small job seems bizarre. Willa Nedeed emerges from the basement holding their deceased son. No one would expect the most privileged and revered home in Linden Hills to be in such turmoil. Nedeed has been keeping his abuse of his wife a secret from neighbors for years, which is common behavior among abusers. The picture of perfection literally goes up in flames, as Nedeed and his wife tussle too close to the fireplace and they, along with the house, burn. As the house burns, Willie and Lester notice the lack of concern among Nedeed's neighbors, who shut their shades instead of assisting Nedeed; the symbolism of this scene invokes considerations of the ways domestic violence operates along class lines. The novel reinforces that class status does not protect against violence.[43] Concerning the neighbors, their place in the neighborhood's socioeconomic hierarchy may have impacted their choice not to respond in this final destructive moment (or in previous moments of domestic violence, if they ever suspected it), as Nedeed is the most powerful citizen and can retaliate and, thus, upset their place in the hierarchy. Additionally, Nedeed's destruction can perhaps elevate their place in the hierarchy and thus be an incentive not to extinguish the fire. This scene connects to overarching points about the role of power and capital in controlling the playing field, facets that the neoliberal paradigm purports are inconsequential because the market is supposedly fair and unbiased.

In the end, the novel delivers its final indictment against the intraracial class antagonism with this burning—ultimately representing the end of an era that fostered divisions. Nedeed's death represents the potential to bring death to the class bias that has reigned in the community and serves as a warning to the other residents who have bought into the same biases.[44] Acutely aware of the dangers of divisions, Willie and Lester double down on their commitment to choose another route, one that omits extreme class bias.[45] The use of "extreme" here concedes there may still be some degree of class bias. Nevertheless, Willie and Lester breach class separation through their relationship, emerging as figures for hope and reconciliation across the working- and middle-class divide in their neighborhoods. Moreover, they represent the broader alliances and conversations between classes that Turner and Naylor hope will take place in the greater African American communities. Ultimately, the narrative's debunking of the myth that a higher class status equates to emotional wellness and happiness is quite apparent in this closing scene, a scene that demonstrates how life is a journey filled with uncertainty and unanticipated endings, no matter the amount of resources people possess.

In *Only Twice*, the Lakeland complex's hidden building problems, including its incinerator and flooding issues, assist in debunking the myth of perfection. Quite shocking to the middle-class Temmy is the condition of her friend's basement apartment in the Lakeland complex and the meager household arrangements. Valerie and her brother, John, the residential janitor, occupy a marginal space even within the building. The basement has a "hallway that smelled of standing water and rotten eggs" and their apartment is "hot and humid" (163). In this scene, Valerie's evaluation of her apartment reflects a contrast with that of Temmy, and she is proud to show Temmy the apartment, "though paint blistered on the cinder blocks and the furniture was a menagerie of old worn pieces and hand-me-down newish ones" (163). The basement apartment could be on Thirty-Fifth Street, instead of in the posh Lakeland complex. Valerie's living space, which is smaller than a maid's sewing room, is unable to accommodate the typical furnishings one would expect in a home. Valerie does not have a bed but rather a pallet that she can unfold at night and put away during the day to conserve space. They are literally boxed in, as there is hardly any outside light from the undersized opaque window. Further, the rusting and protruding wall pipes suggest building code violations. The physical level of Valerie's apartment in relation to Temmy's family's, which is on a top floor, parallels the class hierarchy, as Turner confirms in an interview, noting that with the higher floors "there is the sense that you are ascending, climbing a social ladder."[46] Their being in the same building also reflects the tenuous position of the Black middle-class characters (which is partly a reason for their fears) and class precarity more generally, which connects back to my discussion on delineating class boundaries in the introduction to this book.

Moreover, the presence of this myth of perfection in these novels further shines a light on the standard of living in working-class environments and the intersection between class and race. Unsurprisingly, some people in Black working-class communities are also unhappy about the conditions they experience around them.[47] The stark contrasts between the depictions of the neighborhoods invoke an inquiry about how environments can negatively impact the life chances of certain individuals. The myth encourages the fallacy that people with better circumstances live a life nearly problem-free. Matters of housing remain a part of political debates throughout the United States, and one suggestion for how to level the playing field in this arena is to have mixed-income neighborhoods. Yet, some scholars object to mixed-income approaches as the be-all and end-all solution to improving such neighborhoods. Varying levels of income are already present within Black neighborhoods; the approach of those with policymaking power should be to treat people in these neighborhoods with respect.[48]

Offering hope for cross-class alliances, another myth that the novels present and discredit is the myth that middle-class residents are all alike—a false perspective that hinders people from befriending individuals who have a different class status. The novels reveal the diversity inherent in varying social classes, and individuals who occupy distinct classes hold diverse opinions, perspectives, and experiences. Lester's and Temmy's families, the middle-class halves of the pairs, are familiar with occupying a precarious position among other middle-class people, and their positions shape their perspectives. With a focus on middle-class settings, the funeral wake scene in Naylor's *Linden Hills* and the debutante ball scene in Turner's *Only Twice* debunk this myth. In Naylor's novel, Lester and Willie are performing a short job of removing wallpaper from the bedroom of the deceased Mrs. Lycentia Parker, a resident of Linden Hills; in Turner's novel, Temmy and Valerie are seated next to Temmy's parents, attending the annual ball at the

Lakeland complex. These scenes are significant because they highlight the offending, critical, and anti-working-class voices and illustrate how they play a role in preventing other Black characters from experiencing a decent standard of living and a sense of security in their home environments. In these scenes, the cross-class friends are both present, and they are peripheral to the offensive comments other characters make in the scenes as well as the dissenting voices that challenge the offensive comments. They are the paired, united alliance witnessing the antagonism. Turning the myth on its head, the scenes further illuminate how some characters are opposed to such injustices, thus reinforcing the idea that not all the middle-class characters maintain negative perceptions of the working-class characters—a truth that indicates possible reconciliation.

Witnessing the myth unfold in Naylor's novel, Willie and Lester overhear clear evidence of bias against Putney Wayne at Mrs. Parker's wake. Yet, while there are plenty of negative views, there are dissenting voices in the midst of the acrimony that reveal feelings of sympathy toward Putney Wayne residents. Gathered together to mourn the loss of their neighbor and to console her widower, Mr. Chester Parker, the Linden Hills residents engage in a heated discussion about imposing zoning restrictions for the building of new housing for Putney Wayne residents. Despite knowing about the unsafe living conditions that Putney Wayne residents endure, Linden Hills residents sign petitions in opposition to the project. Even the now-deceased Lycentia opposed the project, as Mr. Parker reveals: "Lycentia spent her last days working on that petition. She would often say to me, 'Chester, I'm going to do everything in my power to keep those dirty niggers out of our community'" (135). Hence, the characters are even using the dead's wishes to maintain social policies.[49]

With Willie and Lester standing at the top of the stairs on break, the narrative continues to expose the myth of monolithic thinking among class-group members. Strategically positioned, the bedroom's location allows Willie and Lester an up-close view of a pivotal conversation during the wake that is representative of the novel's exposure of problematic perspectives about those outside the Linden Hills neighborhood. Naylor's setting and descriptions move from the wider Linden Hills neighborhood to one house on a privileged block in this neighborhood to set the stage for this troubling conversation (127). The novel colors the space with obvious class indicators; for instance, a large chandelier is part of their view from the "set of double stairs" (127). While most of the wake attendees spew vitriolic statements about Putney Wayne residents, Bryan, the councilman for the Linden Hills district, reminds them of the deplorable conditions in Putney Wayne. Unlike most of the attendees, he appears to be somewhat concerned. Still, he cares much more about his reputation than the health of Putney Wayne residents, as he wavers back and forth between trying to appease his enraged constituents and trying to get them to understand the plight of Putney Wayne residents. He stresses that he made an appeal against the building of the new housing even as he explains the need for the new housing, noting the lack of heat and water in the nearly condemned tenements, where the residents' physical health is compromised to the point that a child dies. The council member tries to turn attention to larger, structural issues, while the community members stay focused on the community members' behaviors. Again, intraclass warfare here mostly operates by way of stereotypes that focus on individual behaviors and not systemic patterns. One woman expresses empathy, but she goes on to say how the residents "milk" wealthier neighbors such as herself for "all that welfare and food stamps" (132). Others chime in with complaints and stereotypes that criminalize people from Putney Wayne. For instance, one person shouts, "You fill up the neighborhood with people like that, the next thing you know your TVs and stereos are walking out the door" (133). The scene provides examples of criminalizing people and the physical landscape they occupy.[50] Aside from declaring that they will no longer be safe, they grumble that the students from Putney Wayne will lower the "standard of education" in the nearby schools because "the teachers will be overloaded with a lot of remedial cases and troublemakers" (133). After gaining more insight into middle-class opinions, Willie and Lester remain united in the feeling that it is troublesome that the Linden Hills residents have no concern for the other African Americans simply because they are working class.

Nedeed emerges, in this scene, as a dissenting voice as he boldly affirms that class privilege alone distinguishes him and other Linden Hills residents from Putney Wayne residents. When Linden Hills residents conspire with the Wayne County Citizens Alliance, a white organization filled with racists (137), to block the new housing project, the depth of their disdain for Putney Wayne residents is revealed. Middle-class Blacks allying with whites to exclude or mistreat working-class Blacks is a sad reality, and the size of Black middle classes in the contemporary period has facilitated the creation of such alliances.[51] Nedeed says of the Alliance: "We must give them credit for one thing: they've become civilized enough by now to recognize that there are two types—the safe ones that they feel they can control and trust not to spill tea on their carpets while they use a dozen euphemisms to form a coalition to keep the other type from moving too close" (137–38). The use of "a dozen euphemisms" and "control" provoke thoughts on the ways neoliberal policies claim to allow people "freedom" and "choice," while really limiting them so as to maintain conditions where those with power control the playing field. This language also returns to the ways that neoliberalism obscures the operations of race and racism in its construction of freedom and choice as occurring irrespective of racialization when in fact it is through or by way of racialization that these forces operate. Nedeed has not bought into the stereotypes that Linden Hills residents are "better" than those in Putney Wayne. He expresses a difference in thinking from the other voices in this scene; still, Nedeed makes a deal with racists for his own self-interest—to protect property values in Linden Hills.[52] He knows that the Alliance can "get this entire district red-lined through the banks, and [his] realty company wouldn't be able to finance another mortgage" (138). This decision to work with the Alliance may be the novel's strongest indictment against Linden Hills residents "who have achieved the [American] dream at the expense of their racial identities."[53] In other words, the novel complicates thinking concerning what racial progress looks like in the context of capitalism and the ways race and class intersect in U.S. society, causing already marginalized people (including both middle-class and working-class Blacks) to fight against one another for access to limited resources. Throughout the scene describing the alliance, Naylor inserts lines from Wallace Stevens's poem "Cuisine Bourgeoise." Thomas F. Lombardi notes that the poem "represents a somewhat snide salvo leveled at the middle class, who, Stevens maintained, were quick to forget their roots."[54] The novel does not condemn all social mobility nor does it suggest that working-class African Americans are "the only real" African Americans, as Naylor explains in an interview.[55] Instead, it emphasizes the gravity of intraracial discord by depicting Linden Hills residents as having a better relationship with a racist white organization than with working-class African Americans.[56]

Moreover, the narrative critiques not only intraracial antagonism associated with the myths in the novel but also the larger U.S. society and its troubled racial politics. The narrative expresses that the Linden Hills residents' selfishness or greed coupled with racial inequality in the greater American society greatly influences them, "intensifying both the conflicts and the alliances within their boundaries."[57] Residents never consider joining with Putney Wayne residents to form a sociopolitical mobilizing force or alliance to rectify unjust living conditions and honor the basic human rights of people living in Putney Wayne. Rather, they replicate the exclusions that American society historically has enacted upon African Americans, hoping to not be excluded from gaining a level of power in the wider society.[58] Morrison's *Paradise*, where Black towns are established due to anti-Black exclusion, is an interlocutor here. The characters fail to recognize that their behavior mimics that of those they seemingly despise, the type of people who are members of the Wayne County Citizens Alliance. They are participants in what political scientist Cathy J. Cohen calls "secondary marginalization."[59]

The debutante scene in Turner's novel, in which Illinois senator Bruce Johnson converses with Temmy's father, Thomas Saville, demonstrates a complexity in the feelings of middle-class groups toward working-class people. In a discussion of the upcoming debutante ball, a marker of upper- and middle-class status,[60] Temmy and Valerie are seated at the table with the Saville family when Senator Johnson tries to secure Mr. Saville's vote for a new project to level Thirty-Fifth Street and build another phase of Lakeland in its place. He wants to push the working-class people down a few blocks into public housing (179). He claims that Lakeland is like "a swan in the middle of a pigsty" (178) and that Thirty-Fifth Street needs to become "respectable" (180). The imagery here, invoking animals, reinforces his thoughts about the inferiority of the residents. His comments reveal mean and vitriolic attitudes toward working-class residents.

Reminiscent of *Linden Hills* where the residents talk about voting against the new housing project for Putney Wayne residents, the scene presents, as a dissenting voice, Mr. Saville. Mr. Saville's stance comes as a surprise to readers given that a few chapters earlier he was disrespectful to the maid Miss Lily, exercising his authority over her when she spoke of the imperfections within Lakeland. The senator's lack of concern for the Thirty-Fifth Street residents causes Mr. Saville to be uneasy and confront the senator's prejudices, disclosing his humble beginnings (180). Mr. Saville is psychologically conflicted about remaining quiet concerning the senator's troubling perspective and agreeing with the senator in his disdain for Thirty-Fifth Street residents. He also qualifies the senator's descriptions, noting Lakeland is "subsidized housing," too (179). In fact, he states, "we pay next to nothing in rents. The application makes it clear that our contribution to Lakeland . . . will not be a monetary one, but one in which you add to its aesthetic, academic, and social achievements. . . . Lakeland is a project" (179–80). The use of the phrase "subsidized housing" provokes thinking on the broader project of the welfare state, where neoliberal policies call for a reduction in provisions by the government. His description highlights and boldly compares the similarities in both communities' housing arrangements. In other words, he is saying here that they are not so different. The senator is taken aback by the comments because, even though Lakeland residents have more money than residents on Thirty-Fifth Street, they are not conscious that the Lakeland area is "another ghetto" that looks good on the outside but is deteriorating just like Thirty-Fifth Street, as Turner elaborates in an interview.[61] Furthermore, desiring fairness, Mr. Saville asks if some Thirty-Fifth Street residents would be able to move over to the Lakeland area with the new expansion plans, as he is concerned about all people having fair access to quality housing. While his concern is admirable, he ends his inquiry with a classist point by clarifying whether they will be able to move if they change their behavior (179). Clearly, the rules they currently live by are not sufficient or good enough for Lakeland. Mr. Saville, in this instance, is representative of other middle-class African American characters who feel they have "a sense of responsibility" to help "the less fortunate of the race"; however, he still participates in the history of problematic racial uplift ideology and politics of respectability.[62]

Ultimately, this scene explores and complicates the myth of uniform thinking or claims that all members of a class are alike, weakening ideas about hard-and-fast rules concerning the thinking of class groups. The senator does not envision Thirty-Fifth Street residents as ever being a part of his dream or idea of community. Rather, the scene underscores the "personal conflicts that attend black upward mobility."[63] As this scene demonstrates, Mr. Saville has to determine how he is going to negotiate his new circumstances and whether or not he is truly content with joining in with those expressing such a great level of disdain for working-class people.

A third myth Naylor's *Linden Hills* and Turner's *Only Twice* debunk is that people's circumstances, and specifically, working-class people's circumstances, are solely due to individual behaviors. This myth ignores the reality of structural or systemic inequality, which impacts individual life chances. Those wielding power often get to define what behavior is best or acceptable, and if people are acting in a way contrary to such behavior, accusations that they are the cause of their problems and the problems of the greater society arise. "Racially, economically, sexually, or other marginalized groups are blamed for the decadence and decline of not only the American *city*, but of American *society* more generally."[64] When it comes to matters of housing, in particular, the individual choices of the African American characters have not alone been the deciding factors for determining where they would reside, nor have these choices determined the character or conditions of their neighborhoods. Richard Rothstein writes: "Until the last quarter of the twentieth century, racially explicit policies of federal, state, and local governments defined where whites and African Americans should live"; unhidden public "policy was so systematic and forceful that its effects endure to the present time."[65] Naylor's and Turner's novels present in literary form examples of the effects, including intraracial class antagonism, and the novels highlight a variety of factors that continue to impact Black neighborhoods, emphasizing the importance of addressing housing conditions along a united front.

In Naylor's novel, the circumstances of Putney Wayne residents, including those of Willie and his family, challenge the idea that troublesome or questionable individual behaviors are the sole cause of people's predicaments. While the novel does not focus a great deal on Willie's family, it does offer information on his family background. In the description of Willie's community, *Linden Hills* continues "the spatialization of class inequalities,"[66] as those who lived near Wayne Avenue in Putney Wayne were at the bottom of the class hierarchy. Many Linden Hills residents demonize this area, which boasts liquor stores side by side with churches and a delicatessen that sells marijuana and participates in a form of gambling (23). Similarly, many of them are not fond of or sympathetic to the plights of its residents, such as Willie's family. Willie is one of six children and his father was an alcoholic who abused Willie's mother. Willie recalls: "My mom got beat up every night after payday by a man who couldn't bear the thought of bringing home a paycheck only large enough for three people and making it stretch over eight people, so he drank up half of it" (58). The novel stresses here that not only did his father need help processing his emotions and controlling his behavior, but he also needed more suitable employment. Similarly, having no access to better means, Willie's mother remained in her abusive situation; in fact, Willie believes she stayed because she did not want the stigma of welfare assistance, which she saw as her only other choice due to having no education and needing to care for six children. In his provocatively titled *Yo' Mama's Disfunktional!*, Robin D. G. Kelley describes the correlation between the disproportionate number of mothers who endure physical abuse and seek welfare assistance, as well as how unsupportive government policies often leave mothers with few options other than returning to abusive relationships as a means of survival.[67] In the narrative, Willie's mother, like many others, cannot afford housing on her own, since a lack of formal education has limited her employment options. Aside from quality affordable housing, a living wage, health care, and quality education would help Willie's family. We learn Willie's circumstances affected him emotionally and psychologically, as he would cry when hearing the beatings (27). This impact is a reflection of the psychological strain and trauma that is also displayed in his parents, as psychological and behavioral consequences of inequality do indeed exist.[68]

Circumstances beyond Willie's control as well as his family's and his own personal choices have affected their livelihoods and current class position in life. Lester and Willie recognize that their upbringing and past experiences have influenced the course of their lives. Because Lester finishes high school, he will continue to have access to opportunities, such as having his poetry published, and he also will inherit a house in Linden Hills from his family. Willie, alternately, does not have the same opportunities, as he dropped out of school in the ninth grade, and he does not document his poetry (29). The young men, now twenty years old, share a mutual love for poetry, even though the content of their poetry is quite different. Lester's poems are about sunsets, flowers, and wanting to be like Malcolm X, while Willie recites poetry about "garbage can hide-and-seek. Winos who spoke wisdom," as well as "how it felt to hear your father beating your mother and what the tears looked like on your face" (27). Though he can write poetry, he chooses to memorize it and does not think about how to monetize his gift. The narrative, in this instance, turns attention to the education system and to matters of exposure and career development. At age twenty, Willie is renting a room, hanging with guys tired of looking for work or who cannot find work, and has the same job as a twelve-year-old. He makes choices based on the very limited range of options available to him. Still, some read Willie's path as completely positive and are hopeful about his potential outcomes.[69] Structural solutions, such as a federal jobs program advocated by stratification economists, would be helpful in allowing positive outcomes to materialize.[70]

Despite the different opportunities that may or may not be available to Willie and Lester, they remain united and committed to helping people and not repeating the negative patterns they have witnessed in their communities.[71] Certainly, Willie and Lester agree that systems are not always just, and they believe that "the majority of black folks in this country are poor, have been poor, and will be poor for a long time" (113–14). While a number of Black neighborhoods "are moderate to middle income, not poor,"[72] in reality, "racial inequalities perpetuate the higher poverty rate among blacks and ensure that segregated black communities will bear nearly the full burden of such inequality."[73] Regardless of class differences, Willie and Lester choose to stay unified and become more enlightened during the process, as they receive firsthand insight from working-class and middle-class members on both sides of the marble banister.

While Valerie and Temmy's relationship highlights the larger relationship between the Lakeland community and the Thirty-Fifth Street community in *Only Twice*, it also deflates the myth that the circumstances of the working-class residents are solely their own responsibility by featuring the impending gentrification of the working-class area. Before going through with their demolition plans, Lakeland residents temporarily defy the impulse to dehumanize others after Valerie's tragic suicide. Valerie commits suicide because the local pimp-turned-street-preacher Alfred Mayes has been abusing her.[74] Here, the novel reinforces the stereotype that low class status connects to poor parenting, as Valerie's mother, Ruth, deliberately exposed her daughter to abuse because she experienced it herself and she could not identify ways to break the cycle.[75] Unlike Ruth, the Savilles confront the dangers that could harm their daughter, and they are distraught that Valerie's death might negatively impact Temmy, who remains in a state of shock. Following the revelation of Valerie's death, both neighborhoods express outrage and alarm as they acknowledge that the senseless death of a child occurred right under their noses. Here, the novel delivers an indictment of class feuding and a warning of the constant destruction of Blacks' life chances if it does not cease. Some middle-class characters ignore the larger structural factors at play and, instead, focusing on individual behaviors. Again, Valerie was a liminal figure, a part of both places, and to show respect, Lakeland residents send flowers and money. Yet, they do not attend the funeral, still unable to commit to going to the other side of the fence. This deeply distresses the Saville family, and Temmy is visibly shaken and confused by the absence of Lakeland's residents at Valerie's funeral (261).

With the end of the cross-class friendship between the girls, the novel delivers a final display of antagonism between the two neighborhoods, as Lakeland residents go forward with the plan to demolish Thirty-Fifth Street. The novel exposes the injurious impact of class inequalities, as residents on Thirty-Fifth Street must vacate after the city council gives the Lakeland community permission to expand and build a hotel, boutiques, and eateries (283). This novel forebodes a boon of gentrification that emerges in the twenty-first century. Gentrification occurs at the expense of the working-class characters, and the text suggests a need for cross-class and cross-racial allegiances through the actions of Mr. Saville. This deliberate insinuation of gentrification provokes Mrs. Saville, who was never happy about moving to the Lakeland area, to ask how they can force people out of their places, but she receives no sufficient answer.[76] She realizes that broken systems "can't be fixed, not in any simple way" (258). Mr. Saville's plea to the senator to do something about the stark divisions falls on deaf ears. Perhaps to be conciliatory, the city council gives the gentrification law they passed, which allowed Lakeland's expansion, Valerie's last name: the Nicholae Plan.

As larger structural factors are at play, the people Valerie grew up around on Thirty-Fifth Street, though outraged, recognize they currently lack the power to protect their community. Their housing choices and the influences on their lives are not simply matters of their individual decisions; something like tenant activism and local political participation could help intervene. Turner states in an interview that "there wasn't really an organized body of people on Thirty-Fifth Street who could fight for it" and that "people with the voice and the power, of course—voice means power—are the people who win."[77] The novel evokes matters of self-advocacy, and the display of hopelessness underscores its importance. Ultimately, when people lack "access to powerful networks," they are often "unable to hold institutions accountable" and can "not define the terms of the debate."[78] In these final scenes, Turner's novel invokes the need for increased sociopolitical mobilization among the Black characters instead of intraracial antagonism and neighborhood divides. These factors all tie together to demonstrate the difficulties and complexities of Black upward mobility.

Only Twice exposes readers to the negative and disproportionate effects of gentrification and limits on personal agency as a critique of the myth that the circumstances of working-class residents are a result of only their personal choices. Troubled by the up-close view of working-class people's lives being negatively shaped and impacted by larger circumstances, the Saville family is faced with a moral dilemma and experiences a psychological conflict. Consequently, they decide to move to California to live with a family member temporarily until they can decide what they want to do. While their refusal to participate in the gentrification of the neighborhood reads as admirable, it is important to note that the Saville family makes the *choice* to move, while the working-class residents are forced to relocate. These residents are displaced and denied access to upward mobility, a part of the American Dream. Primarily through the representation of Lakeland residents, especially the Saville family, the novel critiques the American Dream. The Savilles are not at peace with the prejudicial attitudes and warped sense of community; in a way, they wonder if the American Dream is proving to be too costly for them morally. In fact, they are beginning to see the American Dream as elusive, even as the neoliberal paradigm insists the markets are just. This family attempts to offer a model of living outside of class tensions and refuses to embrace class bias any further, but people are always already a part of social stratification in the United States.

Overall, Naylor's *Linden Hills* and Turner's *Only Twice I've Wished for Heaven* provide a literary approach to discussions of intraracial class antagonism and housing inequalities among Black communities through use of the cross-class relationship trope. The spatial imagery complements and illuminates myths that hinder alliances among the working- and middle-class neighborhoods, as the myths encourage invisible barriers that reinforce the physical barriers separating the communities. The novels reveal that one part of the cure for the strife is to expose and question the myths as well as the history behind them, including racial discrimination and fears of continued exclusion from benefits of American citizenship. By debunking myths about the livelihoods and perspectives of different class groups, the novels emphasize commonalities—namely, that the Black middle-class characters have real vulnerabilities despite their class status; not all of them think poorly of the working-class characters; and Black working-class characters' circumstances are shaped by far more than what some deem stereotypical behaviors. The need for a united front between different classes is apparent if upward mobility is to be achieved for larger numbers of African Americans. Further, the friendships between Willie and Lester in Naylor's novel and Temmy and Valerie in Turner's novel offer hope for the future that reconciliation across the class divide is possible and provide insight on navigating cross-class alliances. Both novels illustrate the possibility of healthy cross-class relationships at the same time that they also offer cautionary tales that underscore the dangers of continued fragmentation by presenting the death of a main character at the end of the narratives. While the two friendships consist of young people who, as a group, tend to be more open to others, the novels suggest such lines of communication are possible for mature adults as well. In the end, the novels use the trope to explore the possibilities for alliances and the challenges communities face in overcoming divides. The long history of discrimination in the housing market and the lack of choice in housing opportunities for African Americans connect to historical legacies of the institution of slavery, as discussed in the next chapter.

CHAPTER TWO

Cheap Behavior and Costly Secrets
Taboo Topics in Toni Morrison's Love

> Those who came before us didn't win every fight, but they didn't
> let it kill their vision. It fueled it. So I can't stop, and I'm asking you
> not to stop either. We owe future generations a world free of sexual
> violence. I believe we can build that world. Do you?
>
> —TARANA BURKE, "Me Too Is a Movement, Not a Moment"

As contemporary neoliberal policies began to spread during the 1970s, this period witnessed a rise in challenges to laws related not only to economic violence but also to sexual violence in the United States. Feminist circles advocated for gender-neutral statutory rape laws so that males, who were largely excluded from legal protections for sexual abuse, began to receive state protection. Other campaigns included passage of age of consent laws, close-in-age exemption laws, sex trafficking laws, and, most recently, laws banning nondisclosure agreements in sexual misconduct cases, prompted by the #MeToo movement. This chapter begins with discussion of the latter movement in relation to contemporary African Diaspora literature by women, who have long engaged the "taboo" subject of sexual assault and the secrets surrounding nonconsensual behaviors. Such portrayals are evident from slave narratives to contemporary novels, including Sapphire's *Push*, Alice Walker's *The Color Purple*, Terry McMillan's *A Day Late and a Dollar Short*, Sister Souljah's *The Coldest Winter Ever*, and Gloria Naylor's *The Men of Brewster Place* and *The Women of Brewster Place*. A significant point of contention in sexual assault involves the so-called gray area where people have to prove the behavior was nonconsensual, which is a part of a broader conversation about consent, whether it is implied, coerced, affirmed, or denied. Yet, when it comes to sexual violations against Black women, matters of consent invoke a racial capitalist frame stemming from transatlantic slavery in which the foundation of the Atlantic economy was based on Black women being forced to reproduce capital even as they themselves were also capital. Black women operated simultaneously as commodities and producers of commodities, and their sexual violation was promoted by nineteenth-century capitalist ventures of Europeans. Engaging this history, this chapter focuses on Morrison's *Love* and its inclusion of rape, molestation, and sexual violence in two key relationships that fall in a supposed gray or debatable area.[1] Through depictions of problematic "consensual" sexual relationships and a cross-class relationship trope, Morrison's *Love* calls attention to the continued silence around Black people's historical legacy of sexual violence and commodification while exposing how her imagined society villainizes African American characters who have a working-class status, whether they are survivors or perpetrators.

Morrison's *Love* was published in 2003—three short years before activist Tarana Burke founded the Me Too movement (see figure 2.1). The major initiative of the movement was "to help survivors of sexual violence, particularly Black women and girls, and other young women of color from low wealth communities, find pathways to healing."[2] From its onset, the movement focused on working-class Black women and girls; however, this initial focus shifted when the movement went viral in 2017 after celebrities began using the #MeToo hashtag on social media to address sexual violence in Hollywood. Since then, the movement has decided "to reframe and expand the global conversation around sexual violence to speak to the needs of a broader spectrum of survivors. Young people, queer, trans, and disabled folks, Black women and girls, and all communities of color."[3] Nevertheless, news media continues to highlight well-known figures, who are usually white, and their sexual assault and harassment stories, while ignoring everyday people with similar experiences. These are the people on whom Burke continues to focus; for her the movement is "about the 60 percent of Black girls like me who will be experiencing sexual violence before they turn 18 and the thousands and thousands of low wage workers who are being sexually harassed right now on jobs that they can't afford to quit."[4] While its publication date precedes the Me Too movement, *Love* similarly engages the critical issue of sexual violence. Morrison's novel and other fiction that center sexual violence topics anticipate the movements and social science responses that followed their publications.

Morrison's *Love* refuses to erase the experiences of the marginalized; instead, she places them at the center. The narrative depicts an African American community on the East Coast as it moves through legal racial segregation to the 1990s. It chronicles the lives of two women, Heed the Night Cosey and Christine Cosey, elderly rivals living in the same house who were once childhood friends, as well as the wealthy entrepreneur Bill Cosey (also known as Cosey). Cosey, who is Christine's grandfather and eventually becomes Heed's husband, is the looming figure in the narrative; his connec-

FIGURE 2.1
Founder of the
#MeToo Campaign,
Tarana Burke,
speaks at the
Women's Convention
in Detroit in 2017
(Photo by Chirag
Wakaskar / Pacific
Press / Sipa USA;
Sipa via AP Images).

tion to his family and those in the community is announced by chapter titles such as "Friend," "Stranger," "Benefactor," "Lover," "Husband," "Guardian," "Father," and "Phantom." At age fifty-two, Cosey marries eleven-year-old Heed, who is from the nearby underprivileged neighborhood Up Beach. Their marriage forever fractures the cross-class friendship between Heed and the middle-class Christine. Junior, a working-class outsider, is featured prominently in the novel after Heed, in the present setting, hires her to help secretly change the will of the deceased Bill Cosey. Although Cosey's will declares his house will go to his "sweet Cosey child" (88), it is unclear to whom he was referring. The eighteen-year-old Junior forms a liaison with the middle-class, fourteen-year-old Romen, who does odd jobs around the house of the two elderly women. While the novel presents multiple cross-class relationships, this chapter compares the sexual relationship of Heed and Cosey with that of Junior and Romen in order to demonstrate how the intersections of people's class status with their age and gender work together to shape their experience of sexual violence.[5]

Morrison's *Love* interconnects sexual violence in the present, its roots in enslavement, and its impact on working-class people.[6] The system of patriarchy present in the text also provokes thought on how patriarchy intersects with class or becomes a lens through which to understand class stratification. An essential step in resistance to current-day inequalities is to identify and acknowledge the history and patterns that laid the foundation for the present; Morrison's novel destigmatizes and forces society to engage the subject of sexual violence, particularly related to African Americans. Additionally, the novel critiques the emphasis on female survivors to the exclusion of male survivors in literature on sexual violence by exploring the topic using a female and male character, specifically Heed and Romen.[7] In *Love*, many are outraged by the relationship between Heed and Cosey because of their over forty-year age gap, but some are less troubled about the relationship between Romen and Junior, even though Junior is an adult, according to the law, while Romen is not at the age of consent. The depictions of these two problematic, and supposedly consensual, sexual relationships in the narrative present double standards in relation to several intersections, including age, gender, and class. Is it because the age gap between the second couple is not as large as in the first that the relationship evokes less shock? Is it because Romen is a young male in a society that glorifies young men's sexual exploits that he is not protected from this mature relationship? Does the community in the narrative villainize the perpetrator Junior more than Cosey because she is working class, and he is wealthy? Patriarchy contributes to the uneven reading of the relationships in society.

Various studies on sexual assault argue that the class status of the parties involved is often a factor in how others perceive the assault. Helen Benedict explains that a major misconception about rapes is that they are committed "by lower class men against higher class women."[8] Building on Benedict's work, Tanya Serisier explains that "the more 'respectable' a man is deemed to be the less credence allegations against him are likely to be given, particularly if the woman making the allegations is deemed to be less respectable or have a lower social status."[9] The class status, along with the intersections of gender and age, of the couples in Morrison's *Love* contribute greatly to how the community members respond to the relationships. Ultimately, the novel makes visible and gives voice to the gruesome historical legacy concerning control over the bodies of the African American characters as well as the increased vulnerability of those with a working-class status.

A History of Commodifying Abused Bodies and Souls

Although Morrison's *Love* involves relationships between African Americans, the two cross-class relationships under study in this chapter invoke the long history in the United States of Black people's sexual violation by whites and their overall susceptibility to violence. Drawing on scholarship of both slavery and sexual violence, this chapter asserts that the legacy of this violence continues to inform present-day thinking concerning Black people's innocence or culpability in matters of sexual violence as well as how the sexualization of racism and the racialization of sexism intersect with class-based ideologies. Enslaved Blacks having rights was a moot topic since they were brought to the United States in 1619 and remained a controversial matter after the passage of the Fourteenth Amendment to the U.S. Constitution, which made them citizens and granted them "equal protection of the laws."[10] Blacks did not have ownership, control, or decision-making authority over their bodies. In fact, laws in the growing capitalist enterprise deemed them to be property rather than people.[11] Society objectified Blacks and viewed them similarly to animals that could increase wealth or be value-adding commodities, including when they reproduced. Yet, despite their legal classification, African Americans still enacted agency and bodily control as a way to defy their objectification.

The choice of language throughout the novel reaffirms the troubling nature of the supposed consensual relationships and bolsters the enslaved/enslaver undertones. Toward the end of *Love*, for instance, Heed confesses to Christine: "That hurt, Christine. Calling me a slave. Hurt bad" (188). During one of their many arguments after Cosey married Heed, Christine includes the word "slave." Christine's use of the term "slave" was meant to injure Heed and underscores Heed's powerlessness concerning her relationship with Cosey. Cosey's and Heed's positions in their relationship are like those of an enslaved person and an enslaver.[12] Morrison uses this language to invoke racial and interracial dynamics in association with slavery. For sure, conjuring up slavery in relation to the unequal power relations between Heed and Cosey points directly to the history of racial capitalism where white capitalists abused and profited from enslaved Black bodies. Some see slavery as making either race relations *or* class relations, while others see it as making both, as the discussion in my introduction further expands. Besides this reality, the novel uses other terms, including "sold" (185), "bought" (86), and "gave her up" (105) multiple times in association with Cosey and Heed's marriage. Morrison uses references to slavery and other language associated with objectifying people, especially women, throughout the narrative.

Sexual assaults of enslaved Blacks were almost never characterized as sexual violence because of problematic, racist ideas about the humanity of certain groups of people, specifically marginalized people.[13] Yet, the acts committed against them fit within definitions of sexual assault and abuse. The U.S. government, through its Office on Women's Health, defines sexual assault as "any type of sexual activity or contact that you do not consent to"; also, "it can happen through physical force or threats of force" and "includes rape and sexual coercion."[14] Many enslaved Blacks endured these acts and scores of their free descendants would come to experience them as well. The scenes in *Love* that reference blatant sexual assaults of minor characters, such as Pretty Faye, whom Romen rescues from being gang-raped by teenagers (46), and a woman volunteer being raped by an activist while fighting for Black people's rights (166), keep this theme fresh in the minds of readers. The question of consent is clear in these particular cases. However, when it comes to parties who are in relationship with one another, specifically Cosey and Heed as well as Junior and Romen, it is more complicated; still, both of these relationships exhibit forms of sexual assault. The novel, thus, touches on chattel slavery abuse and sexual violence, displaying the intersections of race, class, and gender in historical and contemporary perspectives.

Furthermore, whether sexual assault was a crime during slavery depended on the identity of the perpetrator. Rape of a Black woman by someone other than her enslaver was only a crime because it was considered trespassing on another man's property.[15] Convicting a white man of rape was virtually unheard of for a considerable time in the United States. Historian Sharon Block writes, "No rape conviction against a white man, let alone a victim's owner, for raping an enslaved woman has been found between at least 1700 and the Civil War" (65). Moreover, in some places, legal protection against rape applied to white women only because laws did not value or see Black women as worthy of this protection.[16] Such legal practices were quite convenient during and after slavery, as many white enslavers used Black women as breeders and felt they had free rein over Black people's bodies.[17] At times, Black men and women were objectified together in such acts, as white male and female enslavers forced enslaved Black men to impregnate enslaved Black women to increase or maintain white men's class-standing.[18] Though not discussed as much as Black women's abuse, sexual violence toward Black men was another feature of slavery. As historian Thomas A. Foster notes, "Enslaved black men were sexually assaulted by both white men and white women"; this assault took "a wide variety of forms, including outright physical penetrative assault, forced reproduction, sexual coercion and manipulation, and psychic abuse."[19] Literature on sexual assault has long explained that sexual assault is not about sexual pleasure; rather, it is about controlling, degrading, and punishing, which are all applicable to men and women.[20] Both of the cross-class relationships reflect controlling behavior on the parts of the male Cosey and the female Junior.

Besides serving as breeders for capitalist profits, enslaved Black women were also subject to rape by their white enslavers, which was quite prevalent on many plantations. Some of these liaisons resulted in biracial children who had to follow the condition of their mothers and be enslaved as well, due to the law.[21] While Heed ultimately is never able to carry a child to full term during her marriage to Cosey, some community members think that Cosey married this "unused girl" (104) so that he could have lots of children to replace his beloved son Billy Boy, who died from walking pneumonia. In essence, they believe Cosey views Heed as a potential breeder of his progeny. The point here is not that Cosey's class privilege equates him to a white enslaver; rather, my analysis is emphasizing the gender, age, and power dynamics of this cross-class relationship and Heed's relative disempowerment as a result. Whether during slavery or after, as fictively portrayed in Morrison's novel, sexual violation of Black women was supposed to benefit someone else, and this representation is also visible in other contemporary African American fiction, such as Gayl Jones's *Corregidora*. Cosey and Heed's cross-class relationship continually evokes slavery, reminding readers of the historical legacy on which the relationship rests as well as the power imbalances due to their class positions.

Stereotypes about Black women's and men's sexual lives as portrayed in Morrison's *Love* are also rooted in historical circumstances. Cosey, Heed, and Junior are either depicted as or rumored to be sexually out of control by community members. Stereotypes concerning Black women, their bodies, and sexuality were the justification for Black women's violation, extending back to slavery when those who claimed people as property "blamed the female slave for the sexual exploitation that she experienced at the hands of her master."[22] Similarly, the supposed sexual predatory nature of Black men was the excuse for hundreds of Black men's lynching by mobs of white

Americans.[23] The irony is blatant when it comes to how whites viewed any form of sexual intimacy, let alone sexual violence, pertaining to white women and Black men. Black men would have never been able to get away with raping white women in the way that white men were able to get away with raping Black women. The Equal Justice Initiative, founded by the acclaimed lawyer Bryan Stevenson, reveals that "nearly one in four black people lynched from 1877 to 1945 were accused of improper contact with a white woman."[24] Lynching was simply another violent control and intimidation mechanism whites, especially those in the South, exercised to terrorize Blacks after the U.S. Civil War.[25]

Regrettably, Black girls and boys also did not (and do not) escape sexual victimization, and Morrison's *Love* details exposure of children to sexual violence in both of the cross-class pairs. To shape perceptions of Blacks in the late nineteenth and early twentieth centuries as an attempt to protect them from the "systemic, racialized violence in the form of lynching and rape," African Americans wrote conduct books that taught parents and their children "protocols of racial etiquette" and to be prepared to "face prejudice at an early age."[26] In many places, Black children were as vulnerable as Black adults to all forms of cruelty and objectification partially because of the adultification of Black children.[27] Some scholars have documented the history of Black girls and teenagers particularly being prey to sexual abuse and exploitation from slavery through the present.[28] This chapter stresses that children cannot consent to sex; today, all states have age of consent laws. Yet, according to the U.S. Department of Justice, "1 in 6 boys and 1 in 4 girls are sexually abused before the age of 18."[29] The cross-class relationships in *Love*, unfortunately, include sex with children, specifically Heed and Romen.

Cosey: A Child Molester or Not?

The cross-class friendship between Heed and Christine introduces Cosey to Heed, as he first converses with and molests Heed when she is on a playdate with his granddaughter Christine at his beachfront hotel. When Cosey sees her shaking her hips to the music from the hotel's bar as she went for toy jacks, he asks her name before he smiles and rubs her chin then nipple to stimulate it. After he walks off smiling, the novel reads: "Heed bolts back down the stairs. The spot on her chest she didn't know she had is burning, tingling. When she reaches the door, she is panting as though she has run the length of the beach instead of a flight of stairs" (191). Clearly, these lines convey that

Heed is traumatized and unaccustomed to such a feeling in her young body. Shortly after and wondering why Heed is taking so long, Christine looks upward to her window to yell for Heed, but instead, she sees her grandfather with his trousers open, masturbating at her window (190). The juxtaposition of these scenes illustrates that both girls experience sexually related trauma, even as Christine is not physically touched. This first interaction between Cosey and Heed affirms the questioning of the consensual nature of their cross-class marriage that comes later in the novel. The experience becomes the girls' earliest costly secret that would affect their lives for decades to come.[30] Self-blame on the part of Heed and shame for her grandfather in Christine's case (192) fracture the girls permanently, and they do not discuss their experiences until they are adults. Heed says in the end that Cosey took her childhood away (194). In this pivotal scene, the novel imitates reality, as scholarship indicates that these are typical emotional responses of violated people and that survivors of sexual abuse and assault tend to know their abusers because they are usually close acquaintances and family members.[31] Cosey, like scores of power-driven people before him, sees an opening and chooses to demonstrate "cheap" or predatory behavior by defiling a young, defenseless, working-class Black girl for his selfish pleasure.

The fifty-two-year-old Cosey sees Heed as a commodity, and the sexual pleasure he imagines gaining from her encourages him to manifest his objectification and violation of her through their cross-class marriage. Just like a purchaser at an auction block assessing the body of an enslaved person, Cosey is strategic in his choice of Heed. The omniscient narrator informs readers: "Only Papa [Cosey] knew better, had picked her out of all he could have chosen. Knowing she had no schooling, no abilities, no proper raising, he chose her anyway while everybody else thought she could be run over" (72–73).[32] That Cosey had a choice of "all" and still chose Heed emphasizes the predatory, abusive intentions that continue to be manifested in bolder ways throughout their marriage.

The intersection of sexual objectification with class status is clear: Heed's class position makes her more vulnerable to Cosey's predatory behavior in that he knows he can get away with it more easily with her. He knows he can essentially buy her from her family. In a capitalist society in which patriarchy provides certain types of benefits, some may see Heed as *needing* Cosey more than he *wants* her because the novel suggests Heed's economic status is better enhanced through her marriage to him than it likely would have been through, for example, work or education. The juxtaposition of Heed with Christine, who struggles greatly despite having some education and a supposed "good" pedigree, makes such a conjecture plausible. The larger fact that Heed can be sold and that selling her economically "benefits" her family even as it overall disempowers her presents more sad commentary on the portrayed patriarchal family. When Heed and Christine converse about their mothers toward the end of the novel, Heed remarks that Christine's mother did not sell Christine (184), and "I heard it was two hundred dollars he gave my daddy, and a pocketbook for Mama" (193). The idea of a human being's value being determined by a monetary amount invokes chattel slavery and/or a dowry, though the latter usually insinuates a different class position from Heed's working-class status. Through the cross-class relationship trope, the narrative is constantly reminding readers about the roots of the current circumstances. As Christine recalls, "Well, it's like we started out being sold, got free of it, then sold ourselves to the highest bidder" (185). Here, the novel alludes to different ways some African Americans participate in "selling" themselves beyond the chattel slavery era.

The neoliberal paradigm has affected protection services for children, who can be vulnerable targets of abusive, predatory adults who practice sexual grooming.[33] With his purchase secured, Cosey engages with Heed in aspects of sexual grooming or, rather, practices that many child sexual abusers use to facilitate their sexual abuse, which evokes questions about the consensual nature of this cross-class marriage. Targeting and obtaining access, gaining the trust of the victim, and controlling the relationship are all parts of grooming,[34] which seeks "to manipulate the child into becoming a co-operating participant."[35] So, is "consensual" an accurate term to describe Cosey and Heed's relationship? Furthermore, techniques in grooming include bathing and wrestling with the child.[36] Not coincidentally, the novel reveals that their wedding night is unlike most others: "Undressing. No penetration. No blood. No eeks of pain or discomfort. Just this man stroking, nursing, bathing her. She arched" (77). The young girl is unaware that he is simply prepping her. She is ignorant, too, about why they "played 'wrestle' in the morning" (128) before she indulged herself with child's play, including coloring books and paper dolls. Juxtaposing these scenes draws attention to the role of patriarchy and the intersections at play in relation to age, gender, and power (i.e., the advantage of class position and physical strength). Cosey's training of Heed to be who he wanted her to be is lost on her.[37] Still, fully aware that Heed is a child when she throws a tantrum at the dinner table one day, Cosey spanks her, treating her like a child in training for womanhood, not a wife (126). The novel holds Heed and Cosey's marriage up for examination, demonstrating an example of Black girls continuing to be commodified and sexually violated while educating readers on the seduction techniques associated with sexual abuse, better known as grooming.

To justify his marriage to this young girl, Cosey boasts that he did not have sex with her until after she got her period (147), which shows he knows it is not "right" for him to be with her. She is a girl, not a woman; indeed, she is a "wifelet" (168). Even Christine acknowledges this when she and Heed are still at odds: "It does something to the mind, marrying before your first period. . . . There's virgins and then there's children" (132). Christine is highlighting the significance of the distinction between virgin and children to emphasize the wrong committed against Heed. Cosey targets Heed and insists on capturing her, which Romen's grandfather Sandler recalls when Cosey describes Heed as if she is a fashion model instead of a child (148). Sandler is troubled by Cosey's marriage to Heed and confused about the description Cosey gives, but he does not voice his thoughts to Cosey. Cosey's position as Sandler's employer contributes to Sandler's silence on the matter. In essence, Sandler's class position hinders his voicing of his thoughts.

Why abusers are not stopped is a question many justice seekers continually ask in the twenty-first century, and Morrison's novel entertains this question as well. Like Sandler, many other characters are outraged by Cosey's marriage to Heed, but there are no real interventions to end his predatory behavior. What is the responsibility of Heed's family and the community members concerning enacting resistance and disrupting the silence? The inaction of characters in Morrison's Love affirms that silence around these matters serves only to perpetuate them.[38] Serisier notes that during the 1970s, "feminist activists began to draw attention to the prevalence of child sexual abuse alongside their campaigns around adult sexual assault."[39] So even as contemporary neoliberalism was gaining its footing in exercising economic and political power over noncapitalist groups, others in U.S. society were advocating for limitations to people's power over other people's physical bodies. The fictive communities in Morrison's narrative espouse a lack of activism concerning these matters.

Instead of working together, the community members villainize and blame Heed and her working-class family, highlighting an intraracial division that seems largely tied to patriarchy. The character L, another character in the novel who is familiar with the private lives of several other characters, expresses the community's view, explaining that "the Johnsons [Heed's family] were not just poor and trifling, their girls were thought to be mighty quick in the skirt-raising department" (138–39). Hence, the novel ties class, gender, race, and sexuality, showing how their intersectionality works to the disadvantage of Heed in this cross-class relationship. This Black community has come to accept the ill treatment of more marginalized Blacks and internalize stereotypes about them. In the foreword to the novel, Morrison mentions "intraracial betrayals" and "class allegiances" in African American communities.[40] Analysis of the novel reveals the presence of these ugly realities in that the middle-class members feel they have to disassociate themselves from working-class characters for self-preservation purposes, as my analysis in chapter 1 also conveys. Furthermore, the community forgives Cosey for everything, and, instead, blames the child for Cosey's interest in her (147), akin to enslaved Black women and girls being blamed for being sexually abused. While problematic, it is not uncommon for people to blame the child, and most perpetrators do not suffer many consequences; hence, the novel encourages that a shift in people's perspectives is needed to help modify these circumstances.[41]

Invoking government provisions or the welfare state, Morrison represents Cosey as crafty, helping more Black people than government programs do in forty years (9). The failure to hold Cosey accountable calls attention to not only class, capitalism, and their intersections with race and Black patriarchy but also Cosey's Black masculinity, which reflects a reality in contemporary society. For example, Bill Cosey's full name invokes Bill Cosby, the celebrity from the television show who represented Black middle-class respectability and economic success but whose behavior in life outside the show offered stark contrasts. This literary representation informs and occludes how Black communities received the news of Cosby's sexual assaults. Like Cosby's, Cosey's power plays a role in why many in the community gloss over his errant ways. Cosey is a complex figure in that the novel presents what some characters consider supposedly redeeming characteristics in him. While his generous acts seem simply to be a part of helping him maintain his power, people such as Heed's family as well as others are grateful for anything he did. They were fully aware that they do not have as much as Cosey and his family and, consequently, believe that they cannot do much.[42] Certainly, Cosey's power and cunning ways played a role in why the community turns a blind eye to Cosey's lewd behavior.

Cosey does in fact simultaneously do very nice things *and* very mean things. For instance, he "didn't mix with local people publicly, which is to say he employed them, joked with them, even rescued them from difficult situations, but other than at church picnics, none was truly welcome at the hotel's tables or on its dance floor" (41), and "he refused to sell land to local people," instead "selling it to a developer cashing in on HUD money" (45). Indeed, the novel skillfully casts Cosey as someone who lacks morals, which he made plainly evident up until his death when he leaves everything in his will to Celestial, a prostitute with whom he had affairs, before the character L changed the will (200).[43] Moreover, Cosey, who has wealth to pass on, shows parallels with the character Luther in Naylor's *Linden Hills*, who owns several homes. Both characters are anomalies in their communities, and the portrayals of these characters' many assets invoke larger conversations about how neoliberal policies continue to hinder Black people's abilities to accumulate and pass on wealth. Ultimately, Cosey and Heed's marriage displays the consequences of the continued practice of devaluing the lives of humans, particularly African American women and girls in this case, which maintains their being disproportionately impacted by sexual violence.[44]

A Woman Perpetrator? The Curious Case of Junior Viviane

While sexual assault is almost always committed by males, female perpetrators exist, and Morrison's character Junior Viviane fits the profile.[45] This section of the chapter takes a slightly different angle, as a result, homing in on the circumstances of the female aggressor Junior. U.S. society tends to view such cases differently from those involving male perpetrators. In fact, many people take abuse by female perpetrators less seriously, which is unfair to male victims. Professor of politics and gender studies Carolyn Cocca explains that "in the 1970s, feminists argued for gender-neutral statutory rape laws so as to encompass young males as victims and to grant formal equality to females, making the crime one focused solely on age rather than on gender."[46] Gender-neutral language concerning rape eventually became the norm by 2000 across all states. Before their cross-class relationship forms, when Junior first sees Romen, she imagines that he is underage and that she would like to be sexually intimate with him (61). The first thing she says to him, referring to Heed and Christine, whom he is helping, is sexually related: "Don't tell me you're fucking these old women too" (62). This immediate boldness, opening the doorway to future sexually explicit conversations, preps Romen. He is fourteen years old, and, once they begin their sexual engagements, which last throughout the rest of the narrative, they keep them a secret because they know people would likely not approve of their relationship for a variety of reasons, including age and class differences.

Like Cosey, Junior is a complex character, and her personal story makes an empathetic person hesitant to condemn her, as her background sets her at a disadvantage. The reason Junior meets Romen is a result of her hustling, trying to make money because she is a runaway no longer connected with her working-class family. Junior's character in *Love* invokes the reality of a welfare state stunted by neoliberal practices, which ultimately results in serious suffering for many people. She comes from the Settlement, which is the antithesis of where the affluent Cosey makes his home (53). The description of her community easily reveals the contrast:

> They built their own houses from other people's scraps, or they added on to the workers' cabins left by the jute company: a shed here, a room there, to the cluster of little two-room-and-a-stove huts that wavered on the slope or sat in the valley. They used stream and rain water, drank cow's milk or home brew; ate game, eggs, domestic plants, and if they hired out in a field or a kitchen, they spent the earnings on sugar, salt, cooking oil, soda pop, cornflakes, flour, dried beans, and rice. If there were no earnings, they stole. (54)

Her family fits the classification of working class in *Class Interruptions*, as my analysis delineates in the introduction, and Heed hires Junior as a domestic worker—an occupation long associated with working classes. As a young, working-class woman trying to escape a community that lives off the bare necessities, Junior finds herself at Heed's and Christine's house responding to a job ad Heed created to acquire help with secretly changing her deceased husband Cosey's will so that Christine is sure to never gain ownership of any of his property. With a "street-life smell" (90) and accustomed to an underground economy, Junior shows up with no job references to offer, but she is grateful Heed still hires her. Not only does Junior desire to escape the hardships of her community, but she also wants to remain free of the vile experiences of her past.

Before she forms a cross-class sexual union with Romen, Junior experiences violence as a minor inside and outside of her home. Her uncles threaten her and physically abuse her, crushing her toes by hitting her with their vehicle. They threaten to "'break [her] pretty little butt' and 'hand [her] over to Vosh,'" who is the "old man in the valley who liked to walk around with his private parts in his hand singing hymns of praise" (57). Her uncles represent an abusive system of patriarchy and its intersections with sexuality and gender are also at play in Junior's history. Vosh, a mentally ill old man, represents a seeming contradiction of sorts with the juxtaposition of holy hymns and public masturbation. This display of religion alongside what some consider sexual deviance connects to the legacy of transatlantic slavery, as they were both attributes of the institution, where enslavers justified all forms of abuse with Bible passages. Escaping from home at age eleven, Junior eventually lands in a correctional institute then prison after an administrator attempted to sexually assault her (117). This part of Junior's history invokes the need for reform in the criminal justice system, as she is sentenced to prison, even though she was defending herself against the administrator. She, in this instance, becomes a part of what scholars call the sexual abuse to prison pipeline, a phenomenon in which the trauma and behavioral reactions of girls, especially young girls of color, who have experienced sexual violence land them in the juvenile justice system.[47] Junior becomes a commodity for the prison system, a modern-day form of enslavement for too many African Americans. When she is finished serving time, some people, such as those in the community in which Romen lives, continue to villainize her.

Perhaps an omen concerning her forthcoming cross-class relationship with Romen, the working-class Junior is persecuted even before she commits a crime or exhibits questionable behavior. From her first appearance in the narrative, Junior is under judgment by those with whom she interacts because of the way she presents herself. Her physical appearance, especially her attire and body attributes, garners much attention from several characters throughout *Love*. The narrative, for instance, reveals the initial perceptions of Junior by (the now middle-class via marriage) Heed: "The girl was not at all what she had expected. Not just the messy hair and tacky clothes; there was some bold laziness in her manner, the way she talked. Like the 'Yeah' she gave to Heed's question" (24–25). Junior's speech and clothing choices meet Heed's disapproval and influence Heed's treatment of her. Sartorial and word choices are signs of social class that people use to judge others,[48] and these class indicators are pertinent because the text uses them to reveal that the characters' assessments of Junior are biased and border on objectifying Junior. The larger significance of the judgment Junior immediately experiences is that it highlights aspects of inequality or social class dynamics that people experience in their daily interaction, which is still unexamined to a large extent.[49] The idea of Junior as suspect remains with key characters throughout the narrative, as the intersections of her class, gender, and age work together to distinguish her and cast her as inferior in the eyes of the others.

To teach Romen responsibility and keep him "out of the sight line of ambitious, under-occupied police"—an evocation of the Repressive State Apparatus I discuss in chapter 3—his grandparents get him a job doing chores for Heed and Christine (15), which is where Junior first sees Romen, whom she describes as the "kid outside" (61). Junior's objectification of Romen is unmistakable, as she suggestively looks at "his crotch, then his face" before announcing to Romen that the women's house has rooms that can offer privacy to her and him (63). Unbeknownst to those around her, Junior has secret plans for the minor Romen at his job in this house.[50] The original owner of the house, Cosey, employed Vida and Sandler, Romen's grandparents, and Vida credits Cosey for their current standard of living, which allows them an apparent lower middle-class position (17–18). Again, Cosey's role as employer and close approximation to the character Luther I analyzed in chapter 1 associates him with the interconnections of capitalism and patriarchy.

Reminiscent of Cosey's predatory behavior, Junior is the initiator and aggressor in their sexual escapades; her behavior is reminiscent of sexual coercion and manipulation. She first manipulates Romen by stroking his ego when she inquires if he is having sex with the Cosey women. Romen, who feels both embarrassment and pride, receives the thought that he could have sex with two women as a compliment (62). This flattery eventually leads to them having a sexual relationship and to Romen being excited about that relationship. They have sex at different places around town, and the narrator reveals Romen's thoughts: "Exciting as all that travel was to anticipate, indelible as this town was becoming . . . nothing beat the sight of a straddling Junior in bed" (115). Yet, sexual coercion plays a role in their relationship as well; "coercion is an issue of power and control."[51] Not "only did [Junior] want him; she demanded him" (113). Concerning their "preplanned spots" to have sex, the novel indicates "the plan (hers) was to make it [have sex] everywhere" (115). Once Romen begins a sexual relationship with her, Junior becomes bolder in her sexual requests, soon asking for sadomasochist behavior (155). Romen describes this behavior as "Weird. Wack" (153), as it makes him feel uneasy. Though Romen does not fit the enslaver/enslaved parameters as well as Heed, his sense of powerlessness, like Heed's, is apparent in this "consensual" cross-class liaison.

When Romen voices his discomfort to Sandler, the advice Sandler gives sounds similar to advice that professionals give when trying to help families and children stay clear of child sexual predators, as he encourages Romen not to ignore his instincts. Yet, before this conversation and unaware that Junior is Romen's sex partner, Sandler wonders if Romen is having sex with a grown woman with free time on her hands, and that does not bother Sandler (112). Romen, whose name is close to Romeo, makes one think of Romeo and Juliet, and I do not believe this is a coincidence on the part of

Morrison. The narrative invokes a critique of Romeo and Juliet laws, or close-in-age exemption laws, which allow someone below the state's legal age of consent to have consensual sex with an older partner who is close in age. In many states with such laws, the fourteen-year-old Romen and the eighteen-year-old Junior's relationship would not be exempt from being prosecuted as a crime.[52] These age choices by the author jolt readers into examining more closely their personal beliefs about age of consent. How old is old enough? While Romen seems to enjoy the sexual activity with Junior at times, he also is confused and a bit uncomfortable, which is evident in his conversation with Sandler and when Junior is being aggressive during certain sexual scenes. Again, the novel invokes the question of what is the responsibility of community and family members to speak up and stop sexual relationships that hinder children in some way, no matter how minor. The novel, in this instance, prods readers to reconsider sexual relationships where the two parties are near in age but still in illegal territory. It is clever that Morrison chooses the ages fourteen and eighteen because this age gap is on the fine line concerning statutory rape laws.

Sex changes Romen, and the only outrage is from his aunt Vida, as many see the relationship as working to their advantage, which is a big factor in why illegal sexual relationships are not obstructed. From the perspectives of his guardians, his classmates, and his employers, Romen's behavior is different. Particularly, his increase in maturity is obvious after he begins having sex with Junior. Fearing that Romen could contract a sexually transmitted disease or impregnate someone as a teenager, Vida urges Sandler to talk to him (112–13, 145). Heed, by contrast, does not see the relationship as problematic, but rather welcomes it for selfish reasons: "Heed thought it a good thing, this baby romance, a way to keep the girl on the premises [continuing the job Heed hired her to do] once she found out there was no way to steal. . . . A little backseat fumbling might loosen up Romen too. Yank him out of Vida's clamp. He was so tight around the mouth. 'Yes, ma'am. No, ma'am. No thank you, I have to be home by streetlights'" (72). Ironically, these lines reveal that Heed appears to have a problem with Romen's modest, respectful behavior. The term "yank" infers that she wants to usher him *away* from the security of his guardians. She seems not to mind him being in harm's way or at least put in a problematic situation. In a capital-driven society, it comes down to profit, in particular Heed's focus on making sure she literally gets her money's worth from Junior. Christine views the matter similarly, believing that "a happily sexed girl would be more likely to stay on" (169). Double standards regarding young men having sex may also contribute to their lack of concern over the sexual relationship, and they did not expect much from Junior because of her class status. Young boys having sex or exerting their sexual prowess is often not seen negatively; in fact, people express the cliché "boys will be boys," meaning that sexual behavior is a part of becoming a man.

Morrison's *Love* highlights the age differences among the two couples to complicate discussions of sexual violence even as they manifest along social class lines. While most readers will say that Cosey and Heed's relationship is problematic, others may be less inclined to say the same about Junior and Romen's relationship because of their ages. Although Romen's and Junior's ages are close in range, Junior, by U.S. law, is an adult at age eighteen. Age, indeed, is more than a number, and it is clearly significant in the novel. When Junior talks to the image of the deceased Cosey, she points out that she ran away when she was eleven, the same age Heed was when Cosey married her (156). They were vulnerable and unprotected working-class girls of whom adults took advantage. Junior later exerts her sexual power over Romen, who was around the same age she was when the administrator in the correctional institute tried to exert his sexual power over her. The fact that Junior has had to endure her history is an important point that should make readers critique the set of circumstances that allowed and facilitated her reality.

Age of consent laws exist because of the mental and emotional development processes of humans. Morrison's *Love* forces readers to examine more closely what is right and wrong concerning sexual activity. Readers may have to ask why the Cosey/Heed relationship makes them feel a level of discomfort they do not feel concerning the Junior/Romen relationship. In essence, the novel is acting in a similar way to the #MeToo hashtag, as it brings attention to various types of sexually violating experiences that have escaped ample and necessary public scrutiny.

Morrison's *Love* ultimately challenges the silence surrounding sexual violence by placing it at the forefront via a cross-class relationship trope and provokes the question: How can people create a world without sexual violence? Given the lack of attention to sexual violence particularly against African Americans—males and females—there needs to be advocacy for this reality to become a part of mainstream conversations so that it is eradicated faster. This absence of focus on African Americans is associated with their long history of being invisible or objectified; eliminating public funding for antiviolence work will continue to hinder the visibility of this reality. Moreover, not until the end of her life and the novel is Heed no longer consistently villainized by community members because of her working-class upbringing. That she is vilified her entire life reveals that overcoming class origins can be difficult. She and her former best friend Christine reconcile right before Heed dies. Their relationship demonstrates the potential or possibility of cross-class friendships but also underscores that communication is essential. Due to her behavior, including harming the two old women at the novel's end, Junior continues to suffer persecution as the novel concludes, however. Still, community members villainized her before she displayed reprehensible behavior. Additionally, that the working-class Heed is a survivor and the working-class Junior is an aggressor convey and affirm that good and bad actors exist in all classes. The novel affirms that people's class position alone should not equate to them being either praiseworthy or culpable. Continuing to develop strategies to resist sexual abuse wherever it exists is necessary. The intersections of people's class position with their gender and race is especially pronounced in the following chapter on educational access in the Caribbean.

PART II | Caribbean Literature

CHAPTER THREE

Beyond the "Class" Room

The Entanglements of Class and Education in Merle Hodge's Crick Crack, Monkey *and Olive Senior's* Dancing Lessons

> I personally see writing stories as not so much an exercise in imagination as a re-imagining of realities that have existed in the past, that exist in the present and will exist into the future.
>
> —OLIVE SENIOR, "Lessons from the Fruit Stand"

> The potential of Caribbean literature for positively affecting the development of the Caribbean is an untapped resource. Caribbean fiction can help to strengthen our self-image, our resistance to foreign domination, our sense of the oneness of the Caribbean and our willingness to put our energies into the building of the Caribbean nation.
>
> —MERLE HODGE, "Challenges of the Struggle for Sovereignty"

Education systems in Jamaica as well as Trinidad and Tobago have experienced many transformations in the post-independence and contemporary neoliberal period, including expansion of formal education to wider segments of the population, curriculum changes to center and reflect Caribbean history and contributions to global advancements, and the institutionalization of standardized testing. The latter has been a subject of debate, particularly over secondary education placement exams, with critics pointing out that overreliance on standardized testing limits the career trajectories, avenues to upward mobility, and life chances of some working-class students.[1] Testing and secondary education placement are central to the plots of Olive Senior's *Dancing Lessons* and Merle Hodge's *Crick Crack, Monkey*, under study in this chapter.[2] The title of this chapter contains a play on the word "class," which is embedded within the name of the central site or domain of education systems—the classroom. The classroom is the face of education systems; it is the contact location between those who teach school curricula and the students for whom the curricula is geared. Students' class background can influence how they perceive the information they are exposed to in a classroom. What students experience and learn in a classroom affects them far beyond that particular setting. Indeed, the classroom is not a neutral space, and the information taught is not value-free.

While published nearly forty years apart by authors born in the same generation, Jamaican author Olive Senior's *Dancing Lessons* (2011) and Trinidadian author Merle Hodge's *Crick Crack, Monkey* (1970) directly engage discussions on the interrelations of class and education. Specifically, they tackle the connection between education and upward class mobility in their portrayal of characters who experience schooling in different socioeconomic environments as well as the impact of that schooling on them and their surrounding communities. Invested in the traditional means of education and respectability as the path to upward mobility, the working classes and the middle classes portrayed in the novels are complicit in the reproduction of social and economic inequalities. With journeys that mirror one another, the protagonist Tee (Cynthia) in Hodge's novel and the character Celia in Senior's novel share similar experiences in their childhood and adolescent years. Focusing on the similarities of these characters, this chapter proposes that Senior's novel ultimately becomes a palimpsest of Hodge's, as it revises and continues Tee's story via the life of Celia in a neocolonial Caribbean setting. The central argument of this chapter is that both novels utilize a cross-class relationship trope to examine the ways people participate in reproducing hegemonic power relations that negatively affect their communities and to offer alternative modes that resist systems that perpetuate social and economic inequalities.

In the first epigraph to this chapter, Senior offers a vital perspective on what literature can do or does do: her view that writing is a "reimagining of realities that have existed in the past, that exist in the present and will exist into the future"[3] is also germane to what literary activism can do and does do. Hodge makes the latter more explicit, in emphasizing the "potential" of literature to affect "the development of" and "building of" nations. Self-determination is fortified by the strengthening of "self-image," and Hodge posits that fiction can aid in "resistance to foreign domination." Senior also ties literature to resistance: she says that she "grew up with a profound appreciation of language as a living object that could be used the same as any other tool or weapon."[4] Literary activism can be a tool, a mode of informal politics, to push back at inequalities exacerbated by neoliberal practices. As Senior stated in an interview, "Politics is intrinsic to everything we do. I feel my job as a writer is to explore the society and to be subversive—to show people different aspects of the society which they might want to think about, as they pursue their daily lives."[5] Hodge further asserts that Caribbean literature is "an important weapon of resistance"[6] filled with "immense political power," and that "there is no fundamental contradiction between art and activism."[7]

Moreover, in an interview about *Crick Crack, Monkey,* Hodge noted that "people in all societies are complicit in whatever system they live under, and don't necessarily see individual injustices as systemic."[8] Awareness is a critical first step in effecting change, and the reality that the characters sometimes participate in their own subjugation is an area that must be investigated if positive change is to occur. Resorting to politics of respectability that only highlight the "good" will not provide a full view of the novels' characters. Still, risks exist when discussing complicity in situations where power dynamics remain uneven in that one can appear to blame the less powerful for their circumstances. "Challenging the boundary between artist and critic" (168), as Dwight A. McBride writes of Toni Morrison, Hodge and Senior engage in critical concerns of Caribbean people through their fiction, which serves the purpose of evoking new ways to view and impact reality or a clear intent to influence it. Senior's creative writing (particularly her poetry) and Hodge's novel, which is one of the earliest postcolonial bildungsroman novels penned by a Caribbean woman writer, reach and influence various audiences, including schoolchildren. The literature of both writers has been featured on standardized exams by the Caribbean Examinations Council (CXC), which is the official institution to administer and monitor standardized testing for a number of Anglophone Caribbean nations.[9] This chapter includes an evaluation of the choices and their consequences made by the various characters in the novels and the decisions of the authors to fashion these characters in this way. Many working-class studies scholars, including Sherry Lee Linkon, Renny Christopher, and Carolyn Whitson, call for literature that will lead readers to revolutionary class consciousness; a candid assessment of the contradictions among classes themselves is necessary to achieve such an aim.[10]

Akin to scholarship across disciplines, such as education, history, and cultural studies, Hodge's and Senior's novels represent the trajectory of education in Caribbean nations spanning from pre-independence to contemporary times and express comparable concerns about the exclusionary nature of education. While *Crick Crack, Monkey* and *Dancing Lessons* reflect the periods they are published in—pre-independence Trinidad and Tobago in Hodge's text and mostly post-independence in Senior's—they reveal strikingly parallel situations in their portrayals of their characters' educational journeys. A number of scholars chronicle the development and influence of education systems in these nations and the wider Caribbean region as well as reveal the intricacies of class status in relation to these systems from their genesis to the current period.[11] A consistent thread in the work of these scholars is the revelation that working-class people continue to be the most disadvantaged in these systems. Education systems ultimately reinforce the class hierarchy even as they purport to provide access.

Access to education has been a challenge throughout history for working classes although education has long been a method to achieve upward class mobility.[12] In his scholarship on Trinidad and Tobago, historian Carl C. Campbell asserts that social change was never an initial goal for school systems; rather, the original goals of educational institutions under colonialism were "to spread Christianity, literacy, and as always in education social discipline."[13] Khitanya Petgrave makes a similar claim about Jamaica's school systems, noting the focus was teaching the Christian religion alongside reading, writing, and arithmetic.[14] After independence of both nations in 1962 and under the tenure of early prime ministers, notably those of Dr. Eric Williams (Trinidad and Tobago) and Michael Manley (Jamaica), the nations underwent a series of substantive educational reforms to promote fairness and access for the wider population. To advance their nations, Prime Ministers Williams and Manley also signed the Treaty of Chaguaramas during this time period. This treaty established the Caribbean Community and Common Market (CARICOM), which promotes economic and foreign policies, for instance, among several Caribbean nations (see figure 3.1). While much progress occurred under these administrations, large disparities in educational attainment continued in subsequent years, and challenges remain. An unfortunate reality is that the quality and type of school a child attends remains indicative of the child's social class background—with schools of poorer caliber being filled with working-class students.[15] With their reflections on such circumstances, Hodge's and Senior's novels engage in a broad discussion on the significance of education via their depictions of school life for Caribbean children and the roles of their families in those experiences.

Crick Crack, Monkey and *Dancing Lessons* are also extensions of a Caribbean literary tradition that explores the theme of education as a transformative tool in characters' lives and can be found in the work of George Lamming, Earl Lovelace, Austin Clark, Jamaica Kincaid, Dionne Brand, V. S. Naipaul, Michelle Cliff, and Erna Brodber, among others. As is the case in Hodge's and Senior's narratives, many characters in the literary works by these authors tend to view formal education as the route to up-

FIGURE 3.1 Jamaica's Prime Minister Michael Manley and Trinidad and Tobago's Prime Minister Dr. Eric Williams sit next to one another in 1973 at the signing of the Treaty of Chaguaramas, which established the Caribbean Community and Common Market (CARICOM) (AP Photo).

ward class mobility, which parallels U.S. thinking. These writers often underscore how people's class backgrounds facilitate or hinder their access to education. Beyond underscoring this fact, as well, this chapter argues that more attention to external forces that shape the characters' lives is necessary if we want to even the playing field.

Extending critical attention to Senior's and Hodge's novels, this chapter contends that both novels engage in a politics of resistance by exposing the complicities and contradictions of working classes and designing characters who disrupt, or can potentially disrupt, unjust systems and reveal alternate routes or methods to combat inequalities.[16] Though the novels suggest education facilitates a person's opportunity for upward class mobility in Caribbean societies, both emphasize that neither education nor class mobility is easily accessible. Each novel probes the failure of the fictive Caribbean nations to enable their people to realize full citizenship or to provide them with adequate opportunities or economic empowerment. Furthermore, the novels suggest a need for focus on structural and behavioral contexts to combat the gross inequalities in social institutions even as this chapter is mindful of using the pejoratively connotated "personal responsibility" that is too often used in neoliberal ideology. My analysis of the narratives reveals that the paired family units in both novels have been interpellated, or "passively, unconsciously drawn into dominant social assumptions,"[17] by British colonial ideology in the case of Hodge's novel and neocolonial ideology in the case of Senior's novel, in that both units see elite education—with the class, racial, and elitism it entails—as unquestionably desirable. The dominant ideology portrayed in the narratives claims that the closer people are to imitating a Western or European lifestyle and partaking of the related cultural accoutrements, the better they are as individuals; but as the novels show, the real effect on characters of going along with this idea negates their African-Caribbean cultural identity and is self-destructive. The character Jadine from Morrison's *Tar Baby* engages in similar behaviors, as my analysis in the epilogue conveys. In essence, the family units internalize cultural assumptions that assist in allowing the society's oppressive hierarchical system to reproduce itself. The novels thus critique both models presented to Tee and Celia—the working-class model and the middle-class model. Still, the novels offer a redeeming space for the working-class protagonists in that the characters make choices in the end that enhance the lives of their families and communities. As in Naylor's *Linden Hills* and Turner's *Only Twice*, the need for intraracial unity despite class differences is promoted in these novels as well.

While Hodge published *Crick Crack, Monkey* in the early aftermath of Trinidad's independence, an effervescent but precarious time for the nation, Senior published her first novel, *Dancing Lessons*, in 2011 during a significantly volatile time for Jamaica, which found itself embattled in global economic problems and serious disparities in education. Unlike the setting of Hodge's narrative, which is in pre-independence Trinidad, Senior's novel is set mostly in the 2000s but also extends back about forty years. Though each author features the theme of education, they approach it in different ways. Hodge's narrative is a bildungsroman where education is a central feature of Tee's experience from childhood to adolescence under the care of her aunts after her mother dies during childbirth. Furthermore, the protagonist of Hodge's narrative is a child whose world is limited by her family life and her schooling. However, the narrative allows readers to obtain a view of the social structures within Trinidadian society via Tee's descriptions of her family and education. In Senior's narrative, education is incidental to her focus on the multiple relationships of the protagonist, Mrs. Samphire. She is a middle-aged woman temporarily living in an upscale retirement home that her adult daughter, Celia, arranges for her to stay at while her house is being repaired from recent hurricane damage. Senior also portrays formal and informal modes of education in her narrative, as Mrs. Samphire acquires informal education from her mother-in-law while Celia acquires formal education through boarding schools and American universities. Mrs. Samphire in Senior's novel is a woman in her sixties who has continually formed opinions about her Jamaican society beyond family and schooling. She and her daughter Celia, whom this chapter compares to Tee, are able to formulate a mature perspective on the operations of governmental entities in their society in a way that a young child cannot. Still, Hodge's and Senior's novels exhibit clear intertextuality, specifically concerning education.

Two of the most significant areas of commonality between Tee's and Celia's lives include their immediate family's class backgrounds and their journey to obtain an education. In both narratives, education for the child is the glue binding the working-class and middle-class family units presented in the novels.[18] The relationship between the family units creates what is best described as a cross-class relationship. In *Crick Crack, Monkey*, the cross-class relationship occurs between Tee's paternal working-class aunt, Tantie, and Tee's maternal middle-class aunt, Beatrice. In *Dancing Lessons*, the main cross-class relationship examined in this chapter is that of Celia's working-class mother, Mrs. Samphire, and Celia's unofficial adoptive parents, the Frasers, who are a middle-class American missionary couple. In both novels, the relationship between the working-class and middle-class family units is antagonistic, and differences in beliefs about child-rearing are significant in both. Child-shifting also is illustrated in the novels; Tee and Celia begin in a working-class background with one set of family members and shift to another set of family members of a middle-class background, primarily in the pursuit of education.[19] The narrator in *Crick Crack, Monkey* guides readers through the episodes of Tee's life in a chronological fashion. In contrast, readers must piece together aspects of Celia's life from childhood to adulthood through Mrs. Samphire's flashbacks and her conversations with Celia. Though there are certainly contrasts between Tee's and Celia's lives, this chapter imagines Celia as the grown-up version of Tee who benefits from an education that is inaccessible to most of her childhood peers.

Aside from drawing on nonfiction by both authors, this chapter also draws on Marxist scholarship, particularly the work of Louis Althusser, whose concept of Ideological State Apparatuses (ISAs) provides a useful framework for looking at the interconnections of the working-class and middle-class units with the school systems in Hodge's and Senior's novels. While 1970 was a pivotal year for Black women's studies, that year also saw the publication of Althusser's well-known essay, "Ideology and Ideological State Apparatuses," in which he explains that ISAs together with the Repressive State Apparatus (RSA) make up the State Apparatus, which the "ruling class" (or those possessing state power) uses to uphold its place in the hierarchy. Describing ISAs as specific institutions, such as schools, churches, families, unions, and media, that advance the ideology of those in power,[20] he argues that the educational ISA is the "dominant Ideological State Apparatus in capitalist social formations" (104). The school, he writes,

> takes children from every class at infant-school age, and then for years, the years in which the child is most "vulnerable," squeezed between the Family State Apparatus and the Educational State Apparatus, it drums into them, whether it uses new or old methods, a certain amount of "know-how" wrapped in the ruling ideology (French, arithmetic, natural history, the sciences, literature) or simply the ruling ideology in its pure state (ethics, civic instruction, philosophy). (104–5)

Thus, the educational and family ISAs—or what he calls the "School-Family couple" (104)—operate by capitalist ideology and reinforce the existing power structures of society.[21] These are the dynamics illustrated in Hodge's and Senior's novels. Clarifying the distinction between ISAs and the RSA as it relates to passivity and force is important, as the ISAs are a more likely vehicle to inculcate power and values because, unlike the police (a part of the RSA), for example, the lack of force (implicit or perceived threat) might obscure how power and interpellation are working.

Caribbean literary scholar Rhonda Cobham-Sander anticipates my supposition that both family units in Hodge's and Senior's narratives are complicit in the reproduction of class inequality, in this case, through education in her analysis of novels by Erna Brodber, Paule Marshall, and Hodge. As Cobham-Sander puts it, "Patriarchy and colonialism may be the bogeyman, but the stories make it clear that the women themselves have participated in reproducing the system, and that the power they now possess to challenge the system has often been won by their complicity within it."[22] She discloses that people can be complicit in reproducing an unjust system, but they can use their complicity, which this chapter reads as the knowledge and experience gained, to change the system. In other words, people do not have to continue participating the same way in a system designed to reproduce their oppression once they obtain power. Instead, they can use the power for good or to challenge the system since they will have "potential for initiating change."[23] In *Crick Crack, Monkey* and *Dancing Lessons*, the working-class characters come to realize they have access to resources (after being complicit) and use them for the betterment of their loved ones. Significantly, however, they use the power primarily within an intimate group of people.

Celia, Mrs. Samphire, and the Frasers in Senior's Narrative

A scene in Senior's *Dancing Lessons* that details Mrs. Samphire's first introduction to other residents at the upscale Ellesmere Lodge retirement home immediately underscores the primacy of education and characters' interpellation by dominant ideology, specifically concerning education. As a result of her now adult daughter Celia's education and eventual fame, Mrs. Samphire gains a level of "status among [her] neighbors" in her working-class community, but that status or privilege does not extend beyond that environment (183). When the director of the home seats Mrs. Samphire at a table for breakfast and introduces her, the first question her fellow residents ask is, "What school?" (107). The residents do not exchange pleasantries with Mrs. Samphire before inquiring about her schooling. Her schooling would determine how they would perceive and treat her; unfortunately, the pleasantries never come. This scene illustrates how these middle-class and upper-class senior citizens have accepted—hook, line, and sinker—an ideology that purports only certain people are "worthy" and should have access to a wide range of resources. The fact that the women ask her about her education before they ask anything else reveals how high a priority education and its signifiers are in their eyes; they privilege education and equate it with a particular class status. Essentially, they are asking her how she got to the retirement home or what (educational) route led her to partake in such a privilege, a place where "the rich people park their parents" (5). Mrs. Samphire is puzzled by their question and confirms that she has not lived a life like theirs, as she expresses, "Such a question had never been addressed to me before. So I had no idea that it was part of the social code, knowing if a new acquaintance had gone to the right schools or not and so was worthy of one's attention. You can see how far removed from present-day reality these ladies are" (109). Hence, the women wonder how she arrived at the same place as them, and despite Mrs. Samphire's thoughts, the ladies are very much in tandem with the "present-day reality" of their society. In fact, they are interpellated subjects, to use Althusser's language, who believe only a specific type of person can or should be at the "top." As Senior elaborates in an interview, "Of course, the ladies at the table are upper class and would look down at her, the way she looks, the way she carries herself."[24] Indeed, the women not only look down on her, but they decide she should be ignored. Her lack of an esteemed education ultimately calls into question her worthiness.

My point with this analysis is not that this scene in *Dancing Lessons* portrays the pursuit and attainment of education as a harmful or unwise undertaking; rather, this scene stresses the point at issue is espousing a set of beliefs that declares people's worth is less valuable if they do not have a certain type of education.[25] People should have the choice and opportunity to decide the type of education they want or that they believe will best serve their livelihoods, and their decision should not warrant degradation or humiliation. Capitalism necessarily circumscribes choice and opportunity in order to maintain class stratification; neoliberalism extends this process by purporting that everyone has or can obtain the same access to the choices, which themselves are designed to have unequal outcomes. People also should not be left to eke out an existence on a minimum wage that does not allow them to make ends meet or provide for their households despite working full time. The novel illustrates that the matters of choice and opportunity are missing in the lives of many of the working-class characters, and there is little respect for informal modes of education on the part of the residents, even though there are many ways to obtain "book" knowledge and different types of knowledge. The narrative conveys that respect for informal education is not embraced by other institutions or cultural forces. Through the course of the novel, readers learn that Mrs. Samphire has had mostly an informal education and that, as a child, she read a lot and enjoyed writing. In an interview about the novel, Senior states, "The thing about her is she's very well read. One of the things I wanted was to demonstrate how books can save you."[26] Mrs. Samphire, regrettably, does not fully recognize the value of her strong informal education until the end of the novel.

While Mrs. Samphire is repulsed by the treatment of the middle- and upper-class characters in the retirement home, scenes about Celia's education reveal she herself is in collusion with the dominant ideology. Mrs. Samphire's focus on her children's education is representative of many working-class people who want their children to have more and better opportunities, as many "poor and minority parents have a high regard for their children's education and see it as a means for improving the children's futures."[27] When the adult Celia inquires how she came to live with the Frasers, Mrs. Samphire notes that it was gradual and that education was certainly a factor (334–35). Celia, a bright child, catches the attention of the Frasers, a white American missionary couple who run the summer program she attends. Eventually, the Frasers, whom Celia calls "Auntie" and "Uncle," become her caretakers and offer to pay for her to attend an expensive boarding school. Similar to the working-class character Tantie in Hodge's novel, Mrs. Samphire allows the child to go.

The working-class character Mrs. Samphire desires to participate in or consent to reproducing relations of domination in her society, instead of wanting her neighbors to also have such things if they desire, which is the fundamental problem with capitalism and neoliberalism. She outright admits her involvement in this venture, stating, "I considered myself a cut above the women in our neck of the woods. Never mind our poverty, they all knew where I was coming from" (304).[28] It is problematic that she treats the other people in her community with the same disdain that the residents in the retirement home treat her. With this narrow-minded perspective that reeks of intraracial class antagonism, she fails to comprehend that her environment, which she currently loathes, could be better if her entire community had access to more resources. As research shows, lack of a sound education "will not only impact negatively on the children's development, but ultimately on the country itself since it would not have the necessary human capital for its development."[29] This scene reinforces that Mrs. Samphire doesn't understand that the community members, the people with whom she shares similar circumstances, could be her allies; they should not be her adversaries. While she is initially reluctant to allow Celia to go away with the Frasers, especially because of Celia's young age, she shamelessly boasts a few years later about her children's schooling. Concerning her son Junior, she states she is proud he attends a boarding school, a "school with boys coming from these rich homes" (68). She is indifferent to the fact that the other children in the community are not able to attend better educational institutions. In fact, she expresses joy and relief that Junior did not hang with the boys in her community.[30] Mrs. Samphire, with a warped and self-defeating perspective, makes no apology for her privileging and esteeming the schools outside of her community that provide formal education.

The novel suggests that rather than looking down on fellow neighbors and displaying false consciousness, or a mindset that causes her to be self-sabotaging, Mrs. Samphire should be wondering about the exploitative conditions of her society that allow her cross-class counterparts—the Frasers—to acquire resources and access to schools that she and others like her have not been able to access.[31] Since first meeting the Frasers, Mrs. Samphire laments, "I could never reverse the way I felt they perceived me, our status unequal at that meeting" (336). Though the Frasers are minor characters in the novel, their role is symbolic, and this chapter associates them with multiple ISAs that Althusser identifies. Furthermore, their involvement in supporting an education system that perpetuates a class hierarchy should not be a surprise, as their occupation as white American missionaries should remind readers of the long and troubling history of missionary involvement in Caribbean education systems.

As the Frasers unofficially adopt Celia for schooling purposes and enjoy having a young child around, their actions reveal their involvement in a U.S. imperialist project. They establish institutions or apparatuses that promote and impose a foreign way of life, notably a U.S. Christian ideology. Underscoring the significance of ISAs, Althusser describes them as "the *site* of class struggle,"[32] and he further explains that the religious apparatus used to be the most powerful. He writes that before the widespread emergence of capitalism "it is absolutely clear that *there was one dominant Ideological State Apparatus, the Church*, which concentrated within it not only religious functions, but also educational ones, and a large proportion of the functions of communications and 'culture.'"[33] In essence, the church moved beyond solely routine church services to influence other arenas of society. *Dancing Lessons* demonstrates Althusser's description here almost precisely as it relates to the Frasers. Evoking the religious ISA, the novel reveals that the Frasers first began with a modest church building, but eventually went on to dominate in several areas, including education, communications, and the wider culture of the society. As (white) Americans, the Frasers assume privileges that allow them to infiltrate and gain influence in the fictive Jamaican society in ways that those in Mrs. Samphire's community never could. They become a part of the domination in the nation and reproduce injustices, as Celia's observations about her educational experiences under their care reveal.

The novel directly references the reproduction of unequal power relations in which Celia's educational institution participated and where Celia fit in the dynamics. The adult Celia's assessment of her early school experiences is clear on this score. Describing the Jamaican boarding school the Frasers put her in as elite and snobbish (121), Celia comments to Mrs. Samphire, "The point of those schools was to ensure that we knew our places in the hierarchy, wasn't it? So . . . I was always somewhere in the middle. Of course the fact that my adopted parents were white and considered rich counted for something with the headmistress and teachers, who were mainly all English themselves" (120). The narrative includes such passages to highlight that the hierarchy in the school system Celia points out is influenced by and mimics the larger hierarchy beyond her school grounds, and just as in society, the school's hierarchy is also marked by racial discrimination. The intersection of class and race are visible in her school experiences. Celia recounts the segregation of the nonwhite students in the school dormitories: "'when it came to things like sleeping arrangements in the dormitories, you can be sure I was safely tucked in with the brown and black girls in our little side room. The main dormitories had to remain untainted'" (120). Schoolchildren like Celia and her peers had to endure being treated like second-class citizens from a young age (121). She explains that these practices were in place when she first began at the boarding school, but that things changed after independence and the practices were no longer in place by the time she graduated (121).

The power dynamics in the cross-class relationship between Mrs. Samphire and the Frasers appear on smaller levels among the students in Celia's school to stress how the cycle of reproduction works and its ill effects. Celia remarks that "poor black people couldn't afford to send their children to those schools anyway" (121) and those who were able to get their children in "weren't going to listen to any complaints from their little ones about how they were treated" (121). These second-class students had no one to petition for redress of their grievances; sadly, they had to accept their circumstances if they wanted to remain enrolled. Celia acknowledges that she received privileges because of her association with the Frasers (120). The students who were marginalized because of their class and race, however, were in a powerless position; their parents did not challenge the system and thus allowed the unjust nature of the power relations to be ingrained in them and to repeat endlessly. The novel later gives an indication of what challenging the system could look like, and Celia learns how to challenge it. The experiences here resemble that of Tee in Hodge's *Crick Crack, Monkey* when she attends the school in Beatrice's middle-class community. Regarding the actual history of Jamaican education, Khitanya Petgrave explains that eradicating the vestiges of the history Celia delineates was of utmost importance to Prime Minister Michael Manley during his time in office, as he "genuinely sought to alter the racial and social profile of the island's schools"[34] because the "island's socioeconomic structure in the twentieth century—still burdened by the legacy of slavery and colonialism—was contingent on race/skin colour, class, [and] notions of inherited and acquired status."[35] But despite everything, the "Jamaican education system remains class-based" in the contemporary period.[36]

Whereas Celia is unknowingly initiated into being a part of systems that perpetuate social and economic inequalities as a child caught between the cross-class relationship of her biological and adoptive parents, exposure to a counter-ideology leads her to critique the dominant ideology of her society. Althusser explains that ISAs are sites where "the resistance of the exploited classes is able to find means and occasions to express itself there, either by the utilization of their contradictions, or by conquering combat positions in them in struggle."[37] Indeed, it is in her school experiences that Celia's perspectives begin to form and change in ways that later help her resist the beliefs of her upbringing. Immersed in the Frasers' way of life, Celia acknowledges that she willingly "adopted their point of view on everything" and only began to think differently when she went away to attend college in the United States (120). Although no one in the circles the Frasers were part of wanted to discuss race, Celia "discovered that [she] was Black" (120) once she temporarily moved away to another country and was able to get out from under the people who reared her. She informs Mrs. Samphire, "It was the 'Black is Beautiful' phase, so I suddenly became conscious of what I was in relation to these white people who had raised me. . . . I was suddenly questioning a lot of things I had never noticed before. And not in a very subtle way, I'm afraid" (123). Celia went from being an active participant in unjust systems to vehemently challenging such systems and the Frasers who were part of them. Proof of her evolving nature is evident when Celia begins to struggle in her interactions with the couple, whom she describes as sophisticated, well-educated Americans (119), as she tells Mrs. Samphire, "I was used to being obedient, so it was a painful time for me—and them too" (123).

Celia's awakening lays the groundwork for her future resistance to systems that promote inequitable power relations and her desire to choose and help others choose an alternative to participating in reproducing hegemonic power relations that negatively affect their communities. Expressing the discomfort, pain, and frustration she often felt with the Frasers, Celia explains she tried to be perfect and asks Mrs. Samphire if she knew the difficulty in trying to live up to other people's ideals (334). Here, she expresses her enlightenment that it is unfair to be forced to operate in a way that benefits others to her disadvantage. She recognizes that she has an opportunity to change such circumstances and confronts Mrs. Samphire for not doing more years ago. Even the most intimate part of her being, her name, became scrutinized and amended to accommodate others. As Celia bawls in a conversation with Mrs. Samphire, "You never even bothered to tell them what name I answered to. They didn't know that name. They didn't like the name I answered to at school, my first name [June]. So I became Celia then, my middle name, a name I have always hated" (328). Similar to Tee, the young Celia experienced affliction around her schooling and "second family" situations that she kept bottled inside on her precarious journey to upward mobility. Yet, Celia reaches a point in her adult life where she is able to and decides to resist any further forms of oppression, and what allows her to do so is access to counter-ideology, particularly Black radical intellectual traditions that resulted in her consciousness-raising.

Revisiting Cobham-Sander's ideas about complicity, my contention is that Celia becomes complicit with an education system that is not designed for her and uses the power she gains to effect change. A character like Celia recognizes that the reality Prime Minister Manley desired was not in existence and chooses to use her elite education to help those in her nation. Yet, individual merit that Manley espoused also needs to be called into question as it alone is not always an avenue to success because the government's role in providing social welfare is key to enacting a level of fairness, which is why a neoliberal frame attacks the welfare state.[38] *Dancing Lessons* particularly demonstrates a politics of resistance through Celia, who becomes a model for many in her nation. In fact, Celia becomes representative of an organic intellectual or a leader who arises from among her working-class community to represent their interests using what Italian Marxist political leader Antonio Gramsci calls civil society or what Althusser calls ISAs.[39]

Celia's association with and "combat position" within the communications ISA, which includes various media such as radio and television, is important. After her school experiences, she returns to Jamaica and, through her career field of communications, infiltrates the nation's media by strategically accessing resources and using tools gathered from abroad to her advantage.[40] Equipped with the necessary means, Celia subsequently helps her biological family and her national family. The communications ISA influences how people see themselves, their nations, and their surroundings; Celia directly affects these portrayals as a well-known sociologist and TV host in Jamaica. Her talk show is called *Quest*, an appropriate name for a character who has been on a journey since the age of five. Through her personal and public quest, Celia changes people's cultural assumptions by giving them a positive image of themselves to view, and, as a result, participates in the rebuilding of her nation. Readers learn that she is on multiple committees and boards and attends conferences (9). She continues to build her knowledge base as well as spread her influence. Celia is able to mature, become a productive member of her society, and enjoy a healthy relationship with her husband and two children. Perhaps Celia's experience or "quest" can be the imagined experience for Hodge's Tee. In presenting features of society people may want to think about, or that can help readers to articulate alternate paths, Senior's novel goes beyond a simple critique of education.[41] Yet it also suggests that reform is not the sole purview of one individual or entity even as Celia asserts her agency.

Mrs. Samphire's transformation over the course of the novel also represents a model for radical, personal change. Through a candid process of introspection, she redirects her energy into privileging her community. During her tenure in the Ellesmere Lodge, she notices the unfairness in the reality that she is protected in that elite environment while most others in the community are suffering hardships, including with drugs, gang warfare, and police brutality (237). The language Senior uses here relates to a dissipating welfare state, where people are turning to other means due to a scarcity of access to resources and being punished for it by legal and extralegal authorities. As Mrs. Samphire ponders, "Poor people. Like those I came from. The ones who couldn't afford to take too much time off from work even when their children were killed" (237). While she previously desired to display that she was a cut above her neighbors, she realizes such a desire is warped and prejudiced. It only serves to continue a cycle of keeping oppressed people in their place. In response, she plans to use her resources to help make positive changes in her community; she envisions, in a sense, becoming an organic intellectual. The emphasis here is that though Mrs. Samphire's reach is not the same as Celia, who subverts the communications ISA, she still has something to offer and contribute to changing the surrounding circumstances. She comes to value her informal education and tasks herself with instructing and edifying others. She reveals specific types of training she wants to offer others, including how to build their own enterprises in their communities and, thus, collectively improve their lives. Although Mrs. Samphire intentionally separates herself from her neighbors in earlier parts of the novel, claiming she is superior to them, she now aims to build alliances with them as well as cross-class alliances with the other residents in the upscale retirement home. The latter alliance begins when Mrs. Samphire initiates a gardening project for the home. The garden-building, in this instance, is symbolic of nation-building. For Senior, the garden is a symbol in many of her works, and gardening, especially small-scale, thoughtful, and diversified gardening, is a form of resistance and a productive alternative to corporate agriculture.[42] Ultimately, the inclusion of cross-class alliances and community-building in *Dancing Lessons* is instructive and a part of the resistance the novel purports to represent for readers.

Tee, Tantie, and Aunt Beatrice in Hodge's Narrative

At the end of her essay "From Juba's Head," Erna Brodber suggests that Hodge's character Tee will be like the character Avey in Paule Marshall's novel *Praisesong for the Widow*,[43] but this chapter proposes that Tee will be like Celia. Avey is the African American protagonist in Marshall's novel who moves from a working-class background to upper-middle-class status and sheds all connection with her Black culture in the process.[44] But then she experiences a reawakening in her sixties and decides to reconnect with her heritage and pass on traditions she was taught as a young person. Although Brodber's connection between Tee and Avey is comprehensible, it is possible to envision a more hopeful future for Tee. Brodber says the "Tee in us can go back, as Avey did, to find our true-true name and after this journey, thus armed, do what we feel has to be done to make our world a better place."[45] However, my chapter submits that the "Tee in us" does not have to wait until she is in her senior years and has spent a lifetime rejecting and being ashamed of her culture. Instead, the "Tee in us" can choose, like Celia, to participate now in building and strengthening our communities, including via subversive means. Hodge's novel uses the character Tee to exemplify the need for education reform because of its importance to the development of a nation beyond perpetual cycles of social and economic inequalities.[46]

During Tee's childhood, Tantie and her community's response to and interaction with the local schools illuminate the lack of a welfare state and how some characters play a part in the reproduction of the very system they despise. *Dancing Lessons* does not provide nearly as much detail about the specifics of Celia's education as *Crick Crack, Monkey* does for Tee, so my analysis in this section takes a slightly different approach. As Hodge's novel describes, Tee's first school experiences are in a working-class neighborhood under the guardianship of her paternal aunt, Rosa (better known as Tantie) because her father travels abroad to England after Tee's mother dies while giving birth to another child. The first school scene in the narrative illustrates Tantie literally racing against other guardians to the government school ("Big-school") to enroll Tee because there are a limited amount of spaces for students. The narrator explains that some of them are actually Tantie's friends, but because they all so earnestly want their individual children to claim a spot in the school, they act as if they do not know each other and enter into a fierce competition against one another. Detailing Tee's school enrollment process, the scene lays emphasis on the struggles Tantie's working-class community experiences to get children in formal schools. They almost assault one another, inflicting bodily harm, as they are a step away from "pushing each other" and even "running over the fallen" (24). The scene represents a failure of the government to provide adequate school infrastructure and accompanying necessities to accommodate the number of children in the community, as all of their children deserve a right to education. The description also invokes for readers the difficult questions of what they should or can do instead; possible answers come later in the novel. In this pre-independence setting, winning independence is an ultimate solution; yet, the novel's final scene suggests resistance capabilities, even if in minor ways.

Opportunity and choice are lacking in this working-class community as they are in Senior's novel, and Hodge's novel emphasizes that inadequate school provisions keep the working-class characters in their place—at the bottom of society with no suitable options. Hodge's novel, in essence, looks toward educational reforms, particularly in relation to the need for expanded (physical and quality) access to school. Hodge says in an interview that an increase in educational opportunities, including to secondary and postsecondary education, occurred after independence.[47] Still, education scholars reveal that the absence of adequate educational facilities and related essentials, which were problems in the pre-independence period, remain problems in the contemporary period to varying extents.[48] In this post-independence era, Trinidad and Tobago, a high-income nation-state in the Anglophone Caribbean, has a government that recognizes reforming various aspects of its education system is crucial for its continued growth in the twenty-first century.[49] Its government also acknowledges that all sectors of the society still do not have adequate access to education, and the Ministry of Education submits that education "not only provides citizens with more employment opportunities . . . but also improves citizens' social status and skills,"[50] even as it simultaneously documents the low performance rates of schools with students from poor backgrounds.[51]

Through Tee's observations of her educational environments, *Crick Crack, Monkey* critiques the inadequacies of Tee's schooling, including the teachers, the curriculum, and the impact on Tee, to demonstrate that Tee and her peers are not being primed to rise above their parents' stations in life, but to maintain the status quo—which evokes Althusser's claim about the educational ISA. Even Tee notices that something is awry with the conditions at the Hinds' school that she attends in Tantie's community. The teacher spends most of her time knitting instead of teaching (27), and shortly after Tee arrives at school, the students are let out for recess after hardly doing any class work. They do nothing meaningful to expand their basic skills. Tee is confused, knowing that she is supposed to be learning to read and write (25–26). An education from a school of such caliber will not pave the way to upward mobility for these working-class students. In fact, the experiences at such a school train them to stay in their place, which is at the bottom of the class hierarchy where they simply reproduce class inequality.

Underscoring Althusser's premise that the educational ISA drills into students the dominant or ruling ideology of the society, *Crick Crack, Monkey* notes the oppressive nature of the schools in Hodge's imagined community, as they inculcate British superiority among other beliefs and behaviors that encourage rejection of Caribbean culture. Through overt references to colonial powers in Tee's school scenes, the novel disavows the primacy or influences of foreign cultural systems within Caribbean societies. The model text for Tee's penmanship lessons reads, "The disciple is not greater than the master" (60), while she and her peers would recite at other times, "Children of the Empire Ye are Brothers All, or sing God Save the King and Land of Hope and Glory" (28). Instead of learning local and national knowledge that will build their self-esteem, the students internalize a sense of inferiority, causing Tee to create an imaginary version of herself, Helen, who represents a foreign culture and way of life (67). Scholars of Trinidadian education June George and Theodore Lewis discuss the significance of the content of learning materials, arguing that "children in developing countries are likely to be more motivated and to be better positioned to learn if their background knowledge and experiences are catered for in the teaching/learning milieu."[52] Such messaging is not subtle in Hodge's narrative, which predates this scholarship by decades.

Tantie expresses cognizance of the dangers of the information to which Tee may be exposed in school, and she despises having to take Tee to the school run by the Hinds family, as she does not approve of what they will expose to Tee. Using Creole to highlight Tantie's social class and level of education, Hodge fashions Tantie to deliver the warning to Tee not to allow the school to put trash in her head, exclaiming, "Jus' you remember you going there to learn book do' let them put no blasted shit in yu head" (25).[53] Tantie cautions Tee and tries to circumvent Tee accepting any teachings to which Tantie would object. While Tantie communicates that Tee should reject the values of the school (and later, Beatrice), Tantie does not provide Tee with clear instruction on what she should do. This scene highlights a fine line concerning education, as guardians want their children to acquire skills that can help them improve their standing, but do not want them to be taught to be a cog in the inequality cycle of society. Althusser expresses that besides children learning "to read, to write and to add" in school, they also learn "submission to the rules of the established order, i.e. a reproduction of submission to the ruling ideology."[54]

Moreover, Hodge's use of a cross-class relationship draws overt attention to the differences between Tantie's and Beatrice's households and lifestyles, allowing readers to view the family dynamics that play a major role in Tee's development of class consciousness as well as her educational experiences. Though both aunts subscribe to class hierarchies that increase their antagonism for each other, they mutually agree that Tee should move and attend the prestigious secondary school St. Ann's, in her maternal aunt Beatrice's community, after Tee performs well on her primary school exit examination and wins a scholarship. Similar to Mrs. Samphire's decision, their decision reinforces that a well-rounded or good quality education is a class privilege. As scholars Loraine D. Cook and Zellynne Jennings-Craig note, success in such examinations "is essential to gain entry into prestigious secondary schools that open the gateway to tertiary education and good employment prospects for the select few. For the others the future brings many hardships."[55] The "select few" and "many hardships" imply a lacking welfare state, insufficient to meet the needs in Tantie's community. Hence, Tantie recognizes that Tee should attend the school in Beatrice's community. Readers witness Tee's transition to living with Beatrice, a lighter-skinned Afro-Caribbean who models herself on English respectability (which brings together intersections of white superiority, sexual chastity, and education), after being under the care of Tantie, a darker-skinned Afro-Caribbean who curses gratuitously, drinks alcohol heavily, and who has quite an active sexual life despite being unmarried—all very much in contrast to the colonial politics of respectability. Unfortunately, Tee becomes increasingly alienated as she moves from Tantie's home to Beatrice's home; she ultimately can be at home in neither.

Under the gaze of the young character Tee, the novel emphasizes that Beatrice desires educational attainment for her family as it can help them participate in reproducing the power relations they witness—where working-class people like Tantie with their "ordinaryness" (105) remain excluded from access to resources Beatrice's family enjoys. In contrast to Tantie's disapproval of the schools in her community, Beatrice is invested in the school in her community and ensures her children take advantage of the privilege of attending the prestigious St. Ann's school. Hodge's characterization of Beatrice aligns with social historical studies of Trinidad concerning education, social mobility, and securing professional occupations.[56] Further, Beatrice reflects the existence of those in society who will always attempt to mimic those with power even as the powerful never allow them access to means to improve their conditions. Accepting European-ness and whiteness as standards for which she must aim, Aunt Beatrice imitates the model of a good woman based on the elite European woman who is a housewife with servants.[57]

Analysis of Tee's time under Beatrice's guardianship reveals that the novel not only shows the oppression of colonial education but also how school systems and families reinforce the color-class hierarchy in Trinidad during pre-independence. Beatrice's adoration of light skin color is also characteristic of some in Trinidadian middle classes during this period. Prestige was associated with lighter skin color and upward social mobility; therefore, it was not uncommon for a darker person to marry a lighter person in hopes of lightening the progeny.[58] The text makes visible the intersections of not only race but also skin tone, class, and gender. Like Tee, one of Beatrice's daughters, Jessica, is darker-skinned because her father, Norman, is darker and complains that the people at school only choose the fair-skinned girls. Beatrice, with a lack of sympathy, exclaims, "The darker you are the harder you have to try, I am tired of telling you that!" (92). Having no desire to see this reality changed, Beatrice continues to play by discriminatory and (self-)destructive rules, which have an ill effect on her daughter and Tee.

Furthermore, the novel illustrates the traumatic experiences Tee suffers from her schooling as well as Beatrice's acceptance of people's hierarchical positioning in society being connected to colorism and color-coding systems associated with having a lighter skin tone. Beatrice praises the white ancestress in the family and informs Tee that Tee's physical appearance does not measure up, specifically stating that Tee may have looked like her beautiful, light-skinned, now-deceased mother if it had not been for the gene pool of Tee's father (90). Tee's physical appearance and the fact that Tee did not grow up in circumstances akin to those of the other middle-class students cause her to suffer the treatment of a pariah. While Tee performs well at St. Ann's, she experiences rejection by academic and extracurricular teachers. For instance, the history teacher Mrs. Wattman, who adores Beatrice's lighter daughter, insists that Tee is a lost cause even though Tee consistently earns top grades (108). Some scholars of Caribbean education note that skin color continues to play a role in educational systems.[59] This is not totally unexpected given that global society still privileges white and lighter skin. Thus, Beatrice's lighter-toned daughter is aware her lighter skin color is a form of capital and that her lighter hue can afford her the benefit of not having to work as hard as others, so she does not take advantage of the privilege of attending a well-resourced school—frequently coming in toward the bottom of the class with low grades yet remaining the teacher's favorite.[60] Commenting on colorism in an interview, Senior states that education "has been the main route out of poverty for dark-skinned people who have had fewer options in this society than the light-skinned. But people perceive different paths—color is seen as one important path which is why some bleach their skins. It's about perception. People perceive other paths, and one of them is race, or in having the right skin color, hair texture."[61] The impact of privileging lighter skin is so strong, some people go to extreme and dangerous measures. While Beatrice is aware of Tee's mistreatment due to her appearance and working-class rearing, it does not seem to be of grave concern to her, as she offers no effective consolation and pressures Tee to conform and try to imitate other middle-class children. Beatrice further abuses Tee verbally, describing her behavior as "ordinariness" and "niggeryness" (105). Ultimately, Tee vacillates between trying to live up to someone else's ideals as Celia does in *Dancing Lessons* and trying to be invisible (114).

Crick Crack, Monkey demonstrates that even with limited resources, Tantie and the working-class she represents can resist existing unequal power relations. In the final scene in the novel, Tantie, recognizing the negative impacts on Tee of living with Beatrice, is motivated to resist in order to protect Tee and allow her to potentially become like the adult version of Celia, who contributes to her society in meaningful ways even as she takes advantage of systems that perpetuate social and economic inequalities. Tee remains a child in need of a guardian throughout the novel and is unable to exercise agency in the way Celia does in Senior's novel. Tantie's peculiar eyeing of Tee during a short trip to visit Tee at Beatrice's home and then abrupt departure signal that it was Tantie who prompted Tee's father to send a plane ticket for Tee and her brother to live with him abroad. Ironically, Tantie previously was firmly opposed to Tee leaving, going on a rampage (121). In this final scene, however, the narrative indicates that Tantie decides the best way for her to intervene and interrupt Tee's further demise is for Tee to leave altogether. Tee returning to her was not a viable option, as her community still lacked quality schooling that could benefit Tee. Moreover, patriarchy and capitalism inform Tantie's position relative to that of Tee's father. He lives abroad with access to greater resources without the women-associated duty of child caretaking that the patriarchal society imposes. This lack of an option also evokes the earlier scene from the novel when Tantie and her friends run against one another to enroll the children in school, and the matter of inadequate school provisions remains unresolved. While the ending is ambiguous as readers do not know what will happen to Tee after she relocates, this chapter envisions the young Tee becoming like Celia—someone who goes abroad and returns to her home country to play an active, positive role—instead of focusing on potential horrors that may await her in Europe.

An earlier scene also displays that Tantie has knowledge of the operation of systems in her society and an ability to resist, and it involves Tantie regaining custody of Tee and her brother from Beatrice when the children were younger. Beatrice uses police force to remove Tee and her brother from Tantie's home, but Tantie takes action and creates a plan to win back custody (34). Tantie says of Beatrice, "Well she know big-shot, yu know, big-shot in all kinda Government office, Father-priest and thing—so she get this paper. But we wipe we backside with she paper . . . [when] I get a statement from Selwyn" (43)—that is, when she receives a reply from Tee's father to a letter that requested he place Tee and her brother in Tantie's care. Tantie is aware of the workings of the law and how to maneuver despite not having the cultural capital and networks of Beatrice. The novel suggests Tantie can make a difference and needs to bring that mentality in approaching other areas in her community. Just as she triumphed in this situation, she can triumph in others even if only in miniscule ways. These two scenes stand in contrast to the early scene where she laments about the lack of school choices: "We marched down to Mrs. Hinds, Tantie muttering all the way her disapproval and disgust blasted government wouldn' build school for the chirren what the blasted government there for but to build school for the chirren now look my cross I have to put the chile by these shift-ers" (24–25). The language in this quote emphasizes, again, the lack of a well-functioning welfare state and Tantie's perspective on it. Tantie has the potential to be an organic intellectual, even as she has not yet fully recog-nized her ability to make more drastic changes in her community.[62] Within a working-class context, community is esteemed and significant as it is needed to combat the ruling body; engaging a counter-ideology is necessary. The cir-cumstances of Tantie's community are reminiscent of the working-class com-munity on Thirty-Fifth Street in Turner's novel, discussed in chapter 1. The students never gain access to better resources, and the same conditions con-tinue until the foreseeable struggle for national independence. Just as in the U.S. context, local schools should not be left to their own devices; a national plan that can offer equal access is essential to the growth, productivity, and functioning of a nation.[63]

THIS CHAPTER CONCLUDES with words from Hodge and Senior that invite resistance to and interruption of anything that seeks to preserve a biased status quo or unhealthy state of affairs. In "Challenges of the Struggle for Sovereignty," Hodge advises that "the power of the creative word to change the world is not to be underestimated."[64] Senior makes a similar point about the power of creative writing, stating that it "can be used as a tool for a wider examination of society as well as for introspection and personal engagement."[65] Both of these novels provoke a range of musings about ways to combat the negative circumstances portrayed. These authors, along with scholars of education, history, and cultural studies, recognize that unequal access to education is a problem, as it stunts the overall development of a nation.[66] Education and class still go hand in hand, and to pretend other-wise is a disservice to all who make up a nation.

In analyzing the portrayal of working-class and middle-class family units as well as institutions of education, this chapter contends that *Crick Crack, Monkey* and *Dancing Lessons* use a cross-class relationship trope to engage in a politics of resistance by not only exposing the complicities and contradic-tions of working and middle classes but also by suggesting alternate routes and designing characters who act subversively to combat inequalities. Through their novels, these writers remind readers of the political power associated with literature. In reality, literature was a part of the European colonial regime to oppress Caribbean people, as it encouraged a rejection of their world that seemed to never measure up to the one portrayed in Euro-pean stories. Senior's novel directly fashions a character (Celia) who makes it her profession to strengthen the image of and build her fictive Jamaican society even as she throws off foreign domination represented by her white American adoptive parents. Hodge's novel represents possibilities for participation in nation-building via the young character Tee who could become a Celia-like figure. Both novels ultimately confront the connection between education and upward class mobility through portrayals of the impact of schooling on characters who experience it in different socioeconomic environments. The right to education, like many human rights discussed in the next chapter, needs continued protection in this neoliberal era.

CHAPTER FOUR

Human Rights and Wrongs

*Violations to a Decent Standard of Living in
Diana McCaulay's* Dog-Heart

> Human rights, whose application is a transnational process,
> offer guidelines for consciousness raising and social praxis
> within global civil society.
>
> —FAYE V. HARRISON, *Resisting Racism and Xenophobia*

The intersection of human rights and neoliberalism has captured the attention of those within and beyond international human rights organizations.
The neoliberalism paradigm undermines the very institutions upon which
economic, social, and cultural rights, in particular, depend. The emphasis
on privatizing, curtailing the welfare state, and having a deregulated global
market are some of its most destructive features. Literary depictions of
these jeopardized rights appear in contemporary fiction, including in Jamaican writer Diana McCaulay's *Dog-Heart*.[1] McCaulay, a native and life-
long resident of Jamaica, does not shy away from the many controversial
issues affecting Jamaican society within the pages of her narratives. Her
debut novel, *Dog-Heart* (2010), is a prime example, as it tackles class prejudices and the gap between different classes, specifically Kingston's "uptown" (middle-class) and "downtown" (working-class) inhabitants, or those
who make up the so-called "Two Jamaicas."[2] The award-winning *Dog-Heart*
is set in present-day Kingston, Jamaica, and chronicles the cross-class relationship between two protagonists: a middle-class woman, Sahara, and a
working-class or inner-city youth, Dexter. While McCaulay's novel explicitly explores class prejudices, it also alludes to the effects of neoliberal globalization on the lives of its Caribbean characters and the human rights
violations that some of them endure.[3] Through the portrayals of Sahara and
Dexter, whose association represents the larger relationship between the
narrative's middle-class and inner-city characters, McCaulay's novel acts as
a cultural lens through which to view the intersections of class relations,
globalization, and human rights. More specifically, this chapter argues that
the use of the cross-class relationship trope in McCaulay's *Dog-Heart* operates to identify and foreground human rights violations as a demonstration

of the limited efficacy of human rights treaties in the novel's imagined contemporary Jamaican society and to offer the fortifying of the welfare state as a solution to specific human rights abuses.

McCaulay's inclusion of the term "globalization" early in the novel alerts readers to its significance and its impact on the lives of her characters. When Sahara details her duties as the manager at Summer Lion, a restaurant that her friend owns, she mentions their use of fresh Jamaican produce. She remarks that using only Jamaican produce has "become a challenge — globalization meant it was now easier to buy seedless grapes than mangoes from local vendors" (20). Although cognizant of the way that globalization influences her particular market choices, Sahara fails to see the ways in which globalization and accompanying (or worsening) structural constraints have affected others in the nation, especially those in Dexter's community. Due to the organization of the novel, however, readers have access to the worlds of both Sahara and Dexter and are privy to the conditions each faces. Organized around a cross-class narrative structure, *Dog-Heart* reinforces the juxtaposition between Sahara's and Dexter's lives by using the two protagonists as alternating first-person narrators throughout the novel.[4] The novel's arrangement facilitates comparisons and contrasts between their personal environments, particularly their material realities, family structures, and worldviews. Furthermore, McCaulay's novel effects a parallel between the lighter-skinned Sahara and the darker-skinned Arleen (Dexter's mother), who are both single mothers; so even though *Dog-Heart* is narrated in the voices of Sahara and Dexter and they present the primary cross-class relationship, Dexter's family is also implicated in that relationship. By exploring Sahara's relationship with Dexter and his family members, the novel provides a fuller view of various predicaments facing the working-class characters. According to a number of globalization and human rights scholars, the conditions surrounding many downtown Jamaican households exemplify human rights abuses; this chapter explores how McCaulay's novel, depicting examples of these abuses in the scenes that feature Dexter and Arleen, represents advocacy for human rights as well as for the restoration or preservation of the dwindling welfare state, which should protect from unnecessary suffering and allow a less unequal playing field.[5]

Through a layered narrative with multiple plot threads, *Dog-Heart* enters a discourse on various types of disparities, as a brief summary elucidates. Dexter's opening scene in the novel, in which he narrates how he and Sahara initially meet, is what first illuminates their contrasting life experiences. Sahara and her teenage son, Carl, are leaving a movie theater at

Sovereign Plaza in uptown Kingston, a place with mainly middle- and upper-class patrons. In contrast, Dexter is at Sovereign Plaza, the place where "plenty rich people go" (14), to beg money of the patrons, which is how he helps to feed his family. Dexter cannot imagine being able to frequent the movie theater as a pastime, while Sahara not only pays to see a movie but also has enough money left over to give Dexter five hundred Jamaican dollars. Speaking in the Jamaican language, Dexter exclaims, "Me can't believe it, no way at all. Nobody ever—*ever* give me five hundred dollar" (17; emphasis in original). Though this amount is roughly equivalent to five U.S. dollars, Dexter's excited reaction lets readers know how large a sum of money this is in his world. Here, Dexter is reminiscent of the character Willie in Naylor's *Linden Hills* who cannot identify with the luxuries of the middle-class characters. The narrative goes on to chronicle Sahara's decision to help Dexter's family and to find sponsors to pay the educational expenses for Dexter and his siblings to attend uptown schools. Because their relationship begins in a community space, the best description for their relationship is a cross-class community-based relationship—albeit a vexed one. Not only do the overall differences in their worldviews present major obstacles for their relationship, but Sahara's preconceived notions about Dexter and his family serve as additional barriers. Despite Sahara's haphazard efforts to help Dexter and his family, the novel closes with Dexter assisting in the kidnapping of Sahara as part of a gang initiation. Ultimately, however, Dexter rebels against his accomplices and allows Sahara to go free.[6]

This chapter underscores *Dog-Heart's* position within a larger framework of globalization and human rights discussions. Over the past few decades, literary artists and an increasing number of scholars from various disciplines have been active participants in the growing debate over the interconnections between globalization and human rights. To define *human rights*, I follow scholar Alison Brysk, who regards them as "a set of claims and entitlements to human dignity, which the existing international regime assumes will be provided (or threatened) by the state."[7] Elaborating on this definition, cultural anthropologist Faye V. Harrison explains human rights as "the morally and legally justifiable claims to dignity, liberty, personal security and basic well-being that all persons can make by virtue of being human."[8] The contemporary phase of globalization—or what Brysk defines as "the growing interpenetration of states, markets, communications, and ideas across borders"[9]—has generated a substantial amount of scholarship concerning the benefits and costs associated with its transnational interactions. One great concern is that the conditions of globalization have led to an increase in human rights violations throughout the world.[10] The correlation between the two is not a simple matter, as various factors ranging from the dynamic process of globalization to the policies of international institutions and corporations play a role. These issues and other socioeconomic and political questions raised in *Dog-Heart* are also part of a larger literary conversation; along with novels like Garfield Ellis's *For Nothing at All*, Olive Senior's *Dancing Lessons*, Oonya Kempadoo's *Tide Running*, Edwidge Danticat's *The Dew Breaker*, and Marlon James's *A Brief History of Seven Killings*, *Dog-Heart* belongs to a rich tradition of contemporary fiction interrogating such issues in the context of neoliberal iterations of globalization in postcolonial Caribbean societies. According to Harrison, Jamaica, in particular, is experiencing a human rights crisis.[11] Significantly, deteriorating human rights affect class positions and neoliberal globalization has contributed to the present-day growth in class inequalities including because of its shunning a functioning or active welfare state.[12]

Structural Adjustment Programs/Policies/Packages (SAPs) are significant, visible features of neoliberalism's presence in Jamaica and many other Caribbean nations. SAPs are established by lending agencies, including the International Monetary Fund (IMF) and World Bank (WB), that Jamaica has been seeking assistance from or has been in connection with since the 1970s. They determine or dictate to a large extent how the nation's economic and political systems will operate.[13] They facilitate a dependency relationship and a national debt cycle at the same time that they discourage social welfare or government programs that aid the nation's disenfranchised. Individual or personal responsibility is privileged over public or collective responsibility in the neoliberal paradigm, which endangers the human rights of vulnerable populations. McCaulay's novel serves to further the emancipatory project of exposing human rights violations in order to rectify them.[14] Since the 1970s, literature has been central to human rights advocacy, being frequently featured in campaigns across the globe.[15] *Dog-Heart* demonstrates what is at stake for segments of McCaulay's imagined Jamaican society in the continued absence or neglect of human rights justice; the novel brings attention to inequalities in an attempt to weaken an unjust status quo and help bring about constructive transformations.

McCaulay's *Dog-Heart* participates in a discussion of human rights as they are outlined specifically in the International Covenant on Economic, Social and Cultural Rights (ICESCR). These have been jeopardized greatly under neoliberal globalization. In particular, the novel engages conversations that question the effectiveness of human rights treaties at the domestic (national) level.[16] Human rights are outlined in the International Bill of Human Rights, which consists of the Universal Declaration of Human Rights (1948), the International Covenant on Civil and Political Rights (1966), and the International Covenant on Economic, Social and Cultural Rights (1966). These documents were adopted by the United Nations General Assembly after the devastation of World War II. The latter covenant, the ICESCR, is under discussion in this chapter, and the chapter's focus is primarily on Article 11, which delineates "the right of everyone to an adequate standard of living for himself and his family, including adequate food, clothing and housing, and to the continuous improvement of living conditions," and Articles 6 and 7, which discuss the right to work.[17] The novel's allusion to this covenant is particularly important because global discussions of human rights tend to pay less attention to the rights outlined in the document; instead, a great deal of conversation tends to focus on civil and political rights.[18] The novel does not allow the rights expressed in the ICESCR to be overshadowed, even as the ICESCR standards are not beyond challenge and some standards may differ slightly depending upon geographical location.

Given that Jamaica ratified the ICESCR in 1975 and all the rights within it are still, to a large extent, not protected, *Dog-Heart* also facilitates a critique of a key human rights monitoring mechanism, which is state reporting. Approximately every four to five years, nations that have ratified human rights treaties must submit a report on their implementation of the treaties to a committee of experts (a treaty body), which then offers recommendations for improvement known as Concluding Observations (COs) in response to the report. While this monitoring system has been in use for decades, the continued failure of some nations to protect human rights raises a question about its relevance and effectiveness.[19] This background on human rights and the monitoring of them lays a foundation for discussing human rights violations depicted in the working-class communities in the novel.

Like a number of scholars, including Deborah Thomas, who notes the class segregation of Kingston's residential districts in her work on violence (103), McCaulay's fictional representation underscores the stark contrasts between the uptown and downtown areas of Kingston and their different standards of living, as she aligns her characters within contemporary class measures and the juxtaposition between Dexter's and Sahara's private lives points out the vast differences between them.[20] Through the descriptions of their family structure and relations, homes, and daily activities, including their means of securing money, readers are able to discern the gravity of the discrepancy in their lifestyles. Where Dexter and his family suffer human rights abuses while Sahara and those in her sphere tend to fare much better, the novel invites a key inquiry about who will ensure that human rights are protected.

The Rights to Adequate Housing and Food

While human rights treaties should protect every citizen in the nation once ratified, McCaulay's novel shows characters that are affected in different ways even within the same national community, resulting in a situation where the aim of human rights work to guarantee adequate housing and food remains "unrealized in practice."[21] This section details comparisons between Sahara's and Dexter's housing conditions as well as access to food and then emphasizes the place of the welfare state. The novel's middle-class protagonist, Sahara, represents what is in effect the control group in McCaulay's narrative exploration of human rights effectiveness, while working-class Dexter represents the experimental group that is radically affected by the failure to ensure that human rights are upheld. The novel shows how the middle class experiences a level of security against the "escalated cost of living" during the current phase of globalization.[22] McCaulay uses the actual Kingston neighborhood of Mona as Sahara's locale, stating in an interview that "Mona is, by definition, a middle-class address. Middle-class, professional."[23] Moreover, McCaulay draws our attention to the issue of color and class. Sahara is of mixed heritage, as her father is an "English missionary" (26), and her mother is an Afro-Jamaican schoolteacher. Dexter describes Sahara as a "browning," a lighter-skinned woman, "who represents the 'uptown' middle-class ideal woman of mixed race," as Patricia Mohammed writes, noting further that "the origin of this ideal [comes] from the 'mulatto' woman bred in slavery."[24] The intersectionality of Sahara's lighter hue (race and color) and her parents' positions in the society (class) afford her benefits that many others are not granted. Besides being white, her father is also a pastor, a position of authority in her childhood community. Although he eventually abandons his family after having an affair with one of the members of his congregation, Sahara continues to have a level of privilege, as her mother raises her with the aid of household helpers in the Mona neighborhood, and Sahara inherits the Mona house after her mother's death.

By portraying Sahara as a person of middle-class rather than upper-class status, the novel reinforces the idea that human rights disparities are not simply a matter of extremes where those who are at the top of the socioeconomic hierarchy have their rights protected and those at the bottom do not.

Rather, McCaulay's more nuanced representation suggests that a more detailed and complex monitoring mechanism is needed because rights violations are not clear-cut. Sahara's descriptions of her belongings disclose that she is not at the top of the social hierarchy. The description of her house, which she labels "modest" (29), and the changing circumstances in the community illuminate her somewhat vulnerable position within the narrative's middle-class Jamaica. As she narrates, "The house itself was unremarkable, three small bedrooms, a living/dining room, small porch, two bathrooms and a kitchen" (37). Reminiscent of Lester's house in Naylor's *Linden Hills* discussed in chapter 1, the house is not lavish, but she is happy with it, and her right to housing appears not to be violated. The UN Committee on Economic, Social and Cultural Rights (UNCESCR), whose job it is to make sure nations are adhering to the covenant, notes in its General Comment 4 that "the right to housing should not be interpreted in a narrow or restrictive sense which equates it with, for example, the shelter provided by merely having a roof over one's head. . . . Rather it should be seen as the right to live somewhere in security, peace and dignity."[25] According to this description, however, McCaulay's character may or may not have adequate housing, in that items are stolen on a regular basis from the houses in Sahara's community from people outside the community. The theft suggests the existence of lack on the part of the thieves who take items to fulfill a need or sell the items to fulfill a need. Sahara claims to be grateful that her car is older, since it will not be of interest to potential thieves. Moreover, McCaulay's novel places Sahara in an ambiguous position within the middle class, which is an uncanny resemblance to some human rights treaties, which use ambiguous language—causing a hindrance to their implementation.[26] Various interpretations to ICESCR terminology lead to various plans of action, which may not all advance the original intended objective. Earlier in the narrative, when Sahara drives away from Sovereign Plaza in her old Volkswagen, Dexter comments that most uptown people drive SUVs. Her ordinary car sheds additional light on her place within the portrayed middle-class community. Nevertheless, although Sahara is not at the top of the hierarchy, she admits that she and Carl enjoy a level of security and privilege that many others do not.

While Sahara's circumstances may complicate ideas of the effectiveness of human rights treaties, the living experiences of her counterpart Dexter and his family on the other side of town in the Jacob's Pen community establish that the existence of human rights treaties alone cannot correct injustice. In the scenes displaying Dexter's housing and access to food,

McCaulay's narrative severely interrogates, as a number of scholars do, the relevance of the rights outlined in the ICESCR, given the reality that they are not being upheld for everyone. Even when nations complete the periodic report and conceal or admit their failure to secure specific rights, the report results in yet another document (the CO) but does not translate into fulfilled rights. Meaningful interventions, particularly rectifying why the nation cannot fulfill these rights, are needed. Yet, this is easier said than done when all fingers point toward economic market-driven neoliberal policies that handicap nations that are already strapped for resources.[27] Dexter and his family members appear to be in a near-helpless situation and unable to truly improve their circumstances. They are struggling just to survive, and their chances of having a better standard of living or achieving upward mobility seem dismal.

The descriptions of Dexter's community display, in fictive form, examples of human rights abuses that the most recent CO document notes are happening in Jamaica. To improve the conditions of the "acute housing situation," the Committee recommends that Jamaica "adopt a comprehensive national housing strategy with a view to ensuring access to adequate and affordable housing with legal security of tenure for everyone . . . [and that the strategy be] developed based on a systematic needs assessment and consultation with and participation by affected individuals."[28] One problem with such a course of action, however, is that the perspectives of those in communities like Dexter's tend to be ignored. McCaulay's name for Dexter's neighborhood, Jacob's Pen, is itself significant in that a pen represents a holding place, usually for animals, and it references a spatial structure dating from slavery, where a pen was used on a type of estate (usually for coffee). Whether or not this is the author's intention, this name symbolizes the conditions in Dexter's community and the devaluing of its residents. Further, how can the nation implement such plans if directives from international lending agencies prevent it, as some governments have reduced capacity to intervene in the housing market as a result of SAPs.[29] By alluding to and highlighting such irony, McCaulay's novel reinforces calls for a thriving welfare state despite it being counter to the neoliberal agenda. A well-functioning welfare state in my analysis is one that offers a "standard of income, nutrition, health, housing, and education [that] enables individuals to thrive, rather than just survive, and is provided as a right, not as charity."[30]

McCaulay's *Dog-Heart* mimics the type of language present in COs, highlighting the redundancy of certain terms in descriptions of Jamaican housing and contesting the effectiveness of the repeated COs that continually use such phrases. Within a particular COs document, the Committee mentions "overcrowded, unsafe and dilapidated housing,"[31] and McCaulay's narrative echoes such terms and is unsparing in its upsetting descriptions of Dexter's surroundings. Not only do the descriptions of Dexter's neighborhood paint a picture of a below-average standard of living, but they also depict an environment that looks like a war zone, which obviously does not meet the standards of adequate housing outlined in the covenant: "The place looked bombed—buildings were windowless and defaced with political graffiti. The rich ones in Jacob's Pen lived in unrendered concrete houses, half constructed, with steel emerging from flat roofs—a second floor planned, even though the ground floor was unfinished" (46). A roof over one's head is not sufficient to merit the term "housing"; yet, Dexter and his family seem to have only a little more than that with their one-room low-cost Habitat for Humanity house built by foreigners that is bare and lacks basic amenities. The scene, focused on those who are supposedly better off than others in the community, describes the poor construction of the housing and invokes wartime images to emphasize the hardships as well as to invoke the presence of the government. Political graffiti alludes to government or political figures vying for the votes of the people in these communities despite not improving conditions. The scene also symbolizes the warlike terror of living in this community and underscores that in times of peace some people are still subjected to physical environs that mimic war conditions.

Among its other inadequacies, Dexter's family's home does not fully accommodate the family's size, and Dexter's narration reveals how the house contrasts with the UNCESCR's normative description of housing, including "adequate privacy, adequate space, adequate security, adequate lighting and ventilation, adequate basic infrastructure and adequate location with regard to work and basic facilities—all at a reasonable cost."[32] In descriptions of Dexter's home, McCaulay plays on the common illegal practice of "stealing" electricity, a practice that the Jamaica Public Service Company, which is the primary electricity distributor in Jamaica, has reported as increasing in recent times.[33] The text reads: "One lamp on dresser near TV. That is where we steal the light. Marlon father—him a 'lectrician—he take light from public service pole on that side a the house" (59). The father of Dexter's younger brother, Marlon, represents the many who use this method due to adverse circumstances that render them unable to pay for electricity. Dexter, who is twelve years old at this point in the narrative, describes a house that survives on theft and is filled with barely functional items. He recognizes the condition of his home and is ashamed as a result.[34] This scene also calls for a critique of stealing electricity. This act can be a type of resistance or subversive tactic to get repair for the economic injury the government has inflicted. Hence, the novel's description of this activity invokes a shifting of how we think about those who actively get their needs met in the absence of the welfare state operating better. Dexter and his family exert much effort to address their needs, but they still fall short due to circumstances beyond their control.

The narrative's use of the cross-class relationship trope also lays the groundwork for critiquing another provision outlined in the ICESCR, as Sahara and her family have access to "adequate food" and the enjoyment of being "free from hunger,"[35] while Dexter's family does not. While the Committee has been collecting reports from nations concerning the right to adequate food since the late 1970s, in 1999 it saw the need to add UNCESCR General Comment No. 12, which expounds on food rights, because the reports were insufficient in allowing monitoring of these rights.[36] It took the Committee a couple of decades to recognize that the monitoring mechanism was not working and to commit to making a change. Simply having ratified these treaties also does not erase the lack of agricultural education, the high cost of importing food, the lack of employment, or the occurrence of environmental conditions such as hurricanes, droughts, and floods—all of which affect food security.

In her portrayals of Sahara's family, McCaulay details scenes of food consumption in a family kitchen setting; such portrayals—that also display class markers—are absent in scenes featuring Dexter's family. Sahara and her now teenage son, Carl, are living alone in the Mona house, where the availability of daily meals is not a concern. Carl goes from complaining that they are having chicken again for dinner instead of steak (26) to saying, "I want french fries, swimming in oil and smothered in salt. With a steak. But I know what I'm going to *get* is an omelette and a salad" (124; emphasis in original).[37] Here, Sahara not only makes sure Carl has food but also that he has healthy eating habits, and they are able to bond over food at times when preparing a meal together. At age thirty-two, Sahara is a single parent who has never been married and the dynamics between the mother and son sometimes become tense and distant. The novel underscores the informal markers of class that dining together signifies, and food also becomes a metonym for a larger ecosystem that interrogates how one type of access feeds into and cultivates another. The intersections of Sahara's racial background and class upbringing work together to put her in networks with people who own businesses, including a restaurant, and who can employ her. Her employment allows her to sustain adequate housing and food for her family. Food insecurity, then, is not a serious concern for this family. In fact, Sahara is secure enough in her circumstances that she is able to bring bags of food to Dexter and his family on a regular basis.

Dexter becomes the novel's poster child for food insecurity, as his family's struggle to obtain food, or rather, to exercise their right to adequate food, exemplifies a continued history of insufficient human rights implementation. The UNCESCR recognized that Jamaica's difficulties in guaranteeing this particular right were "due to the frequency of natural hazards, inefficient farming practices, lack of suitable land, and increases in commodity prices." Yet its suggestion for ways to improve is vague and deficient, amounting to a recommendation that Jamaica "adopt effective long-term strategies aimed at improving domestic productivity in a sustainable manner and building the capacity of local farmers."[38] Neither the UNCESCR nor the state of Jamaica seems to have found a solution, however, and McCaulay's novel depicts potential costs: Dexter, the oldest of Arleen's three children, is largely responsible for providing for the basic needs of his family. In fact, Arleen, who is unemployed, sends him to beg for money every day after school so that they can eat. Still, Arleen is not a shiftless parent, as Dexter describes how she puts the children's needs before her own: "She don't eat so we will have food, she clean, cook and try keep us safe" (63). At each turn, the novel invokes the absence of the welfare state and the resulting deprivations in order to point to the welfare state as part of the solution to rectifying conditions.

The novel also points to the significance of social welfare services by having Sahara play the unofficial role as social worker to Dexter's family. Food becomes money and elicits excitement just as the five hundred Jamaican dollars do in Dexter and Sahara's first encounter. Unlike Carl, who complains of having chicken instead of steak for dinner, Dexter and his family are grateful for cheap fish and dumplings. They express joy when Sahara begins to bring food (53), and their great appreciation for basic ingredients adds to the novel's foregrounding of human rights injustices. Concerning food, General Comment 12 from the UNCESCR stipulates that the "right to adequate food is realized when every man, woman and child, alone or in community with others, has physical and economic access at all times to adequate food or means for its procurement."[39] By depicting that this is not the case in this Jacob's Pen household, McCaulay's novel challenges the practical relevance of General Comment 12 in people's everyday lives, as the descriptions reveal that Dexter and his family do not have "the availability of food in a quantity and quality sufficient to satisfy the[ir] dietary needs."[40] Reviewing compliance and noncompliance with regard to rights every few years, without meaningful suggestions and provisions for their effective execution, will continue to prove a futile endeavor. Sahara's imperfect role as unsupported social worker is insufficient. The novel urges for more meaningful interventions—not a reality in which international lending agencies such as the International Monetary Fund advise that food subsidies be abolished.[41]

The Right to Work and Its Dilemmas

Aside from the rights to housing and food, McCaulay's *Dog-Heart* suggests that a strengthened welfare state can be instrumental in securing the right to work or access to employment. Jamaica's Social Development Commission was established in 1965 by the Jamaica Social Welfare Commission Act, and it has been a part of advancing these rights for citizens, but neoliberalism, particularly SAPs, has led to the erosion of services in many respects. As a result, marginalized populations face limited employment options as well as high food prices and poor-quality housing.[42] While the pairing of the two protagonists allows McCaulay to show that Sahara is gainfully employed, it also reinforces "the global silencing and denial about the true costs of global capitalism" by underscoring Sahara's enjoyment of a sense of security that is absent among Dexter and his family.[43] Once Sahara becomes the breadwinner of her family, she finds employment "at a real estate firm doing their books" (29). She does not make an exorbitant amount of money there, but it is enough to take care of herself and Carl. The covenant's provisions call for people to be able to make a "decent living for themselves and their families," so readers clearly see that Sahara's "right to work" is being satisfied.[44] McCaulay reveals that Sahara is able to secure employment at the firm without prior experience or any formal education beyond "a good early education" (29). Some scholars suggest that Sahara's light skin color plays a role in helping her secure this employment due to the long history of a lighter skin color being associated with middle and elite classes and darker skin color being associated with working classes in Jamaica.[45] The novel parallels Sahara and Arleen, noting that one of the greatest distinguishing factors between them is class and color. In an interview, McCaulay notes that class and skin color are still very much connected in contemporary Jamaica: "If you're middle-class, you're more likely to be light-skinned. It's not a perfect correlation, of course, but if you walk around a downtown Kingston community, most people are going to be dark-skinned."[46] In *Downtown Ladies*, Gina A. Ulysse outlines a four-tier class structure in Jamaica—the lower class, middle class, upper class, and elites—and indicates that the majority Black population is largely a part of the lower class, while the middle class consists of a brown population.[47] For Sahara, then, her skin color "operates as a form of capital."[48] Sahara receives additional benefits that Dexter and his family do not because of her cultural capital and associations with other middle-class people. After the real estate job, Sahara becomes the manager of her friend's restaurant in Liguanea, an uptown Kingston area. Such connections or networking opportunities are vital, especially in a time when jobs are scarce. Not only does the job provide Sahara with stability, but it is also a source of enjoyment for her, which is not what Dexter and people in his area experience concerning employment.

By way of contrast with Sahara's job opportunities, McCaulay's novel demonstrates that the existence of the ICESCR is not alleviating the reality that employment in this period of neoliberal globalization is increasingly difficult to find for a large percentage of Jamaican working-class populations, as represented by Arleen.[49] Among Sahara's greatest frustrations with Arleen is her lack of employment; completely exasperated, Sahara questions in her interior monologue, "Why couldn't she get a proper job?" (186). Her inability to comprehend Arleen's situation leads Sahara to contemplate trying to take Dexter and his siblings from their mother's care (186). Sahara is irritated by and does not understand Arleen's actions, especially why she is not providing more for Dexter and his siblings. Her interior monologues, full of misunderstandings, cause readers to assess Sahara's complaints, scrutinize Arleen more closely, and consider what other factors could be contributing to the current state of Arleen's and her family's lives. Her thoughts provoke contemplation of whether fault lies on the personal level, the level of society, or some combination. Despite Sahara's frustrations, readers can see that Arleen is doing the best she can. Although much of her work is confined to the domestic realm, Arleen appears to gain some money from her sewing.[50] Jamaica has a history of women doing domestic work, which often pays poorly and causes women to struggle to provide for their children.[51] Dexter has responsibilities incommensurate with his age, as a result. Sahara is the neoliberal voice in these scenes, ignoring structural impediments in a way that is similar to the middle-class characters in the funeral wake scene in Naylor's *Linden Hills* discussed in chapter 1. Competitive wage employment opportunities have been limited under neoliberal globalization, as wages have remained stagnant since the 1970s in many places across the globe. The global market, far from being unbiased, is heavily influenced by those with the most capital, yet a neoliberal lens points to personal failure or responsibility when people are unable to find employment or experience upward mobility. A more sustained focus on the structural impediments—particularly in a globalized employment sector where many low-paying jobs are outsourced to the global South—might reframe or suggest possible solutions, including leveling the playing field through government programs that help people become self-sufficient

Focusing further on a lack of understanding in the novel, in an interview, McCaulay discloses: "I wanted [Arleen] to really irritate Sahara, because I wanted Sahara to fail to understand why she was not a better mother."[52] Sahara finds it rather difficult to sympathize with Arleen, although she too is a single parent wanting the best for her children.[53] Perhaps because their situations are so different, Sahara does not recognize the similarities between them. Toward the end of the narrative when Sahara is driving Arleen to St. Stephen's to investigate why Dexter sets fire to a school bathroom, one of Sahara's most candid and merciless observations of Arleen appears, as she describes Arleen as "an ugly woman" with "splayed teeth visible between her lips" and "hair badly creamed and styled" (186). In this scene, Sahara notes that the children had no advantages because of Arleen, but she does not take into account that Arleen, too, lacks advantages and has come from a background of hardship. Arleen's experiences have likely influenced her current situation.[54] Furthermore, what appears to be a lack of grooming, including the unkempt hair, ill-fitting clothes, and unbraced teeth, are all indicators of Arleen's class status; she is unable to afford to spend more on her appearance. Sahara fails to truly see Arleen and her observations seem to indicate that she believes Arleen simply needs to change her actions. Here, we see barriers in the cross-class relationships between Sahara and Arleen.

Sahara appears oblivious to the structural constraints that contribute to Dexter's and his family's situation, and how such hardships are characteristic of an increasingly globalized nation that finds itself unable to guarantee every right within the ICESCR. For many in Jacob's Pen, a real problem is a lack of available jobs, which is due to little or no structural support. This is perhaps the greatest misunderstanding in the cross-class relationship. Sahara does not comprehend that the gravity of the circumstances in Dexter's community is not simply a matter of behavioral impediments. To make a parallel between U.S. and diasporic contexts, there is a long-standing scholarly debate regarding whether social inequalities affecting African American communities are due to individuals' behaviors or social structures; Cornel West, in his well-known *Race Matters*, argues that a balance in this debate is necessary because the two cannot be separated. He explains that "how people act and live are shaped—though in no way dictated or determined—by the larger circumstances in which they find themselves."[55] Presenting this reality in literary form, McCaulay displays the complexities of her characters and their situations. Sahara also believes that getting an education will resolve all of Dexter's problems, but, actually, as McCaulay said in an interview, "the whole question of education is an example of the class divide in that, for the middle-class person, for Sahara, education is the answer."[56] The education system itself is closely tied to class, as discussed in chapter 3, in that those who live in communities with more money attend schools that are better equipped to help students succeed. Sahara fails to see the intricacies in Dexter's family situation and acts as if behavioral factors alone contribute to their predicament. Ironically, readers learn the complexity of Dexter's life and community through Sahara's failure to see the complexity, thus disqualifying her from being the unquestionable moral voice of the novel and highlighting the need for a system that can offer sustained support over the inconsistent goodwill behavior of individual citizens like Sahara.

Although she, too, is a single female who is heading her household, Sahara finds it difficult to sympathize with Arleen, who, representative of many, is being undercut in the job market under the conditions of contemporary globalization. A CO notes that "despite the higher educational attainment of women, their unemployment rate remains more than twice that of men."[57] Yet the topic of gender inequality in Jamaica pervades Caribbean feminist scholarship, so this news is not new. The ratification of the ICESCR has not moved the dial to complete equality, although many women have progressed substantially through the years. Sahara and Arleen share the fact that their color influences their gender vulnerability (Sahara as brown and Arleen as black), and, as single mothers, they also share the gendered position and experience of being vulnerable to men's exploitation. Mirroring a trope that occurs elsewhere in Caribbean women's writing, Carl's father's family, a white family from old money, rejects Sahara because of her color and class, and she is thus abandoned with her son: "In no time I was pregnant and Lester's horrified family had shipped him off to England" (28). She has no choice but to raise Carl alone.

Arleen, Black and impoverished, is even more vulnerable to men's sexual exploitation and abandonment. None of her three children's fathers is assisting her, and women often bear the brunt of social and economic austerity, as they are largely responsible for supporting their families.[58] McCaulay encapsulates these experiences via Arleen's and Sahara's characters. However, although they are both single mothers, the various intersections in Arleen's and Sahara's lives cause them to experience different life trajectories, and Sahara has a very limited perception that does not consider the larger factors at work. The material well-being of women has deteriorated, and gender inequality has increased due to neoliberal globalization, which, consequently, has intensified the "feminization of poverty."[59] McCaulay captures this via Arleen's character in *Dog-Heart*. Yet Sahara simply does not think Arleen is a good mother, since Sahara cannot imagine being in such dire straits. No one in her world has circumstances like those who live in Jacob's Pen.

The role of the government in helping citizens is at the forefront of answers to the questions of why there is a lack of available jobs and why human rights treaties are limited in their effectiveness. Governments are supposed to ensure the productivity of their nations and their citizens. In a scene narrated by Dexter, McCaulay alludes to Jamaica's former prime minister Michael Manley and his Land Lease Program that began during his first term in office: "That same Prime Minister everybody love, Michael Manley, him give land to poor people for growin food. Old people say everybody love that. But instead a farmin, the people sell off every bit a the land and Jacob's Pen don't have not even one piece a dirt leave that could grow a patch a callaloo. People not supposed to sell the land and now the government say everybody who live in the land leases part a Jacob's Pen is a squatter" (96). McCaulay's description here presents a close parallel to what happened in reality, as the program did not experience the success that the government desired. Exemplifying a component of a welfare state, a major purpose of the program was to increase employment for small farmers by providing them with land and resources.[60] It was not enough to bring and keep many people out of poverty, regrettably. Alongside land provisions, resources are needed to sustain the ecosystem, including strong agricultural education and updated or efficient tools to cultivate the land. Although the Jamaican government, as represented here, is not perfect (as no government is), many scholars reveal that the Jamaican government, like many other Caribbean governments, is quite limited in what it can do to assist its citizens because of the regulations of international monetary institutions to which it is beholden due to its debt burden.[61] In other words, the nation's hands are tied. Concerning human rights treaties, some nations simply do not have enough resources to meet the treaty obligations.[62] To get assistance with sustaining the nation's economy—even as it accumulates large sums of debt—the government has to abide by international lending policies that directly discourage or foreclose government intervention in people's personal circumstances.

Again, in pointing to the causes of the Jamaican government's quandary, many scholars cite neoliberal policies, which encourage deregulation, privatization, and unrestricted marketization. Many of the international lending institutions (such as the International Monetary Fund, the World Bank, and the World Trade Organization), which are supposedly helping countries such as Jamaica, have been promoting neoliberal policies for decades.[63] Global studies scholar Jan Aart Scholte is unconvinced of the overall effectiveness of these policies and discusses the disadvantages: "Fiscal austerity to improve 'global competitiveness' has often meant reductions in the amount and quality of state-provided education, housing, nutrition, health care, pensions and unemployment insurance. In sum, neoliberalist globalization has tended to erode the protective shield of the redistributive state."[64] The Jamaican government, like governments of similar debt-ridden nations, has been unable to create sustainable alternatives to the policies suggested and imposed by the international institutions.[65] Many nations in the global South turned to the institutions in hopes that they would receive assistance with economically fortifying the nations, but the policies (which some call austere) ultimately continued and worsened the dire circumstances. These policies affect employment, housing, and food provisions and clarify why Dexter and his family engage in illegal or underground activities (see figure 4.1).[66]

Having little to no other options, Dexter, like many others in his community, turns to illegal activities and participation in an underground economy. Quite simply, the residents of Jacob's Pen are trying to secure money to eat and to live. Some believe this is their only option since they have no other means of obtaining money due to a lack of available jobs. Later in the novel, Dexter contemplates the type of employment he may be able to secure when he becomes older; his list of legal options is limited and includes being a grocery packer, car washer, and security guard (119). Since the novel sets up Carl as a foil for Dexter, readers surmise that Carl's journey in life ultimately will end better than Dexter's, just as Sahara's life path is set to be more fulfilling than Arleen's. The ultimate significance for readers of this

FIGURE 4.1 A woman sells various clothing items in the street of a working-class Kingston, Jamaica, community, participating in an underground or informal economy (author's photo).

structural comparison between Dexter and Carl is to reiterate the key point of the limited efficacy of human rights treaties and to call for a thriving welfare state. Dexter's begging or panhandling is an informal way to get money, and many use begging as a means to try to meet their needs. Many do not qualify for the jobs that may be available because the jobs require some level of skill or education that they lack. The schools in their communities do not prepare them as well as schools in the uptown communities or enable them to thrive and possibly experience upward mobility, which is another way McCaulay represents human rights injustices, including the right to education, outlined in the ICESCR.[67] They also do not have adequate transportation to school because of a lack of buses, so some children have to take turns going to school. Although he does gain access to an uptown school, Dexter comes to believe that an education will not help him and that he needs to seek other means to improve his circumstances.

At the same time, the novel alludes to the reality of dons performing social and economic welfare roles in place of the government.[68] Dexter fears he is getting too old to beg, recognizing that people are less sympathetic the older he becomes. This reality—coupled with the constant humiliation from school officials and other students in the uptown school in which Sahara enrolls him—causes Dexter to turn to friends who are engaged in illegal and gang activities. These males and their performance of masculinity become a model of manhood for Dexter. As Michael A. Bucknor clarifies, "Jamaican masculinity is a matter of social construction and not biological determination."[69] Dexter begins to conform to the models he sees, as they are meeting some of his immediate needs, and he acknowledges that his "life start split in two—the daytime and the night-time. The schoolboy and the big man" (178). It appears that Dexter comes to equate manhood, money, and power with criminal activity, and to the detriment of many, Dexter becomes caught up with people who embody this view. In an interview, McCaulay comments on Dexter's downward spiral: "Who has money in an inner-city community? The local don or somebody who's selling drugs or another illegal activity. In the case of this novel, it's somebody who's doing illegal sand mining."[70] From this point, Dexter's life begins to go down a dark road, and he and his associates are eventually caught by the police and put in jail. Another casualty is Marlon, Dexter's younger brother, who is caught in the crossfire when the police raid their home in search of Dexter.[71] Dexter's character allows readers to see the intersection of masculine expression, class, and race in his downtown community. Those whose performance of masculinity exudes both threat and protection or security become empowered by community members and gain authority both to control (via intimidation and criminal activity) the community and to act as agents of social welfare, fulfilling community members' material needs such as jobs, food, and housing.[72]

Dexter's experience delivers an alternate (though illegal) route to upward mobility, and it demonstrates serious barriers to supposedly traditional routes to upward mobility even when one makes a good effort. Dexter's circumstances restrict his imagination to the point that he is unable to envision a brighter future for himself. Even before his involvement with the gang, Dexter believes he will not have a long or prosperous life, and he recognizes the near impossibility that he will ascend in class. At times in the narrative, he wonders about having another life. After Dexter tells Sahara that he wants to be Carl, she says: "Eventually I realized it was the idea of Carl Dex longed for, not Carl the person. It was the idea of his life. The list of things Carl was and had was long—and Dex would never be or have those things" (160).[73] With her literary portrayal of *habitus* through her character Dexter, McCaulay presents a dismal picture for inner-city communities, filled with human rights abuses and an unending cycle of intergenerational poverty, which receive no help from an absent welfare state.[74]

Climbing over Invisible Walls: Stereotypes, Prejudices, and Misunderstandings

Stereotypes affirm the many prejudices about inner-city people such as Dexter's family and contribute to people's refusal to see their humanity and respect the reality that they are entitled to human rights. This dynamic is apparent in *Dog-Heart*, particularly in Sahara's conversations with Carl and her friend Lydia, who owns the restaurant where Sahara works. In specific scenes with these characters, readers glimpse racial and class prejudices that become invisible walls that blind them to the humanity of inner-city people and hinder potential cross-class alliances or productive relationships between those in Sahara's and Dexter's communities. In fact, Carl and Lydia, representing middle-class attitudes, distinguish themselves from those living in areas such as Jacob's Pen by blatantly stereotyping them. Some scholars, such as Geoffrey Philp and Mary Hanna, write that such characters represent the indifference of the middle classes; on the contrary, this chapter demonstrates that those classes have established and prejudiced ideas about inner-city people. By "breaking class taboos, [McCaulay] exposes what the privileged really think and feel about the Jamaican masses."[75] So opposed are they to people from inner-city areas that both Lydia and Carl—interpellated subjects—strongly try to dissuade Sahara from becoming involved with Dexter and his family. The ISAs, as I discussed in chapter 3, shape their perspectives and contribute to Lydia's and Carl's inability to comprehend the structural inequalities that reinforce class boundaries.

Unsympathetic, Lydia appears to accept that Dexter and his situation are a reality about which neither she nor Sahara can do anything. She also assumes the family would be a danger because of the association of marginalized people with crime, and she questions Sahara about the five hundred Jamaican dollars she gives to Dexter, exclaiming, "That's a lot. Whyever" (22)?[76] Clearly, she is not moved by her friend's generosity, even if there are concerns about a child's well-being. Lydia resigns herself to the belief that this is the way things will always be or are meant to be because this is the way things are now; yet, human rights laws were established to improve and protect people's quality of life. Later, she tells Sahara "Yes, it's sad, we all know that. But what can you do? What can any of us do? Probably all that can be done is what you did—take a basket of food. Maybe take another one at Christmas" (54). The form of aid that Lydia suggests in these lines is that of a quick handout, one that can foster dependency instead of redressing the realities of structural inequality. She is convinced that nothing can be done to help children and families like Dexter's. Coupled with this belief is her fear of danger or "all kinds of trouble" (56), which reinforces her distance. Lydia does not suggest any other way in which Sahara could possibly be of assistance. Instead, because of the perceived perils, she removes herself from any involvement with making individual decisions that can lead to societal changes. When Sahara responds with the story about a boy who throws a few washed ashore starfish back into the sea despite his father's protest that he will not be able to help all of them, Lydia retorts that the story is a fairytale. Yet, the story is instructive in that it encourages individuals to do whatever they can to help because it indeed can make a difference. Sahara, like the little boy, is trying to help save as many lives as she can, literally and figuratively. She recognizes her privilege in her society and is now trying to extend a helping hand.[77] Still, the novel makes clear that Sahara's lopsided or uneven efforts are not sufficient. A larger safety net is needed. Lydia, who also occupies a place of privilege in their society, is able to turn her head in the other direction without remorse; just like the father in the story, she refuses to acknowledge people like Dexter and his family.

Like Lydia, Carl stereotypes inner-city people and even blames them for their own circumstances. McCaulay strategically introduces a discussion of class in a scene detailing one of the many shouting matches between mother and son. Carl disapproves of her "dangerous" involvement and states that she does not "know what ghetto people are like. [She] should see how they behave in school—the girls are slack and the boys have knives. They're always in trouble" (88). Given that Carl attends a school in an uptown area, it is unlikely that all of the "ghetto" females and males enrolled in his school are "slack" and carry knives.[78] His statement may be a description of a few inner-city students attending his school, and he has used it to generalize an entire segment of his school's population. Becoming more infuriated later in the conversation, Carl continues his tirade, shouting "They bring it on themselves! Why don't they work hard at school? Why don't they get jobs? Why do the girls get pregnant before they're sixteen" (88). Interrupted by Sahara's reminder of her teenage pregnancy and that he has Black blood coursing through his veins, Carl flinches and states: "It's nothing to do with those children being black. It's to do with where they are from, their *class*, their *attitudes*" (89; emphasis in original). Though Carl claims he is not talking about their race but rather their class, the reality that those in the inner city are Black underscores the role of intersectionality concerning people's position in society, and it also emphasizes the difficulty of discussing race without considering class and vice versa.[79] In the scene, Sahara expresses bewilderment about Carl's litany of abuses, which reminded her of her white racist Aunt Gladys, even though Carl does not remember the aunt. Sahara concludes that he has such beliefs because her racist Aunt Gladys was in his gene pool (90). However, that some of his words are reminiscent of Lydia—"they'll be criminals on the street" (89)—reveals these may be pervasive stereotypes that are common among those outside of the inner city. His peers, whom McCaulay describe as being from a "wealthy family" (45), appear to be influencing him in greater ways than Sahara.

Although Sahara does not voice pejorative statements like Lydia and Carl, who ignore inner-city people's humanity, Sahara is a complex character that McCaulay uses to shine a light on the reality that people can still possess prejudiced beliefs even when this is not detected in their overt behavior. Her compassion and decision to assist Dexter and his family are admirable and certainly exhibit her courageousness. Despite objections from those closest to her who firmly oppose helping certain people just because they are from inner-city areas, Sahara chooses to continue with her undeveloped plans of assisting. Still, Sahara also has classist beliefs (of which she may be unaware, however). The first time Sahara brings groceries to Dexter's house, she has thoughts akin to those of Lydia and Carl. In fact, Sahara's thought process is similar to Lydia's, in that she wonders if the neighborhood people are going to rob or harm her in some way. She assumes that because they live in Jacob's Pen, they are violent; again, the novel associates crime with class status. Once she arrives at Dexter's home, and Marlon hugs her in gratitude for the food, she, "to [her] shame, wondered what [she] might catch from this boy" (47). At least, here, she is aware of her prejudiced mindset.

Additionally, Sahara, who was reared by her paternal aunt, whom she despised for being racist, has offensive thoughts about Black people as well. Her feelings manifest most blatantly in the novel during a scene with Arleen and a school guidance counselor at St. Stephen's, Dexter's high school. While in Mrs. Darby's office with Arleen, Sahara expresses that she "could smell the two women—Arleen, metallic and poor, Mrs. Darby powdered and perfumed, but *the black smell* was there underneath" (190; emphasis added). Sahara is repulsed by what she calls "the black smell" that apparently all Black people emit. Even though she notes that she herself was sweating, she does not mention anything about her own odor or if what she smelled possibly came from her body. So although the school official was higher in class than Arleen, she is still Black and is not immune from Sahara's racist thoughts. The final sentence in this scene alludes to slavery and how "slaves had been horrified by the smell of white people" (190). McCaulay's inclusion of this sentence confirms that Sahara's concern is also one of racial difference. Moreover, McCaulay admits she was deliberate in casting Sahara as racist: "The way she behaves in some instances is racist, dismissive, and condescending. I didn't want her to be a saint or a savior. She's just a regular person. She's a regular person with regular prejudices from her upbringing and from living in a place like Jamaica where such notions are . . . permeating everything."[80] Perhaps Sahara has such feelings because of her own insecurities about her racial background. In high school, where she first begins to think about race, Sahara wonders whether she is Black because she "knew [she] wasn't black on the inside" (65). She never saw herself as being a part of the group of students who were "black-blacks" and who talked about "slavery and a whole bunch of isms—colonialism, imperialism, racism, tribalism" (66). Sahara's lighter skin color allows her privileges in her society, but the privileges do not quell her insecurity about her mixed racial identity.

Despite the classist and racist beliefs that have shaped her worldview, Sahara makes efforts to overcome these invisible walls and becomes involved with Dexter's educational pursuits because she recognizes it is a human right to have a sound education. The overall differences in Sahara's and Dexter's worldviews present major obstacles, however. Sahara insists that education alone is the answer to Dexter's problems, despite the classism within the education system. It is not a value neutral system, as so many Caribbean scholars have explained and as discussed in the previous chapter. On the first day of school at Holborn Prep, the other students tease Dexter and Marlon, calling them Big Foot and Baby Big Foot after Dexter takes off his shoes to play football (105). He is not socialized in middle-class social habits, and he already stands out from the other students because, as he observes, "them is all brownins, some light, some dark. None a them is black" (98). Dexter's high school principal, Mr. Bancroft, also reinforces racial and class stereotypes when he says to Sahara: "I know you mean well, Mrs. Lawrence, but it's hard to help these people. In all my years of teaching, I've seen only a handful of boys like [Dexter] take school seriously and do well. It comes down to character and not many of them have it" (194). Mr. Bancroft has preconceived beliefs or expectations about students like Dexter and, unfortunately, Dexter realizes the expectations. These school incidents allude to the subtheme of violence in the novel, as such treatment is a type of violence.[81] Wanting to avoid further violence in her life, Arleen, who has only a primary education, is aware of the prejudicial treatment of which school officials are capable and appears intimidated in their presence, even lying to them (69). The novel suggests perhaps this is the reason she does not visit her children's school, and maybe it is not that she simply does not desire to be involved with their education.[82]

Ultimately, McCaulay's *Dog-Heart* uses a cross-class relationship trope to express the fact that the mere existence of international human rights law does not guarantee the protection of human rights, and she thus adds a literary approach to discussions that interrogate the effectiveness of human rights treaties, as the narrative advocates for an effective welfare state. McCaulay's fictive account of contemporary life for some communities in Jamaica reveals ways in which some rights outlined in the ICESCR are disregarded. The result of inadequate employment opportunities and other circumstances is that some people's basic necessities are not met. McCaulay's narrative enlightens readers to the fact that Dexter faces critical circumstances, including sometimes not having enough to eat, which will not be solved by simply attending school in uptown. In fact, Dexter thinks, "Miss Sahara think she can make us into uptown children. She think if we learn how to read and count, learn how to behave, get expose to *opportunity*—she always talkin about *opportunity*—make uptown friend, then we will be like uptown people. I sure it not going go like that" (118; emphasis in original). The text's emphasis on the word "opportunity" reinforces the glaring lack of opportunity in Dexter's life. Dexter cannot imagine how attending school will help him have a better life because it does not provide the immediate results, such as adequate housing and food, which he needs. Thus, a disconnect exists between Sahara and Dexter concerning his needs and the avenue to have them met. Yet beyond their relationship looms portrayals of pressing national circumstances that are tangibly affected by the ever-changing global community.[83] In the end, McCaulay's *Dog-Heart* promotes deeper understanding of the limited role of human rights treaties in alleviating substandard conditions and evokes human rights concerns that Jamaica and many other nations in the global South are facing. The depictions of the conditions and human rights violations in this chapter feed into the next chapter's discussion of contemporary imperialism.

Epilogue

Romance across (Class) Borders and Have Some Post-Class

> However, my silence, like all our silences about class, easily
> becomes part of the collusion, part of our acquiescence and
> participation in unjust economic practices, an unwitting
> support of class elitism.
>
> —BELL HOOKS, *Where We Stand: Class Matters*

> The [Occupy] Movement has heightened the urgency and visibility
> of the issue of economic inequality. Ninety-nine percent is not only
> a number now, it is a symbol, a discourse, an idea.
>
> —MATTHEW BOLTON, EMILY WELTY, MEGHANA NAYAK, and
> CHRISTOPHER MALONE, "We Had a Front Row Seat"

Neoliberalism and its entanglements with contemporary imperialism and neocolonialism impacts even the most intimate aspects of our lives. Romance, though seemingly a light-hearted affair in the opinions of some, can be influenced by capital-driven ideologies and practices. Cross-class relationships, particularly cross-class romances, are quite familiar in contemporary popular culture in the United States and the Caribbean, featuring prominently in sources ranging from films and television shows to songs, magazine issues, and internet blogs.[1] During periods of economic turmoil, such as the Great Depression and the Reagan era, movies featuring cross-class romances multiplied. However, when there is no economic crisis, films featuring such relationships are still not difficult to find, as the cross-class romance has been a staple of the industry throughout almost cinema's entire history.[2] Such romances appear in several contemporary Hollywood box office hits featuring actresses and actors across racial and ethnic backgrounds, including *Crazy Rich Asians* starring Constance Wu, *Maid in Manhattan* starring Jennifer Lopez, *Pretty Woman* starring Julia Roberts, *Jumping the Broom* starring Paula Patton, and *Good Deeds* starring and produced by African American movie mogul Tyler Perry (see figure E.1). Similarly, African American and Caribbean fiction also demonstrates a history of portraying cross-class romances; yet, a happily-ever-after end-

FIGURE E.1 A movie advertisement for *Jumping the Broom*, which chronicles the impending marriage of a couple from different class backgrounds (Sony Picture Home Entertainment).

ing is not always present as is the case in the aforementioned films. Rather, African American and Caribbean writers employ a cross-class relationship trope to interrogate deeper socioeconomic and political issues. This chapter looks at Caribbean writer Oonya Kempadoo's *Tide Running* (2001) and African American writer Toni Morrison's *Tar Baby* (1981), novels that are exemplary in their depictions of the featured cross-class romantic liaisons.[3] These two novels (with a wide publishing time frame) are representative models of cross-class romance portrayals that demonstrate how some fiction has long moved beyond short-term goals of tickling people's fancy, as displayed in smash-hit films, to illustrating how matters of class are tied to the larger discourse of imperialism, including U.S. imperialism, that pervades contemporary life.

Morrison and Kempadoo are from different generations and backgrounds, yet their texts unite in depicting troubling continuities for people of the

African Diaspora. Still, the publication dates of the novels as well as the setting of *Tar Baby* in the early post–civil rights years, in comparison to the setting of *Tide Running*—closer to the turn of the twenty-first century—influence my analysis, as the contexts and portrayals of these continuities take on different dimensions. With particular attention to the final scenes of the novels, I argue that the embattled and unstable cross-class romances in the two novels, which ultimately fail in the end, are emblematic of both unresolved tensions concerning the foreign relations between the United States and Caribbean nations and the precarious standard of living among some people of the African Diaspora. Further, these rocky romantic relationships unsettle and thereby expose the social hierarchy to reveal the extent to which contemporary society is reproducing the asymmetry and disempowerment of traditional colonialism and maintaining the legacy of slavery. Although critics note the novels emphasize the slavery and/or colonial historical context of the United States and Caribbean, this chapter asserts that the authors unveil the continued exploitation of the Caribbean and (segments of) the U.S. Black population beyond the enslaved past, revealing that even though legal slavery and colonialism are over, the lived experiences of Black populations still reflect that history, as slavery's legacies emerge in the texts via characters' living conditions, employment opportunities, psyches, and overall positions of power.[4]

The novels initiate a first step in the solution to halt anti-Black racism and discrimination, which is to excite or help readers to become cognizant of the ways neoliberal and racial capitalist ideologies impact all parts of people's lives, encouraging readers via the open-ended structures of the novels to determine and take succeeding steps against continued antiblackness. To be sure, these novels present a literary critique of and resistance against imperial powers, and by shedding light on neoliberal imperialism and the associated working-class conditions, Kempadoo's and Morrison's narratives invoke thoughts on furthering the process of full liberation for the fictive Black populations. To resist contemporary class injustice is to resist neoliberal imperialism, which stands to continue contributing to present-day growth in class inequalities, as my analysis in previous chapters conveys.[5] Drawing on the troubled history of anti-Black racism, Kempadoo's and Morrison's novels expose how we have yet to reconcile it and its legacy in the current period, thus aligning with postcolonial studies that expose the long history of U.S. imperialist practices and their continuities in the contemporary period. Despite the history of U.S. imperialism, the association of the United States with imperialism is often not discussed at great lengths.[6] This association is often ignored or denied, but postcolonial studies, expanding in the 1980s and 1990s, emphasize the importance of empire, including U.S. empire, in the making of modernity and contemporary global structures just as it also critiques the legacies of empire.[7] Carole Boyce-Davies and Monica Jardine discuss the imperial relationship between the United States and some Caribbean nations, highlighting the essay "American Imperialism and the British West Indies" by Caribbean feminist and socialist Claudia Jones: "This early analysis of the role of U.S. colonialism and imperialism is one of the first to literally name 'American imperialism' (as its title identifies) for what it is—a task still difficult even for current intellectuals and activists, as they flirt with various terminologies."[8] While often under the guise of peacekeeping, U.S. policies with some nations and territories, including Caribbean nations throughout the twentieth century up to today, are best described as imperialistic, as seen through, for instance, the country's military presence abroad, the influence of its economic power and trade agreements, and its political influence on foreign governments.

This chapter employs Julian Go's succinct definition of imperialism as the "process by which [empires] are established, extended, or maintained," while being mindful of the fact that this process can be subtle and involve less obvious forms of control.[9] Both *Tide Running* and *Tar Baby* showcase various forms of imperialism instead of continuing the exclusion of the United States from imperialist discourses.[10] Novels from the United States have participated in a culture of U.S. imperialism throughout the nation's history. Hence, literature has a history of fostering empires, as some writers openly put forward imperialist viewpoints.[11] While some scholars discuss the presence of imperialist adventures within American novels, Morrison, in her nonfiction text *Playing in the Dark*, critiques the romance genre and highlights the role of race in American romance novels.[12] Through the explorations of the cross-class romances and their connections to working classes, Morrison and Kempadoo both convey that imperialism adversely affects the quality of life and class positions of their Caribbean and African American characters.[13]

A brief summary elucidates general similarities and differences between the two cross-class romances. Set in present-day Tobago, Kempadoo's *Tide Running* exposes the troubled dynamics of a cross-class romantic partnership among three partners. The love triangle in Kempadoo's novel involves Cliff Dunstan, a twenty-year-old working-class Tobagonian and a married couple, Peter and Bella, who are long-term middle-class visitors to Tobago.

The interplay of class and skin tone/color features prominently in Kempadoo's novel, as Bella is mixed-race from Trinidad and Peter is a white Englishman who formerly lived in Trinidad.[14] Meanwhile, Morrison's *Tar Baby* details the cross-class romantic liaison between two African American characters, Jadine "Jade" Childs and William "Son" Green. The primary setting of Morrison's novel is the fictive Isle des Chevaliers in the late 1970s where white U.S. citizens, Valerian and Margaret Street, vacation in the "oldest and most impressive" (10) house on the isle, L'Arbe de la Croix. Jade, who is the middle-class, Sorbonne-educated fashion model and niece of the Streets' African American butler and maid, meets Son during a visit to the house for the Christmas holiday season. Son, a stranger who has escaped to the island to avoid capture in the United States, is originally from the small, working-class, all-Black town of Eloe, Florida.

As in *Tar Baby*, the house in Kempadoo's novel, a contemporary "great house," is a significant site in that many of the romantic escapades take place there, and its breathtaking appearance leads Cliff to fantasize—to a dangerous degree—about having a U.S. movie "film-style" life. Once the relationship between Cliff and the couple escalates to a sexual one after they invite him to their house, Cliff transforms for the worse and the novel closes with him in jail awaiting his court date for stealing from the couple. The Streets' house in Morrison's novel is a major site that is pivotal in the novel's construction of the social hierarchy among the characters, particularly because it is essentially a re-creation of a great house on a plantation; it also shows the continuity of slavery and colonialism in the contemporary period. With an unresolved ending, Morrison's novel concludes with the protagonist Son separating from Jadine and riding off with mythical horsemen. The endings of the narratives, or the outcomes, are evidence that the intersectionality of the African-descended characters' identities work together to create vulnerable and precarious life experiences.

The setting of the final scene in Kempadoo's *Tide Running* is significant because it reminds readers of the literal, physical presence of colonial vestiges in the present moment and its continued devastating impact on the lives of those in Cliff's community. The scene includes an old fort built by former European colonizers that is now used as a jail to imprison the working-class protagonist Cliff.[15] Yet, while the narrative ends with this prison-fort erected by European colonizers, *Tide Running* is replete with references to the influences of U.S. imperialism in Trinidad and Tobago. U.S. imperialism over the Caribbean, in many respects, has taken the place of European colonialism.[16] The U.S. occupation of Trinidad and Tobago during World War II and its invasions in other Caribbean nations, such as Grenada, bolsters such a claim, and *Tide Running* demonstrates the imprint of the United States on life in its fictive Trinidad and Tobago. The U.S. military's presence on the bases it established on the twin-island republic affected the economic and cultural fabric of this Caribbean nation.[17]

Although the relationship between Cliff and the married couple does not begin as a sex tourism arrangement, sexually exploitative undertones—a continuity of colonial privilege and slavery—are present in the cross-class relationship.[18] Sex tourism is a legacy of slavery and colonialism in the region and has become a growing industry under imperial powers. This form of tourism is a part of the wider tourist industry in which multiple segments of Caribbean societies participate, as tourism is intertwined in the economy of Caribbean nations. The novel plays on the racialization of sexism and sexualization of racism that is part of the discussions of sex tourism in the Caribbean.[19] The threesome relationship invokes the need to interrogate the term *romance*. Is a romance an accurate description of this relationship? It does not appear so to me. Cliff is barely out of his teen years, while the couple is middle-aged, and he is a young man embattled by the disadvantages of his society at the same time that the couple benefits from the inequalities. Readers immediately are able to decipher Cliff's class status by descriptions of his home, including the lack of food, the dilapidated kitchen counter "that the wood ants [are] eating out" (7), and the lack of running water. It is not clear how or why the couple begins the threesome, other than to achieve sexual gratification. In an interview about the novel, Kempadoo is not bashful in admitting that "the gaps and connections, opportunism or not, that [take place] between the classes that share a society became the story" (112).[20] Sex is the form of Cliff's exploitation and labor, and Bella and Peter feel entitled to Cliff's body and sexual labor. Invoking transactions, the novel reads: "Now tourism is the trade, the new crop. But still it brings people who have to be served, white people expecting something in return for the Yankee dollar" (116). Payment to Cliff by the couple comes in the form of paid restaurant meals, excursions with the couple, and nights spent in the luxurious Big House. Cliff is infatuated with his access to the couple, and he ponders, "Peeta and Bella in they clean house. I eating dinner with them. Knife and fork shining under table lamp, black night outside, and the li'l boy laughing" (202). The "li'l boy" is Peter and Bella's young son, who is unaware of his parents' sexual interactions (or, rather, transactions) with Cliff. Rather than altering his socioeconomic position, the couple offers temporary relief or escape for this young man who is participating in a (sexual) line of work in which both men and women partake to make ends meet.[21]

The final scene in *Tide Running* is an indictment of the contemporary conditions some Afro-Caribbean characters face in Trinidad and Tobago, particularly working-class populations. Akin to their ancestors, many still confront being fettered with iron, locked up, and in need of true liberation. The novel's conclusion presents evidence of new forms of enslavement, as it ends with Black suffering and immunity for those who played a part in it. The middle-class protagonist Bella and Peter never suffer because of the decisions they make concerning their cross-class romance with Cliff, but Cliff suffers tremendously. Cliff is a young man in need of guidance, but Bella and Peter see him as a source of sexual pleasure. They are not interested in seriously mentoring him, despite being aware of his circumstances. This reality becomes clearer in this final scene, particularly when Cliff's mother tells Peter that Cliff needs guidance, "Cliff need somebody to follow. . . . 'He need a man.' Looked at Peter direct. 'Cliff like you a lot. He talk plenty 'bout you. Come to admire and respec' you'" (212). In response, Peter scoffs, "Cliff's twenty, he's not a little boy anymore" (212). While in jail, Cliff muses: "Scraps. Is scraps I feel like too. Beat-up hand-me-down police scraps. Like how you does feel when the swelling gone down from a bruise—a shadow'a real pain left in you flesh. Weaken you bones. Poor-me-one magger dog with bare ribs showing, bathing there. Trying to wash the smell away" (214). Cliff has these musings while sitting in jail because he stole from the couple. Arguably, the couple also steals from Cliff; yet, they remain free from a jail cell. While they do not steal material things from Cliff, they rob him of his youth and the innocence he had when he first met them. Cliff is surprised and becomes pleased with himself when the couple invites him to their house for the first time: "Me they talking to, eh! Hear things. 'Come around some time if you'd like.' Visit them. Is me they talking to. Not no small boy, no poor-ears fella from Plymuth. Like as if I have me car and house same like them. . . . I smile and watch them looking out still" (48). Although the language here indicates Cliff's pleasure, the language Kempadoo uses in the jail scene underscores the sense of helplessness he feels. Cliff is brutally beaten by the police before they incarcerate him, and even Peter acknowledges this abuse and punishment is not befitting the crime, and he states, "No. They have no right to beat him" (207). He is in an objectified state, feeling and looking like a battered animal. Still, Peter and Bella objectify Cliff before the criminal justice system—a part of the Repressive State Apparatus mentioned in chapter 3 of this book. The mention of pain and bruising on his body further evokes not only the prison-industrial complex of the contemporary period but also the bitter enslaved history of Africans. Readers do not know what his fate will be in the end, but this closing jail scene, where Cliff lies battered and bloody like his African-descended ancestors, indicates it will not be good.

Moreover, U.S. cultural imperialism is represented in the novel by the entertainment, food, and clothing choices characters make. Television shows operate as overt references to U.S. imperialist influences, and many of the shows Cliff watches, including commercials of U.S. restaurants with global franchises, offer U.S. portrayals of what people's lives *should* be.[22] As Cliff puts it, "Foreign is a place that have a thing for everything. Not like here" (178). Recognizing that his material conditions are lacking and believing that he as an individual is lacking, he fantasizes about foreign people, which draws him to the married couple. Enamored by the images of American people that he watches, Cliff eventually believes he can reenact what he sees on TV when his relationship begins to grow with Bella and Peter. Kempadoo never shows Bella and Peter indulging obsessively in trite TV shows; they see their reality as a paradise. Bella and Peter have completely different circumstances from Cliff and his family who are operating under a cloud of U.S. imperialism that dramatically impacts their cultural and economic worlds. Bella muses: "The house, our holiday haven from Trinidad city life, seduced us into its womb, promising peace of mind, crime-free living, and the blue Caribbean Sea. . . . And now the haven sheltered us from things unknown and deep" (64). Bella is oblivious to firsthand experience with serious hardship: she is *sheltered* by the house and from the circumstances Cliff is unable to circumvent. Cliff's gaining access to Bella and Peter's grand house is akin to some enslaved Africans being granted access to the "Big House." Cliff sees this as a privilege. The privilege allows him to imagine himself as a celebrity. When he—adorned in his U.S. name-brand clothes and shoes—first visits the house, he is literally speechless.[23] Cliff details his experience in the house as if he were famous: "We starring now. I move me famous foot. You know how much people go pay for me two-foot to be in a ad? For me to wear a Nike trackpants? Thousands'a U.S. dollars. Better yet if I smile and say, 'Just do it.' Millions. I watch me brother, Magic, relaxing, chatting in the talk show. Everybody like he. But I have the looks. Watch me nuh" (57). Despite his meager circumstances, Cliff is deluded into believing his worth is defined by how much access he has to things "foreign." With these references to U.S. sports gear and figures, the novel makes clear Cliff is trying to mimic what he sees as the "Empire."

The cross-class romance is also haunted by the portrayal of the two-island state's relationship with the United States. The Trinidad-Tobago divide in the novel operates as a microcosm of the larger United States–Caribbean divide. The couple is representative of imperialists, even as Bella and European people continue to enjoy colonial privilege in Tobago. Even though Trinidad and Tobago should be equal given that together they make up the two-island nation, Trinidad—bigger, wealthier, more modernized in Western terms—plays the part of the United States to a degree. The unequal relationship between Cliff and the couple parallels the unequal relationship that exists in the Republic of Trinidad and Tobago and demonstrates how various intersections, including race, skin tone, class, and geographical location, affects people's lives. Cliff is acutely aware of the differences between the two islands, so much so that he and his family view Trinidadian people as privileged foreigners. "When them Trinis come over to Tobago, they look like they come from Foreign. Even when they ain' wearing all the Ray Ban and beach wrap and sporting Carib Beer towel, something does make them look like Foreign" (17). The various descriptions of "Trinis" such as this one in the narrative, including Bella, provoke a broader conversation about intra-national, intraracial, and interethnic relations. Though the relationship between Trinidad and Tobago is not imperialistic in the way that the United States' relationship is with Caribbean nations in general, the inclusion in the novel of Tobago's disadvantages underscores the vulnerable positions of Cliff and his community. Ultimately, Kempadoo's novel leaves readers with a sobering reality concerning the fate of many of those who share Cliff's working-class status.

In the scholarship on *Tar Baby*, there is less examination solely on how the differences apparent in Jadine and Son's relationship initiate a discussion about the various working-class populations within the novel, specifically the Caribbean working class in Isle des Chevaliers, the African American working class in Son's hometown, and the African American domestic workers, Sydney and Ondine.[24] Their romance is connected to and/or influenced by these groups, and my analysis offers an investigation of how the cross-class romance between Son and Jadine highlights the imperial thread in the narrative in relation to the various working-class populations. My focus here is on the communities to which the cross-class romance brings attention. The final scene of *Tar Baby*, which may be described as idealistic and dreamlike in that the protagonist Son rides off with mythical horsemen, presents an unresolved ending that emphasizes the continued disconcerting situations and circumstances of some African American and Caribbean populations. In fact, the ending indicates that the subpar conditions that these characters' lives illuminate continue in the contemporary period.

The final scene of *Tar Baby* involves Son's interactions with the local Caribbean working-class population, specifically Gideon, Therese, and Alma Estee, who work at the Streets' house. Jadine and Son begin to become more intimately connected after a picnic date, but Christmas dinner, destroyed by a conversation about none other than the working-class locals, foretells of future trouble between the couple. The current living conditions of these workers beg for a discussion on contemporary imperialism because their conditions so closely resemble those of the past.[25] Their circumstances reveal they are still impoverished and powerless to a large extent in that they are dependent upon jobs offered by Valerian Street, whom many scholars describe as a modern-day colonizer.[26] Their house is small, encompassing a "cot where Therese slept at night, the floor where Alma Estee sometimes slept and the tiny bedroom where [Gideon] did" (154). Highlighting their distress, Gideon divulges that Therese nearly starved to death (154) after her baby-nursing services were no longer needed, and he tells Therese earlier in the narrative that he is starving to death.[27] Even Son recognizes when he eats the meal Therese prepares at their house that "the delicacies had cost them" (150). The dependency—a familiar term in imperialism discourses associated with economic underdevelopment—that Gideon, Therese, and Alma Estee possess in relation to the Streets is obvious to Son.[28] This knowledge, along with the revelation that Valerian recently fired them after a long history of exploiting their labor, causes Son to become enraged at the Streets' Christmas dinner:

> Although [Valerian] had taken the sugar and cocoa and paid for it as
> though it had no value, as though the cutting of cane and picking of
> beans was child's play and had no value; but he turned it into candy,
> the invention of which really was child's play, and sold it to other
> children and made a fortune in order to move near, but not in the
> midst of, the jungle where the sugar came from and build a palace
> with more of their labor and then hire them to do more of the work
> he was not capable of and pay them again according to some scale of
> value that would outrage Satan himself and when those people wanted
> a little of what he wanted, some apples for *their* Christmas, and took
> some, he dismissed them with a flutter of the fingers, because they

were thieves, and nobody knew thieves and thievery better than he did and he probably thought he was a law-abiding man, they all did, and they all always did. (203; emphasis in original)

While this passage alludes to days of formal slavery and colonialism, it also highlights similarities between the past and the present. During both, the labor of the natives is what sustains the whims of the more powerful and it all fuels a capitalist system. The beginning lines of this passage reiterate how the products and the labor associated with the products have "no value" to Valerian.[29] Hence, the value and subjectivity of those performing the labor is not of concern to him either. He plays with their lives just as a child plays with candy before devouring it. Valerian devours the livelihood of these workers for daring to take and eat some apples without his permission. Their employment is jeopardized because they took food, which is needed substance that would ensure their continued labor for him. Severe punishment for daring to take more of the master's food was common during slavery. Valerian is concerned only about his ultimate profit, which is a "fortune." The last phrase of this passage, "they all always did" refers to the unwillingness of (former) colonialist powers or those who have profited and continue to profit from the colonial enterprise and modern-day imperialism to admit their oppressive actions. In *How to Hide an Empire*, Daniel Immerwahr discusses a history of the United States profiting from its various forms of dominance in its relations with many nations and territories, and the Streets represent this reality. Yet, Son is incensed further in this scene when Jadine defends Valerian, which foreshadows the irreconcilability between Son's and Jadine's worldviews. Earlier, Gideon tried to offer Son advice about Jadine, whom he calls "yalla," referring to her light skin color: "It's hard for them not to be white people" (155). Rather than skin color, Gideon is really referring to Jadine's disassociation with all things Black. Jadine's supposed refinement from school and her other experiences have shaped her to identify with or be more like the Streets.

Morrison's use of a cross-class relationship trope illuminates far more than the romance between Son and Jadine. Son shares a sense of kinship with the three working-class groups in the narrative, even as he and Jadine upset the overall hierarchy of the Streets' house because they are not a part of the house in the same way as the other characters. Yet, Jadine, along with her aunt and uncle, views herself more highly than she does the local residents and Son as well. She and Son, in the end, cannot reconcile their contrasting class perspectives and value systems, so they part ways. Son, unlike

Jadine and her family, respects the other working-class characters, while Jadine and her family participate in the marginalization of the locals and continue the imperial relations embodied in the Streets. At the close of the novel, readers see that Gideon's and Marie Therese's roles in the narrative are quite significant, as the novel ends with Son rejoining them. Gideon warns him to stay away from Jadine, perhaps because he sees her as being a tar baby who will entrap him, while Marie Therese ensures that he stays away from her by leading Son to join the mythic Chevaliers.[30]

When Son and Jadine visit his hometown, Son compassionately sees similarities between the conditions of all the working-class populations, while Jade is not only unsympathetic to their circumstances but also judges the hometown of her romantic partner as a place with "no life there. Maybe a past but definitely no future" (259). The physical attraction between them—which is further aroused after their private picnic near the Streets' home—makes them decide to go away together, but Jadine sees lifelessness in the space in which her partner's family ended up living. The house in which Son was reared is just as small as the one he visited while going for a haircut with Gideon. The narrator reveals he did not remember the house being so tiny: "It had seemed so large and sturdy compared to the Sutterfield shack he and Cheyenne [his ex-wife] had. . . . It wasn't as big as Ondine's kitchen" (246). Despite the limited space in the two-bedroom house, Son grew up in it with his mother, father, and four siblings, and the enclosed space probes his memory of the similar conditions shared by others. While working-class African Americans are no longer confined to domestic jobs like Ondine and Sydney, the novel invokes thoughts about why so many people still have to depend on unstable jobs where their livelihoods are in constant jeopardy. Even as the term *imperialism* is synonymous with U.S. foreign policy in some circles, the United States has a history of African Americans being characterized as "refugees" or foreigners, and some argue the circumstances of African Americans have resembled those of people in Caribbean nations subject to U.S. foreign policy.[31] *Tar Baby* reflects the ongoing reality of unfortunate shared experiences between African Americans and Afro-Caribbean populations that are associated with the seemingly uncontrolled power structures of the United States.

A cook and a butler respectively, Ondine and Sydney—Jadine's aunt and uncle—share similarities with the people of Son's hometown in Eloe, Florida, as well as with the locals who work for the Streets. Through them, the novel reveals parallels between U.S. domestic and foreign relations concerning working-class populations. The novel elucidates the parallels between the

African American and local Caribbean working-class populations and their dependency on the Streets. Further, both the Eloe community and Jadine's aunt and uncle have meager living conditions just like the locals. Sydney and Ondine are aware of the inequalities and hierarchy that exist even in the Streets' house, as Ondine quips that it is "not as grand" (160) as upstairs when she sees Son surveying the room she shares with her husband. Contrasting greatly with the rest of the house, their living quarters contained "second-hand furniture, table scarves, tiny pillows, scatter rugs and the smell of human beings. It had a tack permanence to it" (160). Much like the local community members, Ondine and Sydney are also dependent on the Street family, as they have been serving the Streets for years and are too old to find employment elsewhere. The Streets also control their livelihoods—the key to their existence.

Although Ondine and Sydney are aware of their own vulnerable position and dependence, they still treat the local Caribbean population and Son as if they are lesser, exhibiting intraracial antagonism. Their U.S. citizenship gives them privilege over the local residents, which continues a centuries-long power relation. They believe the intersections of their nationality, race, and class places them in higher positions than both the natives and Son—the outsider. They are also living in the largest house on the island, and their status as in-house workers of the Streets affords them privileges that the local people, and likely those in Eloe, cannot access. In their poor treatment of the others, Ondine and Sydney try to reproduce or mimic the imperial power structure that exists in the Streets' household in a way that is similar to Cliff in Kempadoo's novel.[32] Representative of internalized racism, they mimic the Streets and treat the others as if they are inferior.[33]

Ultimately, U.S. imperialism operates in Morrison's *Tar Baby* and Kempadoo's *Tide Running* to complicate discussions of class by introducing how U.S. imperialism influences class relations and inequalities within the African Diaspora. The novels explore how new articulations of imperial power impact relations between middle-class and working-class Afro-descended characters. This is important not only to the larger project of combatting and annihilating various inequalities but also to the enterprise of quelling intraracial antagonisms in order to move forward with an expanded, more united front. Readers see how postcolonial figures, such as Bella and Peter, engage in imperial-type exploitation of Cliff and how African Americans such as Jadine, Ondine, and Sydney take on demeaning perspectives of wealthy white Americans toward both other African Americans (Son) and

Afro-Caribbeans (Gideon, Marie Therese, and Alma Estee). In the case of *Tide Running*, there is the additional issue of an internal asymmetry within the nation of Trinidad and Tobago that allows Trinidadians, particularly those of lighter skin tone, to enjoy the privileges associated with former colonizers and tourists benefiting from imperial power. In many respects, the two white patriarchal figures in the novels, Peter and Valerian, are similar, taking no responsibility for their roles in the situations that transpire, including being generators of the strife. Moreover, since the cross-class romances in both novels fail, Morrison's and Kempadoo's novels indicate that issues concerning class inequalities are long battles not easily resolved. Their discourse on class presents readers with a grievous perspective concerning the life chances of some individuals with a working-class status. The cross-class relationship trope that is manifested through the supposed romances of Son and Jadine as well as Cliff and the married couple juxtaposes the stark differences in the material realities between the parties and allows the novels to participate in exposing contemporary struggles of working-class life and their associations with modern-day imperialism. This exposure then permits the novels to compel from readers a response—now having awareness of its wide and transnational existence.

BEFORE COVID-19 CAME to Miami, Florida, in 2020, it was already ravaging the New York City area, which, along with Miami, has the largest concentration of Afro-Caribbean residents in the United States.[34] As in Miami, death rates from the coronavirus among the Black population in New York City are disproportionate. This is not a coincidence; instead, it is the result of the interconnected foundation laid by factors such as long-standing systemic racism, racial capitalism, and neoliberalism in all of its many dimensions, as stated earlier. These are just some of the factors that work together to shape people's class standing. The contemporary world is not in a *post*-class state; class still matters very much. My use of the term "*post*-class" concerns this book's focus primarily on inequalities, disparities, and inequities around, for instance, subjects of housing, education, and employment, which are core areas associated with class position and are highlighted during the COVID-19 pandemic. With the election of Barack Obama, the first Black president of the United States, some people assumed (and some continue to assume) that the United States is a post-racial society in a post-racial world. This is flawed thinking, to say the least, and the U.S. presidential administration that followed Obama's and shook the world because of its constant disregard for norms is evidence that various identities, including class status, matter and impact people's everyday lives. Indeed, the forty-fifth U.S. president and his administration played on racialized class anxieties to stake its policies, including its election campaign platforms.

My play on the phrase "have some class" in the title of this epilogue does not refer to the particular behaviors or personal tastes of people. Instead, it refers to the need for us to have some more studies of the reverberations of class position in people's lived experiences. The fiction explored in this book demonstrates how the intersectionality of class with gender, race, ethnicity, and geographical location, for example, influences the choices and circumstances of the characters' lives. *Class Interruptions* foregrounds literary portrayals of situations African American and Caribbean working classes confront, centering the growing class gaps or increasing class inequality in public discourse. Although some people take issue with literary discussions on Black working classes because of the stereotype and erroneous information that all Black people are working class, *Class Interruptions* refuses to ignore the need for continued explorations of these populations and the reality of their existence. No matter how fragile the subject of class, we must discuss it so that injustices do not continue to be hidden.

During 2020, in the midst of the coronavirus pandemic, Trinidad and Tobago, Jamaica, and the United States held elections for their national leaders in August, September, and November respectively. While Prime Ministers Keith Rowley of Trinidad and Tobago and Andrew Holness of Jamaica won reelections, former vice president Joseph R. Biden emerged as the winner in the U.S. election—a hotly contested election where rioters supporting the forty-fifth U.S. president ignited an insurrection at the U.S. Capitol on January 6, 2021, which led to that president's second impeachment (see figure E.2). Rowley and Holness offered congratulations to Biden with the former stating he looks forward to strengthening bonds with the United States, given the nations' "joint economic and security connections," and the latter noting hopes for "continued strong bilateral relations with [its] largest trading partner," at a time when both economies were in need of stimulation due to the pandemic.[35] These nations face additional challenges in the areas of employment, housing, schooling, and other domestic issues due to COVID-19, but the most focus globally remains on President Biden's plans to mitigate further fallout from the virus within U.S. borders and beyond. Many of the U.S. citizens who voted for Biden also expect a brighter future and desire a shift from neoliberal policies that extend from capitalist greed; yet, a drastic shift that can rectify a four-hundred-year legacy of Black people operating as labor and capital to enrich and fortify the

FIGURE E.2 Rioters supporting the 45th president of the United States scale the walls of the Capitol in Washington, D.C., on January 6, 2021, before vandalizing the building and looting congressional offices (AP Photo/Jose Luis Magana).

wealth of others is too high an expectation for one presidency, just as it was for Obama's eight-year presidency. In other words, Biden will not be upending capitalism, even if many believe some of his policies may work to lessen the blows of various -*isms*.

It is, however, as good a time as ever to begin such a shift to achieve these aims, as these nations can determine now where they stand or what they want for the future of their populations in a post-pandemic world. Cultural critic and feminist theorist bell hooks emphasizes the importance of people knowing where they stand on issues of class in contemporary societies. She reveals that the motivation for writing *Where We Stand: Class Matters*, published nearly two decades ago, was the impending threat of major class warfare in the United States that was spurred on by the ever-widening gap between the rich and poor. An appropriate step to take to eliminate the disproportionate rates, according to hooks, is to know "where we stand" on matters of class. Addressing intersectionality, hooks notes that "class conflict is already racialized and gendered."[36] Knowing "where we stand" is not only an individual or personal responsibility, to use a trite phrase of neoliberalism, but also a charge for nations to make domestic assessments and to work for change to create just socioeconomic systems where people's basic needs are met no matter the intersections of their makeup. Aiming to make the world anew, not as it was pre-pandemic, is an admirable goal for nations to have.

The highly stratified extremes we are witnessing today came about with the onset of contemporary neoliberalism in the 1970s. Societies made and are making the "choice" to continue with destructive neoliberal ideologies and practices, and thus they can make the choice to stop and instead offer alternatives. Governments can stop choosing inequality and start choosing to require paid sick leave, to raise the minimum wage so that full-time workers never have to seek food benefits from the government or stand in food bank lines, to impose market rules that prevent predatory behavior from private equity firms, to provide affordable health care, and to ensure basic services for everyone, for example.[37] *Class Interruptions* amplifies the need for such choices, as the fiction it explores speaks to the issues of our time. The writers advocate for a (re)imagining of societies and equip readers with ample "free food" for thought or increased knowledge about inequalities African Diasporic communities face. Imagination is critical during this time, as a rallying call from the Movement for Black Lives (sometimes referred to as the Black Lives Matter Movement) explains: "Everything in our lived experience was once imagined and created." In essence, we have to get to the work of imagining and working toward "a life rooted in freedom and dignity for Black people."[38]

This book demonstrates how African American and Caribbean writers use what I call a cross-class relationship trope, a literary technique that pairs two characters from different class backgrounds, to participate in multiple discourses, and the fiction in *Class Interruptions* ponders solutions to inequalities in the areas of housing, education, sexual violence, and other state-sanctioned abuse. This trope exemplifies the importance of coalition-building and alliance-building; in fact, relationships represent the beginning of or foundation of the solutions to address these matters. The reality of imperfect alliances should not be deterrents, as fractures can lead to further insight. The fiction advocates for people to see themselves and others in different ways and to imagine new ways of thinking to help generate solutions to inequalities. A part of changing the narrative and wider culture around class involves increasing people's class consciousness and their awareness of their possible complicity in the skewed state of affairs. Mind shifts can lead to greater advocacy for structural changes.

In this contemporary period of neoliberalism, when standards of living are constantly in flux, continued explorations of portrayals of working classes are needed. Literature is playing an increasingly important role because it is one form of public discourse that takes on class and has done so consistently, even before civil rights and independence movements—events that had the promise of improving standards of living for African American and Caribbean communities. *Class Interruptions* engages serious concerns African American and Caribbean women writers reflect in their writing—concerns that are also shared with millions of others in these societies—which is of particular importance because of the lack of other venues in which working-class portrayals receive serious attention. The absence of sustained public attention to the lived experiences of working classes needs to change. There are a number of possible directions for future studies of literary portrayals of class and the cross-class relationship trope, including its use by male writers. Also, there can be closer examinations of the middle-class spaces in novels that feature this trope as well as studies investigating the presence of the trope in other genres, such as the short story, which would allow comparative studies on its various uses. The prevalence of the cross-class relationship trope in other bodies of literature (other than African American and Caribbean) was not in the scope of this book, but the ideas offered here certainly can be expanded to address class issues in other spaces. *Class Interruptions* expands the research on issues of class in general and working classes in particular; it can be an entry point to conversations on these topics and encourage additional studies that seriously engage dismantling inequalities.

In the past ten years since the Great Recession (2007–9), news headlines from conservative and liberal U.S. outlets continue to focus on "the middle class" with headings like "In the Middle Class, and Barely Getting By," "Why the Future of America's Middle Class Is So Financially Fragile," and "Shrinking Middle Class Threatens Global Growth, Stability." These articles, with debates and commentary on the suffering of the U.S. middle class, are reminiscent of the news articles that appeared during the Recession. Though segments of some nations' economies have experienced a rebound since then, many people continued to suffer, and COVID-19 has resurfaced or exacerbated serious conditions. At some point, we have to wonder how long nations will be able to sustain continued growing inequalities. Silence about working-class predicaments is typical of far too many people, and the gross misrepresentations as well as the character assassinations of working classes are hindrances to pathways for improved circumstances. In her documentary *Toni Morrison: The Pieces I Am*, released shortly before her death in 2019, Toni Morrison says, "I'm not sure that people understand that poverty was not shameful as it is now." Shaming people for circumstances that stem from structural inequalities instead of addressing root causes is a practice we must end. Since the Recession, movements such as the Occupy Movement and the Movement for Black Lives have brought attention to various injustices, including class injustice, within and beyond the United States. Though the 99 percent versus the 1 percent is a commonplace phrase at this point, *Class Interruptions* urges us to move past these numbers to the actual lives the numbers represent.[39]

Acknowledgments

A lot goes into writing a book, and I am grateful for every person who helped me in any way move this project from conception to physical manifestation. Fortunately, there have been many people with whom I have engaged along this journey, and I would like to thank some of them here. My mentoring network and wider community of national colleagues have been instrumental every step of the way. The guidance, insight, and kindness of Faye V. Harrison at the University of Illinois at Urbana-Champaign, Amy Ongiri at Lawrence University, and Leah Rosenberg and Apollo Amoko both at the University of Florida were of tremendous help in the early stages of this project. They offered me spaces of intellectual safety as I bounced ideas off of them and played around with different approaches to the project as a whole. Their advice on ways to expand my ideas always proved fruitful in the end. Despite her work being outside of my primary areas of specialty, Faye was someone on whom I could always depend to offer a wealth of knowledge about key parts of my book. I greatly appreciate her for always "sticking it out" with me and for being a person I can confide in concerning a wide range of professional and personal matters. Like so many others, I am a happy beneficiary of her gift of mentoring.

Years ago, I discovered writing can sometimes be more "fun" when I am surrounded by other hardworking writers—cue in writing groups and accountability partners! It was a pleasure to participate in writing groups for brief periods during different phases of this book. Usually, my desire for such groups was when I felt I needed a shot of writing adrenaline. I actually forgot who first introduced me to the world of writing accountability partners, but I am so grateful to whoever it was. Thanks to Rhonda Williams—whose research area is math—for our many writing sessions in the early days of this project. Despite our different fields, success was our common goal. It was a pleasure to meet Michelle Boyd a few years ago and participate in her Inkwell residential writing retreat, Composed. I am thankful for that summer connection in the woods (despite my up-close encounter with a black bear—lol) because it ultimately resulted in Michelle as well as other great scholars becoming resources for me, including Ifeoma Nwankwo and Kim F. Hall. I also participated in the Sisters of the Academy (SOTA) writing retreat while I was a Provost's Postdoctoral Scholar at the University of South Florida. I am appreciative of the help from and continued connections with sister-scholars. While I was a postdoctoral fellow at the University of San Diego, I participated in faculty writing sessions as well; I am thankful for the colleagues I came to know at that institution. By far, one of the most wonderful professional development experiences that aided my writing and research productivity for this book was with the National Center for Faculty Development and Diversity's Faculty Success Program. Thank you, Kerry Ann Rockquemore! I feel forever indebted to you for all the information I gained and the fantastic connections I made through this organization, including folks such as Naomi Greyser, Anthony Ocampo, and Badia Ahad (who helped me "bootcamp" my book proposal and revise parts of the manuscript).

The University of Pittsburgh, along with many other institutions, organizations, and foundations, provided funding for various parts of this project. I would like to thank my departmental colleagues at the University of Pittsburgh (including the chair of the Department of Africana Studies, Yolanda Covington-Ward, for her leadership) and colleagues in several departments and offices across the university for support and fellowship. I extend thanks to the dean's and provost's offices at Pitt for much support. Funds from the dean's office paid for me to participate in the Inkwell residential writing retreat. The dean's office also awarded me research funds for the manuscript and nominated me as one of two people to represent the university in the National Endowment for the Humanities Summer Stipend competition. I am thankful, too, for the book subvention provided by the Dietrich School, via the Richard D. and Mary Jane Edwards Endowed Publication Fund. The Junior Faculty Research Leave for a semester and the dean's nominating me for participation in the provost office's inaugural Institutional Mentoring Program Across a CommuniTy of Color (IMPACT) were also valuable to me. The two Hewlett International Grants from the University Center for International Studies and the Global Studies Center Faculty Research Grant were significant in enabling me to do further research in the Caribbean and receive feedback on different parts of my project. The World History Center Grant helped cover expenses related to the book. Supported by the Andrew W. Mellon Foundation, the Collecting Knowledge Pittsburgh's "Work Forces: Mobilizing the Visual and Material Cultures of Labor" workshop assisted me with thinking more broadly about the scope of my work.

I am grateful for my time in Atlanta, Georgia, at Emory University where I spent my Ford Foundation Postdoctoral Fellowship year working on this book. Researching and living in Atlanta was a wonderful and needed experience for me. I would like to extend thanks to Dwight A. McBride, Michelle M. Wright, Carol Anderson, Valerie Babb, Meina Yates-Richard, Michelle Y. Gordon, Carol E. Henderson, Jericho Brown, Andra Gillespie, Rhonda Patrick, Courtney R. Baker, Shante Paradigm Smalls, and Barbara McCaskill. Some of the organizations and offices that have supported my research in its earliest stages deserve mention as well, including the Modern Language Association (South Atlantic), the Working-Class Studies Association, the Florida Education Fund, and the University of Florida's College of Liberal Arts and Sciences and Department of English. It excites me that so many others have agreed that my project is a worthwhile venture.

Thanks to the people who helped me with my book publishing jitters and inquiries; some of those include Alisha Gaines, Kevin Quashie, Deirdre Cooper Owens, Aneeka A. Henderson, and Ashley D. Farmer. At various points on my journey, people have made the sun's rays shine brighter on me. I want to thank the following people—in no particular order—who have either helped me in some way (including through their wonderful friendship!) or who have produced awesome scholarship that kept me interrogating my ideas and ultimately facilitated my intellectual growth: Jerrilyn McGegory, Maxine Montgomery, Maxine Jones, Robert J. Patterson, Carol Boyce-

Davies, Meredith Gadsby, Tera Hunter, Herman Beavers, Stacie McCormick, Tanisha C. Ford, Andreá N. Williams, Marlo David, Marlon Moore, Natanya Duncan, Angelique V. Nixon, Stephanie Y. Evans, Ayesha Hardison, Kim Blockett, Koritha Mitchell, Cynthia A. Young, Monica Coleman, Darryl Dickson-Carr, Candice M. Jenkins, Elizabeth Metzger, Vernetta K. Williams, Donovan Ramon, Yomaira Figueroa, Marquita Smith, Maria Rice Bellamy, Yolanda Martínez-San Miguel, Hadassah St. Hubert, Sonali Perera, Trimiko Melancon, Kelly Baker Josephs, Joseph Entin, Nicholas Coles, Sherry L. Linkon, Michele Fazio, Betsy Leondar-Wright, Treva Lindsey, Samantha Pinto, Brittney Cooper, Dean Makuluni, Christina Greene, Craig Werner, Stanlie James, and the late Nellie Y. McKay.

Also, I give great thanks to those who offered me feedback and facilitated my research while I was in residence at the University of the West Indies, Mona, in Kingston, Jamaica, especially Nadi Edwards, who is such a kind-hearted person, as well as Khitanya Petgrave, Carolyn Cooper, Michael A. Bucknor, Anthea Morrison, Carolyn Allen, Verene Shepherd, and Kimberly Robinson-Walcott.

For their interviews and communication with me, I offer great thanks to the writers appearing in this project: Olive Senior, Diana McCaulay, Merle Hodge, and Dawn Turner. Thank you to Sharon Burney, Keisha Brissette, and Natalee Cole for also allowing me to interview them about their work in my earliest stages of prepping for this project.

Thank you so much to the awesome University of North Carolina Press and its team! Lucas Church is a stellar editor and demonstrated his deftness with editorial business from my very first interaction with him. I give a huge shout-out to the anonymous readers for helping make my project so much better. Thank you to the *Journal of West Indian Literature* for allowing me to use a version of the article I published for my book chapter on McCaulay.

I cannot possibly name everyone, but know I am grateful, and I count it a blessing that there are far too many to name. Bunche Park, North Dade, and NM folks—y'all shaped me; thank you! I give special thanks to my McKnight family for their support and belief in me. Finally, I say thank you to all my loved ones—and give the biggest thanks to those right in my face! Thanks for your unwavering faith in me, encouragement, patience, cheers, and prayers throughout this part of my life's journey. Jeremiah 29:11.

Notes

Introduction

1. See U.S. Census Bureau, Quick Facts. The website notes that as of July 2019, the population is 2.7 million and 15.7 percent are living in poverty. Later in this chapter, I explicitly discuss class categories (e.g., working class, middle class, poor, working poor) and various definitions of class.

2. See Viglucci et al., "'A History of Broken Promises.'"

3. See Jones, "Florida's Failed Pandemic Response."

4. For a discussion of racial capitalism as a cause of the racial and socioeconomic inequities displayed within the pandemic, see Pirtle, "Racial Capitalism."

5. Examples of book publications on the subject of class in these disciplines include Gest's *New Minority*, Isenberg's *White Trash*, Wolff's *Century of Wealth in America*, Franko and Witko's *New Economic Populism*, Desmond's *Evicted*, Fields and Fields's *Racecraft*, and Stiglitz's *Price of Inequality*.

6. Throughout this book, the term "Caribbean" refers to parts of the Anglophone Caribbean, specifically Jamaica and the twin-island nation Trinidad and Tobago. The phrase "Black women" refers to women of the African Diaspora, especially African American and Afro-Caribbean women. The phrases "post–civil rights" and "post–independence" signify the long contemporary period from the 1970s up to the 2010s and appear interchangeably at times. Discussion of the second renaissance appears later in this chapter.

7. Some of the novels examined in this book are not canonical, but class analysis is still essential to all the novels under examination.

8. See Lauter, "Under Construction," 68; and Christopher and Whitson, "Toward a Theory of Working-Class Literature," 74.

9. See Johnson, "To Remake the World." Scholar of prison abolition Ruth Wilson Gilmore also asserts that capitalism is "never not racial" ("Abolition Geography," 225). Katie Donington further explains that scholars believe "that slavery and colonization were the foundations of racial capitalism. The recent upsurge of interest within academia of the relationship between capitalism and slavery traces its roots to [Eric] Williams's pioneering arguments about the role slavery played in the development of the systems of global capital, industrialization, and the emergence of free trade" ("Eric Williams' Foundational Work").

10. Robinson, *Black Marxism*, 2. See also Hudson, "Racial Capitalism and the Dark Proletariat," for a thorough discussion of the different ways the concept of racial capitalism has been used historically. Additionally, Smallwood, "What Slavery Tells Us about Marx," details Karl Marx's (lack of) attention to the real significance of slavery in capitalism.

11. See Melamed, *Represent and Destroy*, 39.

12. For more on neoliberalism, see, for example, Harvey, *A Brief History of Neoliberalism*, Hong, *Death beyond Disavowal*, Brown, *Undoing the Demos*, and Ferguson, *The Reorder of Things*.

13. See the scholarship of Darrick Hamilton, a forerunner in the field of stratification economics, including "Neoliberalism and Race."

14. Hamilton, "Neoliberalism and Race."

15. Kelley, *Yo' Mama's Disfunktional!*, 9. More recently, Kelley writes in his foreword to Henry A. Giroux's *America at War with Itself*, "While many of us are fully familiar with neoliberal policies that have redistributed wealth upward, ripped away any real safety net for the poor, and promoted capital flight, outsourcing, and free trade policies that destroy the environment and reduce much of the world's labor force to semi-slavery, we are less familiar with policies and practices that cultivate popular ignorance, that reduce the body politic to civic illiterates, and that privatize what ought to be an open and vibrant public sphere" ("We Hold the Future," xiv).

16. See McDowell, *"The Changing Same,"* preface, and Kuhn, *Structure of Scientific Revolutions*. Again, many scholars use the term "second renaissance" to describe the proliferation in texts by and about Black women, including Madhu Dubey and Caroline Rody, who also uses the term to describe the increase in African American and Caribbean women's writing in the late twentieth century. See Rody, *Daughter's Return*, 9–10; and Dubey, *Black Women Novelists*.

17. The second renaissance is also germane to this project because it coincides with the critical and theoretical shifts in Black literary studies during the 1970s, as expressed in a number of critical texts. Concerning the year 1970, Stanlie M. James, Frances S. Foster, and Beverly Guy-Sheftall, editors of *Still Brave*, write that it "was a significant year for the emerging concepts of race/gender/class and intersectional approaches to the study of women" (xiv). Dubey, in *Black Women Novelists*, elaborates on the Black women's literary renaissance, or the "second renaissance' of the 1970s" (1), describing it as a critical moment in literary history when novels and critical works by authors such as Toni Morrison, Alice Walker, and Toni Cade Bambara began to gain widespread scholarly attention and "engendered a burgeoning and vigorous black feminist critical discourse" (1). Also, Hena Maes-Jelinek and Bénédicte Ledent observe a similar progression among Caribbean women writers, asserting that "if the emergence of a new generation of novelists may be viewed as one of the main developments of Caribbean literature since the seventies, the long-awaited recognition of writing by women was an even more striking phenomenon" ("The Caribbean Novel from 1970 to 1995," 177). Furthermore, the 1990s began to realize the aspirations noted in the genesis of Black women's studies that emerged from Black (or Africana) Studies, as a substantial increase in publications and scholarship on Black women emerged inside and outside of the academy in that decade. See James, Foster, and Guy-Sheftall, *Still Brave*, xxvi–xxvii, n14; Mitchell, *Within the Circle*; Griffin, "Key Texts in African American Literary Criticism"; and Smiles, "Popular Black Women's Fiction."

18. James Smethurst notes the dominance of poetry and drama publications during the Black Arts period (*Black Arts Movement*, 5). For connections between BAM and the twenty-first century, see Crawford, *Black Post-Blackness*. *Class Interruptions* acknowledges scholarship produced within and about the preceding literary and cultural arts

period of BAM and CAM that began in the 1960s in association with the genesis of the field of Africana Studies for providing a foundation for this project. Given that discussions of class were widespread in this period, the shift away from extensive class-focused scholarship in the contemporary period is ironic. Bill V. Mullen provides an examination of the absence of class portrayals in contemporary African American literary criticism and credits BAM, which he calls "a de facto working class cultural movement" ("Breaking the Signifying Chain," 152), for putting forth detailed analyses of working classes. He argues that a framework of race has displaced class and that, beginning with the slave narrative tradition, critics most often see slavery as making race instead of class (148). Mullen's argument resonates with the claim Guyanese historian and political activist Walter Rodney made decades earlier in his noted *The Groundings with My Brothers*, where he observed that the enterprise of slavery in the West Indies was based, first, on economics but race soon played an extensive role in the system (25). Additionally, several scholars note the reality of class differences among Black people during slavery, including attention to mulattoes, or mixed-race individuals, who were often "house slaves" with more privileges and who formed an upper class or Black elite after emancipation. See Lacy, *Blue-Chip Black*, chap. 1; Andrews, *Slavery and Class in the American South*; Cole and Omari, "Race, Class and the Dilemmas," 786–87; and Robinson, *Black Marxism*. Moreover, Amy Ongiri notes that the praise of working-class culture during BAM was "very much in keeping with the Black Panther Party's elevation of 'the brothers on the block' to vanguard status in radical African American politics" (*Spectacular Blackness*, 23). The "brothers on the block" referred to what Karl Marx called the "lumpenproletariat," in this case, African Americans who were severely disenfranchised and often chronically unemployed. BAM coincided with the Black power movement and U.S. civil rights movement in many ways. Examining this reality, bell hooks, in *Killing Rage*, observes that "a major difference in the agendas set by the movement for civil rights and militant struggles for black power was caused by different class perspectives" and that "the values shaping this struggle [the civil rights movement] were fundamentally bourgeois" (163).

Like BAM artists, Edward Kamau Brathwaite has long praised the culture of Caribbean working classes and co-founded, along with John LaRose and Andrew Salkey, CAM (1966–1972) in London, which was similar to but not as well known or large as BAM. CAM was significant in bringing together writers, artists, painters, filmmakers, actors, and musicians of Caribbean descent; it was also male-dominated like BAM. Brathwaite affirms the use and evolution of "nation language," a language he identifies as the language of slaves (enslaved Africans) and servants (*History of the Voice*). Along with George Lamming, who also exalted the peasant novel and folk narrative, Brathwaite championed the idea that the 1960s were the foundational years of Caribbean literature (erroneously). Scholars such as Leah Rosenberg have revealed that the history of Caribbean literature begins well before the 1960s. See Rosenberg, *Nationalism and the Formation of Caribbean Literature*; Brathwaite, "The Caribbean Artists Movement"; and Walmsley, *The Caribbean Artists Movement, 1966–1972*.

19. The most popular writing of that time did not center on women characters or women-centered concerns. A number of scholars who examine BAM refer to the widespread discussions of class in the creative writing of that period as well.

20. See McCaulay, "Uptown and Downtown," 99.

21. Morrison, *Lecture and Speech*.

22. As a result of its multidisciplinary frame, this book is in dialogue with a number of scholars, including literary and cultural studies scholars with recent publications in the area. Over the past few years, various texts highlighting class concerns from literary and cultural studies fields have been published, including Andrews, *Slavery and Class in the American South* (2019), Jenkins, *Black Bourgeois* (2019), Merish, *Archives of Labor* (2017), Robinson, *Dreams for Dead Bodies* (2016), Perera, *No Country* (2014), Lawson, *Class and the Making of American Literature* (2014), A. Williams, *Dividing Lines* (2013), Lawson, *Downwardly Mobile* (2012), Tokarczyk, *Critical Approaches of American Working Class Literature* (2011), Marsh, *Hog Butchers, Beggars, and Busboys* (2011), Murray, "The Time of Breach" (2010), Wilson, *More Than Just Race* (2009), Boyce-Davies, *Left of Karl Marx* (2008), and Dow, *Narrating Class in American Fiction* (2008).

23. See A. Williams, *Dividing Lines*, 13. Williams further explains that in the antebellum period, African American literature displayed more harmonious relations between Black classes. Williams also evokes the Black women's club movement of the late nineteenth and early twentieth century, which was very aware of class differences. In *Too Heavy a Load*, Deborah Gray White discusses the National Association of Colored Women (NACW), one of the largest assemblies of Black women's clubs throughout the nation, whose motto was "Lifting as We Climb" and was based on an ideology of racial uplift. Angela Y. Davis critiques the belief of the mostly middle-class leaders of the club movement that their behaviors should be followed: "What was and remains problematic is the premise that middle-class women embody a standard their poorer sisters should be encouraged to emulate" (*Blues Legacies and Black Feminism*, 43). See also, Brooks, "Looking to Foremothers for Strength."

24. A. Williams, *Dividing Lines*, 3.

25. See Lang, *Black America in the Shadow of the Sixties*.

26. See Thorin, *The Gender Dimension of Economic Globalization*, Collins, *Black Feminist Thought*, and Pearce, "The Feminization of Poverty."

27. David Harvey writes of the tumultuous period that "the turn to neoliberal politics occurred in the midst of a crisis in the 1970s, and the whole system has been a series of crises ever since. And of course crises produce the conditions of future crises" ("Neoliberalism Is a Political Project").

28. *Class Interruptions* focuses on more recent relationship dynamics between classes while recognizing that the writers build on the work of their literary foremothers. Even before the 1970s, Black women writers made their mark on the Black literary canon and addressed a number of matters related to Black people's lived experiences. Black women writers such as Jessie Fauset, Zora Neale Hurston, Paule Marshall, Gwendolyn Brooks, Dorothy West, and Ann Petry strategically delineated a class-conscious reality in their writing. Literary critic Mary Helen Washington identifies Alice Childress's 1956 novel, *Like One of the Family*, as the first proletarian novel by a Black woman ("Alice Childress, Lorraine Hansberry, and Claudia Jones," 202). Washington notes that Barbara Foley erroneously calls Margaret Walker's *Jubilee* (1966) novel the first proletarian novel by a Black woman because many do not know about Childress. Hurston's *Their Eyes Were Watching God* (1937), which focuses

on the protagonist Janie and the working-class community around her, receives much fanfare, but her other writing, including the short story "The Gilded Six Bits" (1933), also spotlights class by highlighting a community enthralled by a flashy newcomer who is laced with gold pieces, which turn out to be fake. While Caribbean women writers did not gain much recognition for their writing until the 1970s and 1980s, a collective of Caribbean women writers, including Una Marson, Louise Bennett, Vera Bell, Judy Miles, Clara Maude Garrett, and Sylvia Wynter, made inroads within the literary arts. Some also tackled tough subjects concerning the reality of the masses in their nations. Marson and Bennett, for instance, boldly addressed race and class issues not only in their thematic choices but also in their decision to break from using standard English to using the language of the folk or "everyday" people in their creative writing. The literary successors of these earlier generations of writers continue to blaze their paths and use a deliberate pattern with the cross-class relationship trope to convey and highlight an awareness of class difference. For information about Caribbean women writers, including poets, gaining recognition and becoming more widely read since the 1980s, see essays in Bucknor and Donnell, *The Routledge Companion to Anglophone Caribbean Literature* (especially Edwards, "Sylvia Wynter: Insurgent Criticism"), as well as volume 2 of Arnold, Rodríguez-Luis, and Dash, *A History of Literature in the Caribbean* (especially Maes-Jelinek and Ledent, "The Caribbean Novel from 1970 to 1995," and Baugh, "A History of Poetry").

29. Lacy, *Blue-Chip Black*, 23, 30. John Russo and Sherry Linkon discuss that nearly half of Americans consider themselves to be working class ("Introduction," 10). Also, several more recent financial market and business news articles observe that most Americans erroneously identify themselves as middle class. For instance, see Martin, "70% of Americans Consider Themselves Middle Class—but Only 50% Are."

30. See Lacy, *Blue-Chip Black*, chap. 1, for a discussion of indicators.

31. Lacy, *Blue-Chip Black*, 35–42.

32. For outlines of class stratification systems in Caribbean nations, see Ulysse, *Downtown Ladies*, 13; Maingot, *Gordon K. Lewis on Race, Class and Ideology in the Caribbean*; and La Guerre, "A Review of Race and Class in the Caribbean."

33. While national governments usually do not offer definitions of terms such as "class," "working class," or "middle class," some national governments do offer a definition of poverty based on income levels of their citizens.

34. Lauter and Fitzgerald, *Literature, Class and Culture*, 3–4.

35. Lauter and Fitzgerald, *Literature, Class and Culture*, 3.

36. Pierre Bourdieu's work on taste, cultural capital, and habitus, as in *Distinction*, is significant to my discussions of class. Scholars who have extended Bourdieu's ideas on these matters include Ortner, "Bourdieu and 'History'"; Young, *Embodying Black Experience*; and McMillan Cottom, *Lower Ed*.

37. Michael Zweig describes the capitalist class as people who "own and control businesses of all sizes" (*Working Class Majority*, 13), and he underscores levels of power between capitalists. The middle class "includes professional people, small business owners, and managers and supervisors who have authority over others at work," while the working class consists of people who are "skilled and unskilled . . .

[and] share a common place in production, where they have relatively little control over the pace or content of their work" (*Working Class Majority*, 3).

38. For instance, Zweig believes they should be looked at together (*Working Class Majority*, 78) while Vivyan C. Adair believes they should not because someone from a background of generational poverty faces different circumstances than someone with a stable low-paying job; see Adair, "Class Absences."

39. In the introduction to *New Working-Class Studies*, Russo and Linkon discuss the place of "systems of power, oppression, and exploitation" in working-class studies (11).

40. Coles and Zandy, *American Working-Class Literature*, xxii.

41. Russo and Linkon, "Introduction," 11.

42. See Hamilton, "Neoliberalism and Race."

43. In *What's Class Got to Do with It?* Zweig writes, "Power exists as a relationship between and among different people or groups. This means that we cannot talk about one class of people alone, without looking at relationships between that class and others. Working class studies, then, necessarily involves the study of other classes, most importantly the capitalist class. But in working class studies, we look at all classes in society from the point of view of working people—their lives, experiences, needs, and interests" (4).

44. Erik Wright conducted a study among capitalist countries aimed at examining the likelihood of friendships across class boundaries. He found the least permeable class boundary is between the working class and the employer/capitalist class. The most permeable class boundary is between the worker and the supervisor or the working class and the middle class. See Wright, *Class Counts*.

45. Collins, *Black Feminist Thought*, 61. See also the following foundational articles: Crenshaw, "Demarginalizing the Intersection" and "Mapping the Margins"; Beale, "Double Jeopardy"; and King, "Multiple Jeopardy."

46. hooks, *Where We Stand*, 8.

47. See Barriteau, *Love and Power: Caribbean Discourses on Gender* and "Relevance of Black Feminist Scholarship," as well as Mohammed, *Gendered Realities: Essays in Caribbean Feminist Thought* and "Towards Indigenous Feminist Theorizing."

48. For more on the topic, see Pearce's work, "The Feminization of Poverty" and "The Feminization of Ghetto Poverty." Also, bell hooks elaborates, explaining that "women of all races and black men are rapidly becoming the poorest of the poor" (*Where We Stand*, viii).

49. Carole Boyce-Davies, in *Left of Karl Marx*, notes that it was the norm that Black feminist scholars would use race and gender approaches in their scholarship during the 1980s and 1990s (4).

50. Darrick Hamilton further explains, "In addition to wages, wealth disparity, and mass incarceration, black Americans face other obstacles to economic inclusion such as vulnerability to predatory finance, municipal fees, shortage of affordable housing (and the instability associated with evictions), food insecurity, environmental injustice, and climate gentrification. These vulnerabilities disproportionately fall on women, blacks, and other nonwhites. Their education, employment, and earnings are more precarious and they tend to have more caregiving and financial responsibilities" ("Neoliberalism and Race").

51. Jarrett, *Representing the Race*, 9; Iton, *In Search of the Black Fantastic*, 4.

52. Kelley, *Race Rebels*, 33.

53. Russo and Linkon, "Introduction," 6. They note that analysis of literature as a source for understanding working-class experience has become a dominant approach in studying working-class culture.

54. Harper, *Abstractionist Aesthetics*, 2; emphasis in original.

55. Robert J. Patterson writes, "Cultural production and politics work dialogically, and . . . [they] both help us to understand the past and the present and to imagine the future" ("Dreams Reimagined," 5).

56. Trimiko Melancon discusses how the fiction of Black male writers, particularly protest fiction writers such as Richard Wright, James Baldwin, and Ralph Ellison, centered mainly on male protagonists (*Unbought*, 24).

57. Patterson, "Dreams Reimagined," 6; emphasis in original.

58. Connolly, "This, Our Second Nadir"; Iton, *In Search of the Black Fantastic*, 19.

59. Hamilton, "Neoliberalism and Race"; Strong, "Interview with Darrick Hamilton."

60. Harrison, *Outsider Within*, 112–13.

61. Harrison, *Outsider Within*, 119–20; emphasis in original.

62. A. Williams, *Dividing Lines*, 3.

63. Keizer, *Black Subjects*, 8.

64. A. Williams, *Dividing Lines*, 4.

65. Taking a similar perspective, Melancon argues that Black women's fiction is not simply imaginative; rather, it speaks to the sociopolitical climate in which it was produced (*Unbought*, 13). Moreover, Patterson observes, "The solutions black cultural production offers often require us to invoke our imaginations and think outside of the norms that the existing sociopolitical order disciplines us to call upon when we imagine or think about black freedom" ("Dreams Reimagined," 6).

66. Christopher and Whitson, "Toward a Theory of Working-Class Literature," 72. Additionally, Janet Zandy is not bashful about the intent of her scholarship; she proclaims that her text is indeed political (*Calling Home*, 8).

67. See Wright, *Physics of Blackness*, for a discussion on the need to have more inclusive definitions of Blackness and to move beyond a "Middle Passage Blackness," which continues to be the "most frequently discussed, published, and assumed epistemology" when defining Blackness (12).

68. The novels I examine in this book project are Gloria Naylor's *Linden Hills*, Dawn Turner's *Only Twice I've Wished for Heaven*, Toni Morrison's *Love* and *Tar Baby*, Diana McCaulay's *Dog-Heart*, Merle Hodge's *Crick Crack, Monkey*, Olive Senior's *Dancing Lessons*, and Oonya Kempadoo's *Tide Running*. A few examples of some other novels with a sustained cross-class relationship—but not discussed in this book—include Paule Marshall's *The Fisher King*, Sherley Anne Williams's *Dessa Rose*, Octavia Butler's *Fledgling*, Zee Edgell's *Beka Lamb*, Michelle Cliff's *Abeng* and *No Telephone to Heaven*, Erna Brodber's *Myal*, Andrea Lee's *Sarah Phillips*, and Jamaica Kincaid's *Annie John*. This trope appears in some novels by male writers as well as in other genres, such as the short story, by both men and women. Examples are Ernest J. Gaines's *A Lesson Before Dying*, David Bradley's *The Chaneysville Incident*, John Edgar Wideman's *Brothers and Keepers*, Randall Kenan's *A Visitation of Spirits*, Walter Mosley's Easy Rawlings Series,

James Alan McPherson's "The Story of a Scar," Alice Walker's "Everyday Use," and Toni Cade Bambara's "The Lesson," "Mississippi Ham Rider," and "The Johnson Girls."

69. See Patterson, "Dreams Reimagined," 10–11, and Rosenberg, *Nationalism and the Formation of Caribbean Literature*. Moreover, African American and Caribbean creative writers have delineated working-class culture in literary works for well over a century in both the United States and English-speaking Caribbean nations. In fact, working-class characters or characters representative of what some called "folk" or "peasant culture" were common and popular features of literature in countries such as Jamaica and Trinidad and Tobago; see Rosenberg, *Nationalism and the Formation of Caribbean Literature*, 1–12. While there are exceptions such as Richard Wright's *Native Son* (1940) and Ann Petry's *The Street* (1946), which gained literary fame, mainstream U.S. society frequently deemed working-class portrayals as part of an alternative literary tradition. See Coles and Zandy, *American Working-Class Literature*, xix–xx. During specific times in U.S. history, such as the Depression era of the 1930s, the U.S. mainstream "embraced" literature about working classes (i.e., proletarian literature). Africana Studies opened the door for the mainstreaming of African American and Caribbean literature.

70. Keizer, *Black Subjects*; Rody, *Daughter's Return*.

71. Harvey writes: "Resistance to neoliberalism can occur in a number of different ways" ("Neoliberalism Is a Political Project"). And Faye V. Harrison writes: "Despite neoliberalization's pervasiveness and interpenetration with governmentality, globalization and the opportunities it creates for networks of transnational communication and solidarity have opened up new spaces for resistance and counterhegemonic action" ("Anthropology Interrogating Power and Politics," 17).

72. Collins, *Black Feminist Thought*, 274.

73. Leith Mullings discusses countermodels in *On Our Own Terms*, 94–101.

74. Lauter and Fitzgerald, *Literature, Class and Culture*, 2.

75. See Aneeka Henderson, *Veil and Vow*, for discussion of the relationship between neoliberal policies and marriage.

76. Pattillo-McCoy, *Black Picket Fences*, 28.

77. For more on colorism and Caribbean societies, see Stuart Hall, "Pluralism, Race and Class in Caribbean Society" and "Race, Articulation and Societies Structured in Dominance."

78. Concerning Black male youth culture, Caribbean writers in this project present a more dismal picture than African American writers in suggesting extreme hopelessness among these young men. Each of the Caribbean novels depicts criminal activity among young Black men.

79. See Patterson, "Dreams Reimagined," for discussion of this paradox in the post–civil rights era.

80. See Hamilton et al., *Umbrellas Don't Make It Rain*. In his scholarship, Hamilton also discusses gross disparities in inherited wealth among Blacks in the United States. See, for instance, "Neoliberalism and Race."

81. See Zweig, *The Working Class Majority*, where he also explains that people must be proactive to combat the continued declines (64–69).

82. Ulysse, *Downtown Ladies*, 13. Decades earlier, Margaret Bass noted that the Black population remains "the largest and poorest racial group in the West Indies" ("Race, Class, and Gender," 133).

83. Working-class studies is a multi- and interdisciplinary field, encompassing disciplines such as literature, economics, labor studies, anthropology, and sociology. In general, working-class literary studies focuses on literature identified as "working-class literature," which refers broadly to literature that focuses on the experiences of people in the working classes. Please note that *Class Interruptions* does not classify the novels under consideration as working-class literature per se, but it does assert that these novels overlap with working-class literary traditions. Still, some people classify the writing of some authors discussed in this book, particularly Gloria Naylor and Toni Morrison, as working-class literature. See Coles and Zandy, *American Working-Class Literature*, and Zandy, *Hands*, 91. Zandy asserts that working-class studies emerges during "a critical moment, a time of ruthless economic disparities, of disappeared jobs and struggling cities and towns, of political and corporate oligarchies, and fear of America's vulnerability and its imperialistic power" (*Hands*, 3). Moreover, both Black women's studies and working-class scholarship privilege an intersectional analytical approach. As scholar of working-class studies Michelle Tokarczyk notes, intersectional analysis, borrowed from Black feminist thought, is a common approach among working-class literary critics (Tokarczyk, *Class Definitions*, 14). This approach is not the only instance in which working-class studies discourses intermingle with Africana Studies discourses. Zandy refers to W. E. B. Du Bois's concept of double consciousness in her explication of working-class writers who move into the middle class: "For writers who were born into the working class and aspire out of it through education or professional jobs, the connecting link back to a community is sometimes tangled or even lost. These writers come closer to a sense of what W. E. B. Du Bois speaking of race, called 'two-ness,' being in two worlds at the same time and belonging to neither of them" (*Calling Home*, 12). She also invokes the term "passing" in reference to people attempting to conceal their class origins. It is easier to pass concerning class, but not so much when it comes to race for most people. For more on interconnections of race and working-class literature, see Balthaser, "The Race of Class."

As a result of the far-reaching history of overlaps between Black cultural thought and leftist traditions, *Class Interruptions* also easily engages with leftist and Marxist discourses as well as scholarship dealing with a global focus, building on the works of scholars such as Carole Boyce-Davies, Sonali Perera, and Janet Zandy. For more on these topics, see Robinson, *Black Marxism*, Mullen and Smethurst, *Left of the Color Line*, and Orr, *Transforming American Realism*. Ultimately, this project agrees with working-class studies forerunners such as Zandy, who recognizes that such studies deepen "class analysis and provides a space for reciprocal visibility across divisions of race, ethnicity, citizenship, and geography" (*Hands*, 3). Highlighting various intersections, Boyce-Davies's study of Trinidadian-born Claudia Jones examines the trailblazing efforts of this radical Black woman who identified as "a communist of Marxist-Leninist orientation" and placed Black working-class women at the center of her efforts (*Left of Karl Marx*, 5). She explains how Jones used several avenues (e.g., editorials, poetry, and political essays) to forward her agenda against various forms of oppression. Ultimately, Boyce-Davies models how to consciously insert the transnational into larger discussions of Black feminist thought while emphasizing the import of class and left history. *Class Interruptions* builds on Boyce-Davies's discussions and extends analysis more broadly to the representation of these ideas in the fiction of Black women writers.

84. See A. Williams, *Dividing Lines*, 6–7, and Coles and Zandy, *American Working-Class Literature*. Rhonda Cobham-Sander discusses middle-class authors and how their experiences and use of folk culture are different from working-class authors in the conclusion of her essay "Revisioning Our Kumblas."

85. Coles and Zandy, *American Working-Class Literature*, xxii.

86. Lamming, "Occasion for Speaking," 39.

87. Lubrano, *Limbo*, 2.

88. During my doctoral studies, I spent a fellowship year (2012–13) as a specially admitted research student in the Department of Literatures in English at the University of the West Indies, Mona, in Jamaica. While in Jamaica, I was able to conduct literary fieldwork, or ethnographic research—to borrow from the fields of anthropology and sociology. Some of the literary and cultural spaces and places that offered fruitful exchanges included the monthly fellowships of the Poetry Society of Jamaica hosted at the Edna Manley College of the Visual and Performing Arts; local theater venues including the Pantry Playhouse, the Theatre Place, and Centre Stage Theatre; literary arts and music festivals such as Kingston Pon Di River; and lecture series and book launches by writers such as Paulette A. Ramsay and Curdella Forbes staged at the University of the West Indies, Mona, campus. Additionally, I had the opportunity to volunteer with the Sistren Theatre Collective, a Jamaican working-class organization of women that began in 1977 and confronts class issues using literary avenues with the goal of exposing and eradicating the serious situations that working-class women face, including domestic violence, sexual abuse, and teenage pregnancy. I worked with their young adult community ambassadors and at a primary school in a working-class area, Drewsland Primary. Aside from Sistren, I volunteered around town independently at schools in different areas, including the uptown schools of Campion College (high school) and Mona Preparatory School (primary school) as well as the downtown Dunoon Technical High School. For more on Sistren, see Ford-Smith, *Ring Ding in a Tight Corner*; Sistren, with Honor Ford-Smith, *Lionheart Gal*; and Green, "On a Knife Edge" and "Sistren Theatre Collective."

89. I was able to examine unpublished writing by writers who currently identify as working class or who have recently emerged from a working-class background. The interviews provided me with a context for understanding the positions of writers. A key difference between their work and the largely canonical novelists in *Class Interruptions* is a lack of direct concentration on class issues; they are distinct from the canonical writers in terms of genre, status of the writer, and attention to the theme of class. There can be no comparisons of their use of a cross-class relationship trope because they do not use it. What probably accounts most for the difference is the question of audience. The works I examined by these authors are unpublished, and

none has the kind of following that the more widely read canonical writers studied in this book have. They also differ from the other writers in this book in that none of them have completed novels; instead, they write short stories, poetry, and drama.

Chapter One

1. For more on this topic, see Taylor, *Race for Profit*, and Rothstein, *The Color of Law*.

2. Dawn Turner's former name is Dawn Turner Trice; her former name appears on the novel's cover. Also, page citations for the novels will be made parenthetically in the text.

3. I use the words "neighborhood" and "community" interchangeably throughout the chapter. However, some scholars, such as sociologist Mary Pattillo, describe neighborhoods as parts of a community: "broadening the analytic framework suggests that poverty neighborhoods are in fact one part of a segregated black community that also consists of moderate-, middle-, and sometimes high-income neighborhoods" (*Black Picket Fences*, 209).

4. Within the Nedeed family, there are multiple Luther Nedeeds, as each generation gave birth to a son and named him Luther Nedeed. Luther Nedeed, the current "Luther's double great-grandfather" (2), purchases the land, which seemed uninhabitable or useless to the local whites, during the 1800s. After building himself a house at the bottom of the hill near a cemetery, he establishes a funeral business and has enough money to build wooden houses along the hill to rent out.

5. After Nedeed's creation of the Tupelo Realty Corporation and his renting of the houses to the residents for a 1,001 year lease, the process of choosing residents becomes more selective. Money is not always the qualifier that ensures residency in Linden Hills. Thus, the novel highlights various class markers other than simply money (15).

6. A. Williams discusses the "Great Migration narrative" or the "migration novel," which she defines as "an African American literary subgenre overtly preoccupied with the politics of space and mobility" (*Dividing Lines*, 82). In her discussion, she explains that economic and geographic mobility are aligned in such narratives, with characters moving from the U.S. South to the Northeast or Midwest oftentimes for employment opportunities (*Dividing Lines*, 89).

7. While the characters Lester and Willie in Naylor's novel are twenty years old, Temmy is eleven during the time of the main events in Turner's novel (the year 1976). Altogether, the narration that Temmy delivers about her experiences in Lakeland took place "nearly twenty years ago" (3) around 1994. Temmy is delivering a retrospective narrative in 1994, about her experiences in 1976.

8. See McKittrick, *Demonic Grounds*, Woods and McKittrick, *Black Geographies and the Politics of Place*, Said, *Orientalism*, and Williams, *The Country and the City*. McKittrick's work focuses directly on people across the African Diaspora. Edward Said and Raymond Williams use phrases such as "imaginative geography" and "knowable community," respectively, to characterize depictions of place within literature. Eric Bulson examines space within modern fiction with a focus on literary maps. He argues

that maps are significant to the way scholars theorize the various effects of spatial representation on readers (*Novels, Maps, Modernity*, 15). See also A. Brown, *The Black Skyscraper*.

9. A. Williams, *Dividing Lines*, 80.

10. A. Williams, *Dividing Lines*, 83.

11. A. Williams, *Dividing Lines*, 80.

12. A. Williams's articulation of the narrative strategy of "mapping class" also complements Marxist geographer and theorist David Harvey's ideas in *Social Justice and the City* about the relations between a city's space and the social processes that take place within that particular space. In his discussion of cities and urban planning, Harvey refers to "spatial consciousness" or the "geographical imagination" and explains that "this imagination enables the individual to recognize the role of space and place in his own biography, to relate to the spaces he sees around him, and to recognize how transactions between individuals and between organizations are affected by the space that separates them" (24). Regarding spatial consciousness, he writes that "the way space is fashioned can have a profound effect upon social processes" (24).

13. Although rich and illuminating, the existing body of scholarship on Naylor's and Turner's novels leaves room for me to incorporate a more rigorous examination and expansion of the novels' value and role in critiquing class relations among African Americans. Concerning *Linden Hills*, most scholars investigate the novel's structure and its resemblance to Dante's *Inferno*; they also focus on the external influences on residents in Linden Hills, such as the broader society's definition of success or the American Dream. Others concentrate on the type of community disconnect residents experience as they ascend the socioeconomic ladder, taking examples from the Nedeed family, and more specifically the Nedeed women. I especially want to note the critique of scholars regarding the representation of space in the novel. Luke Bouvier's discussion of space concerns a critique of "the black/white binary opposition" ("Reading in Black," 142), while Maxine Montgomery's examination, in *The Fiction of Gloria Naylor*, focuses largely on the domestic space with close examination of what she regards as the "house-home dichotomy" (21). Bouvier discusses the construction of Linden Hills as a space of "absolute blackness," or a valorization of blackness in opposition to the "white" half of the binary. Montgomery notes that the fictional geography is masculine and argues that Willa, Luther Nedeed's wife, whom Nedeed locks in the basement, possesses the potential to dismantle the patriarchal house (22), since Montgomery believes the basement represents a "space reserved for the subaltern" (34).

In contrast to *Linden Hills*, Turner's novel has generated substantially less scholarly attention, although critics have looked at key topics in the narrative. Some scholars focus on the depiction of the young protagonist Temmy's coming-of-age experience. Others highlight the overall meaning of community among African Americans as well as the relationship between Temmy and the ancestor figure of Miss Jonetta, who acts as a guide for the protagonist. Regarding spatial features in the novel, Corinne Duboin observes that Turner "incorporates spatial imagery . . . into her narrative to express her critical views on a mainstreaming black middle class that disconnects itself from the 'black folk'" ("Writing the Fragments," 63). In a similar manner, Lean'tin Bracks asserts that the middle-class Black characters earnestly separate themselves from the lifestyles and conditions facing the working-class residents of Thirty-Fifth Street ("Dawn Turner Trice," 455).

14. Turner reveals in an interview that "the setting for *Only Twice* was based on the community of [her] childhood, which was very much fragmented by class" (Turner, untitled email interview by Robin Brooks, November 28, 2012).

15. Pattillo, *Black on the Block*, 299. Pattillo's former name was Pattillo-McCoy, but *Class Interruptions* uses Pattillo throughout.

16. Several research studies, such as those conducted by The Eviction Lab at Princeton University, reveal that "the lack of affordable housing sits at the root of a host of social problems, from poverty and homelessness to educational disparities and health care" (Desmond, "Questions & Answers about Eviction").

17. Pattillo notes that an increase in studies on Black middle-class neighborhoods appeared in the late 1980s and early 1990s ("Black Middle-Class Neighborhoods," 307).

18. In their research on class within African American communities, psychologists Elizabeth Cole and Safiya Omari note that enslaved mulattoes, or mixed-race individuals, received better treatment "by virtue of their light skin and blood relations to the White, slave-owning class." After emancipation, many in this group continued to experience privileges and a higher status than other African Americans, forming an upper-class Black elite ("Race, Class and the Dilemmas of Upward Mobility," 786, 787).

19. Pattillo, *Black Picket Fences*, 13; Pattillo, "Black Middle-Class Neighborhoods," 305–6.

20. Pattillo notes that with the onset of the Great Migration and the subsequent formation of Black residential neighborhoods in northern cities, a Black middle class consisting of entrepreneurs and professionals began to grow (*Black Picket Fences*, 17). She also points out that contrary to a prevailing misconception, "the black middle class continues to live near and with the black poor" (*Black Picket Fences*, 13). Cole and Omari describe "a 'new Black middle class,' which came of age after the restrictions of Jim Crow began to lift, and consequently had access to a wider range of occupations, residential neighborhoods, and opportunities to purchase goods and services" ("Race, Class and the Dilemmas of Upward Mobility," 787). Additionally, African Americans acknowledged class differences even during segregation. As A. Williams writes, "Even when segregation forced African Americans to share public space, those spaces could be cordoned off by invisible class lines that were less obvious to outsiders" (*Dividing Lines*, 90).

21. Because of its focus, this chapter adds to a body of scholarship that examines such fiction, including Madhu Dubey's *Signs and Cities* and Yoshinobu Hakutani and Robert Butler's *The City in African-American Literature*.

22. According to Pattillo, "Blacks of all socioeconomic statuses tend to be confined to a limited geographic space, which is formally designated by the discriminatory practices of banks, insurance companies, and urban planners, and symbolically identified by the formation of cultural and social institutions" (*Black Picket Fences*, 25).

23. Chicago Housing Authority, "History."

24. See Pattillo, *Black on the Block*, chaps. 5 and 6, for discussion of Lakefront Properties public housing in Chicago. Pattillo further explains that the late 1960s was "the early period of black suburbanization" in Chicago (*Black Picket Fences*, 24).

25. Pattillo observes that "the current intraracial character of the conflicts does not absolve whites or governments" (*Black on the Block*, 182).

26. Pattillo, *Black Picket Fences*, 202.

27. Concerning middle-class Blacks, Pattillo discusses "the simultaneity of mobility and marginalization in American society" (*Black Picket Fences*, 209).

28. Pattillo, *Black on the Block*, 85; Pattillo, *Black Picket Fences*, 215. Pattillo further reveals that "unlike most whites, middle-class Black families must contend with the crime, dilapidated housing, and social disorder in the deteriorating poor neighborhoods that continue to grow in their direction" (*Black Picket Fences*, 6). See also García, "Historically Illustrating the Shift to Neoliberalism in the U.S. Home Mortgage Market."

29. Harvey, *Social Justice and the City*, 24. Pattillo explains that "African Americans, like other groups, have always tried to translate upward class mobility into geographic mobility, but remain physically and psychically close to the poorer neighborhoods they leave behind" (*Black Picket Fences*, 23). In many regards, this statement characterizes the Tilson family.

30. Lawrence O. Graham discusses the history and role of debutante cotillion balls among African American elites (*Our Kind of People*, chap. 3). Michelle Tokarczyk discusses class shame in fiction and among writers (*Class Definitions*, 22), as does Rita Felski ("Nothing to Declare," 38–39). The national nonprofit organization Class Action discusses shame among upper classes as well, observing that "upon becoming aware of their economic privilege, wealthy people can suffer from the guilt, shame and depression often associated with the realization that they may not feel like they deserve what they have, and that much of what they have may have come at the expense of other people" (Class Action, "About Class").

31. Jim Sidanius and Felicia Pratto's definition of legitimizing myths is useful here. Such myths "consist of attitudes, values, beliefs, stereotypes, and ideologies that provide moral and intellectual justification for the social practices that distribute social value within the social system" (*Social Dominance*, 45).

32. See Pattillo, *Black Picket Fences*, 28. Pattillo also observes that "class, status, and lifestyle are real axes of distinction in the black community that are perhaps heightened by the spatial proximity of, and interactional networks that exist between, blacks of varying classes" (*Black Picket Fences*, 209).

33. Pattillo discusses this reality among Black middle classes concerning Black working-class people (*Black on the Block*, 95).

34. See Durante and Fiske, "How Social-Class Stereotypes Maintain Inequality."

35. Leondar-Wright, *Class Matters*, 88.

36. In her analysis of Naylor's novel, the late Black feminist and literary scholar Barbara Christian asserts that "Willie and Lester are not opposed to each other's values" and observes that "Naylor may be suggesting that genuine friendship between men who share similar values . . . is critical to the African-American community's search for empowerment" ("Gloria Naylor's Geography," 372).

37. Pearlman and Henderson, "Gloria Naylor," 71.

38. Christian asserts that "Linden Hills is characterized as a group of houses that never becomes a community, a showplace precariously kept in place by the machinations of one wealthy black patriarchal family" ("Gloria Naylor's Geography," 349).

39. Bracks, "Dawn Turner Trice," 456.

40. Duboin elaborates on the fence as a metaphor ("A New Voice," 117). Duboin also writes that "Trice integrates the fence as a metaphor for the social and cultural divide between the black urban underclass at a dead end and upwardly mobile African Americans who ultimately, ironically, marginalize themselves further in their collective effort to conform and gain respectability. Thus, more than a physical borderline that separates the inside from the outside, the fence materializes binary oppositions between 'we' and 'they,' 'unity and dissolution, ascent and downfall, good and evil" ("Writing the Fragmented," 68).

41. There are multiple cross-class relationships in the novel. The main ones are between Temmy and Valerie and Temmy and Miss Jonetta.

42. While Lester and Willie are performing odd jobs throughout Linden Hills to acquire money during the holiday season, they find themselves in the midst of a crime scene at one point, as Laurel Dumont, a well-to-do resident, has deliberately leaped to her death from a bedroom window (249). Lester and Willie express disbelief that someone did not "get her to see a shrink" (256). Whereas matters of mental health and seeking counseling can be taboo among Black communities, Naylor's novel reiterates that such matters extend beyond class lines and are critical for all people. See Ward et al., "African American Men and Women's Attitude toward Mental Illness."

43. For more on this topic, see Assari and Jeremiah, "Intimate Partner Violence."

44. For sure, "it is not only this individual Nedeed who causes the destruction of this artificial world; for years, Linden Hills has been rotting from the inside" (Christian, "Gloria Naylor's Geography," 360).

45. Engles notes, "This novel's closing images, of the fall of the house of patriarchy and of two alternatively inclined men escaping Linden Hills to walk off into a new year, also suggest a fresh start in terms of resistance to several forms of anticommunal pressure" ("African American Whiteness," 676).

46. Duboin, "A New Voice," 119. Duboin also observes, "Trice uses the high-rise apartment building, divided up into codified spaces, as a metaphorical representation of social hierarchy" ("Writing the Fragmented," 61).

47. Pattillo, *Black on the Block*, 294.

48. Pattillo issues a "call for policymakers to treat poor and black communities fairly as a focus for advocacy, as places that are already mixed income and still underresourced, as places that absorb voucher-holding families that do not make 'mobility' moves, and as places with functional social networks, rational modes of behavior, and respectable moral codes that deserve consideration and nurturing rather than wanton dismantling and transformation" ("Investing," 42). On a related note, Pattillo argues, too, that people should be able to prosper where they are (*Black Picket Fences*, 217), and she underscores the role of discrimination in neighborhoods: "The fact that a neighborhood's racial makeup is frequently a proxy for the things that really count—quality of schools, security, appreciation of property values, political clout, and availability of desirable amenities—attests to the ways in which larger processes of discrimination penalize blacks at the neighborhood level" (*Black Picket Fences*, 30). While both novels offer a broad myth of perfection, they also portray myths that allude to more specific matters such as the ones Pattillo names here.

49. See Mbembe, *Necropolitics*. Pattillo, *Black on the Block*, 84–85, 288–90, discusses the behaviors of working-class people from the perspective of those with a middle-class status or who are "better off."

50. Pattillo, *Black on the Block* asserts that "there is an easy slippage from criminalizing individuals to indicting the physical landscape believed to spawn such bad individuals, frequently the public housing project" (*Black on the Block*, 264).

51. See Pattillo, *Black on the Block*, 300, for more on the topic of middle-class Blacks forming alliances with elite whites.

52. In her analysis of Dunbar's writing, A. Williams makes an observation that can apply to Naylor's decision to "unite" the Linden Hills residents and the racist white organization that does not want any Blacks near them, but especially working-class Blacks. Williams writes, "Dunbar uses the strategy of mapping class to delineate intraracial distinctions, but while doing so, he also presents the physically and economically mobile black subject as the source of concern for both white and black Americans" (*Dividing Lines*, 96). In this scene, Linden Hills residents are a concern for the Putney Wayne residents as well as the white organization.

53. Collins, "Narrative Structure," 290.

54. Lombardi, *Wallace Stevens*, 106.

55. Bonetti, "An Interview with Gloria Naylor," 47.

56. Tim Engles asserts that the novel "critique[s] various aspects of the African American pursuit of materialism and class status" ("African American Whiteness," 665).

57. A. Williams, *Dividing Lines*, 101. Christian reminds us that "Linden Hills [has] been created by racism, or more precisely, as a result of the effects of racism on their founders" ("Gloria Naylor's Geography," 351).

58. Christian, "Gloria Naylor's Geography," 352.

59. Cohen, *The Boundaries of Blackness*.

60. Graham, *Our Kind*, 46.

61. Duboin, "A New Voice," 117.

62. Pattillo, *Black on the Block*, 104–5. Also, they are still closed in and limiting themselves, and Lakeland, as Duboin explains, "perpetuates oppression, segregation and exclusion" ("Writing the Fragmented," 62).

63. A. Williams, *Dividing Lines*, 102.

64. Pattillo, *Black on the Block*, 264; emphasis in original.

65. Rothstein, *Color of Law*, vii–viii.

66. A. Williams, *Dividing Lines*, 102.

67. Kelley, *Yo' Mama's Disfunktional!*, 83.

68. See Markus and Stephens, "Editorial Overview: Inequality and Social Class."

69. Bouvier optimistically highlights Willie's future: "Willie is a producer—both a worker in Linden Hills and a composer of poems who memorizes them all and refuses to write them down. He thus avoids a certain alienation from his poetic creations, refusing to part with them and run the risk of a certain commodification" ("Reading in Black," 147). Like Bouvier, Maxine Montgomery emphasizes Willie's hopeful future and describes him as "an emerging artist and cultural historian" (*The Fiction of Gloria Naylor*, 36). Montgomery suggests that Willie is Willa's alter ego (24), as Naylor tells Montgomery in an interview that Willie and Willa are "two sides of the

same coin" (86). She further argues that Naylor "scripts the feminine" (32) through Willie, meaning that Willie is able to tell Willa's story, and this is possible because Willie and Willa are both "existing on the margins" (32).

70. See Hamilton, "Neoliberalism and Race."

71. Michael Lynch remarks that they both share the desire to become "poets with a sense of fidelity to disadvantaged blacks" ("The Wall," 192).

72. Pattillo, *Black Picket Fences*, 25.

73. Pattillo, *Black Picket Fences*, 30.

74. The narrative reveals that the minor character Ruth, Valerie's mother, who is a part of Mayes's New Saved congregation, has been allowing Mayes to sexually abuse Valerie. In fact, she has been "selling her own child" (203) to men who want sexual favors so that she can support her drug habit. For a discussion of literary portrayals of Black maternal figures and stereotypes associated with Black mothers in African American literature, see David, *Mama's Gun*. For a broad discussion of portrayals of religion and spirituality in African American literature, see Moore, *In the Life and in the Spirit*.

75. Duboin suggests that Turner "portrays politically and economically disempowered parents who end up yielding to environmental pressures, thereby furthering urban violence" ("Writing the Fragmented," 73). Moreover, various forms of abuse, including sexual abuse, occur at all class levels; still, Turner deserves commendation for addressing the difficult subject of child abuse.

76. While Mr. Saville came from a working-class background, Mrs. Saville was reared in an (upper) middle-class family. See Summers, *Black in Place*, and Prince, *African Americans and Gentrification in Washington, D.C.*, for discussions of gentrification.

77. Duboin, "A New Voice," 121.

78. Pattillo, *Black on the Block*, 225.

Chapter Two

1. Page citations for the novel will be made parenthetically in the text.

2. See "History & Vision."

3. "History & Vision."

4. Burke, "Me Too Is a Movement."

5. Examples of other cross-class relationships in the novel include Cosey and Sandler Gibbon's "friendship" and the marriage of May and Billy Boy (Cosey's son). Family and the father's role in particular are other points of interest for scholars. Charting the resemblance of Bill Cosey's name to that of Bill Cosby, who played the nearly perfect father on the popular sitcom *The Cosby Show*, Mary Paniccia Carden argues that Morrison is disputing "the notion that the father-dominant model of home and family is a panacea for the problems afflicting many African American communities in the twenty-first century" ("'Trying to Find a Place,'" 131). A basis of her analysis is racial uplift ideology and American racial politics more generally. Mar Gallego details Cosey's failure in fatherhood and as a family leader; she extends her analysis to another common topic in the scholarship: the violence of patriarchy. She asserts that "Morrison continues her critique of black patriarchy and unequal gender

relations in the family" in the novel and that "African Americans' adoption of a patriarchal model is reckoned as the greatest source of conflict in the text" ("Love and the Survival of the Black Community," 94). Focusing on patriarchy's role in intergenerational conflict and abuse, Evelyn Jaffe Schreiber suggests a wider influence beyond solely Black families: "The interpersonal dynamics in *Love* point to the damaging narrative of patriarchal power in American culture" ("Power and Betrayal," 106) as a whole. In a similar manner, Susan Neal Mayberry connects patriarchy to laws created by white men in American society and examines the effects on Black men ("Laying Down the Law of the Father"). Looking more in depth at laws of segregation and desegregation specifically, Lucille P. Fultz explores the aftermath in African American communities and notes that "Morrison invites a studied critique of the promises, successes, and failures of desegregation" ("Love: An Elegy for the African American Community," 95). Most closely associated with my approach to Morrison's *Love* and its portrayal of toxic masculinity, Tessa Roynon's work interrogates representations of rape in three of Morrison's novels, seeing them as Morrison's "contribution to current feminist re-theorizing of rape" and "sites of resistance to sexual violence" ("Sabotaging the Language of Pride," 39, 51).

6. The scholarship on Morrison's *Love* has focused on a variety of topics, but some topics are more prevalent than others. One concerns the friendship between Heed and Christine and its destruction by Cosey's marriage to Heed; Pin-chia Feng examines their friendship from childhood to adulthood as she reads Morrison's novel as a "double female Bildungsroman" ("'We Was Girls Together,'" 39). As J. Brooks Bouson examines the friendship of the women, she concentrates specifically on the "damaging impact of the color-caste hierarchy on black identity" ("Uncovering 'The Beloved,'" 358), noting the darker and lighter skin tones of Heed and Christine, respectively, and their complementing working- and middle-class statuses. While she describes this hierarchy as an unpleasant secret among African American communities, other scholars concentrate directly on secrets held by characters in the novel and their impact on the characters' lives. For instance, Carolyn Denard details the "trope of silence" in the novel and its connection to characters' secrets, claiming that love is a reason people keep secrets ("'Some to Hold, Some to Tell,'" 91). Katrina Harack, in addressing secrets, focuses on memory and the trauma associated with certain memories of the characters ("'Not Even in the Language They Had Invented'").

7. Carolyn E. Cocca, who examines matters of gender and law, explains that "even though many states have gender-neutral laws, the idea of male as aggressor and female as victim pervades the discourse as well as the prosecutions" (*Jailbait*, 16). Similarly, scholar Tanya Serisier observes that "media representations of sexual violence tend to almost exclusively focus on cisgender male perpetrators and female victims, ignoring male victims, female perpetrators, transgender victims and perpetrators, and same-sex sexual violence" ("Sex Crimes," 10).

8. Benedict, *Virgin or Vamp*, 15.

9. Serisier, "Sex Crimes," 7.

10. U.S. Constitution, Amendment XIV, Section 1, July 9, 1868.

11. Franklin and Moss, *From Slavery to Freedom*, 140.

12. Heather Duerre Humann further explains that "rather than entering into marriage as a partnership, by marrying young Heed, Cosey bought the pleasures of a 'slave-owner'" (*Domestic Abuse*, 130).

13. See Hortense Spillers, "Mama's Baby, Papa's Maybe," on the impertinence of the idea of consent in the context of slavery.

14. U.S. Department of Health & Human Services, "Sexual Assault."

15. Franklin and Moss, *From Slavery to Freedom*, 141.

16. Cocca, *Jailbait*, 11.

17. Additionally, historian Estelle Freedman discusses how Southern laws pertaining to rape during slavery excluded enslaved and free Black women, but that there were some exceptions, such as a Georgia statute that outlawed raping enslaved women (*Redefining Rape*, 28).

18. Jones-Rogers, *They Were Her Property*, 21.

19. Foster, "The Sexual Abuse of Black Men," 447. Lamonte Aidoo also discusses the history of sexual abuse of Black men during slavery in Brazil, in particular, in *Slavery Unseen*.

20. Benedict, *Virgin or Vamp*, 15.

21. In *Killing the Black Body*, Dorothy Roberts explains: "Legislation giving the children of Black women and white men the status of slaves left female slaves vulnerable to sexual violation as a means of financial gain" (29).

22. Hine, *Hine Sight*, 28.

23. According to Africana Studies scholars and historians Darlene Clark Hine and Earnestine Jenkins, "As racism grew in the nineteenth century, it was accompanied by the development of stereotypes and racial myths. Among the most pervasive and deeply embedded stereotypes is the black man as the rapist of white women" ("Black Men's History," 38).

24. See "History of Racial Injustice." Many have questioned the validity of the rape claims concerning Black men against white women, including the Black foremother, journalist, and activist Ida B. Wells-Barnett, who famously wrote on this topic in pamphlets such as *A Red Record* (1895).

25. See "Lynching in America," as well as Mitchell, *Living with Lynching*. Additionally, see McCormick, *Staging Black Fugitivity*, for a discussion on contemporary dramatic performances that highlight the legacies of slavery.

26. N. Wright, *Black Girlhood*, 134–35.

27. For more on the adultification of Black children, see Epstein, Blake, and Gonzalez, *Girlhood Interrupted*.

28. See scholarship by historian of African American history Wilma King, such as "Prematurely Knowing of Evil Things."

29. U.S. Department of Justice, "Raising Awareness about Sexual Abuse."

30. Concerning this scene, Feng writes, "Both feel their experiences are beyond communication because their prepubescent sexuality has been excited, and they are afraid of contaminating the purity of their friendship" ("'We Was Girls Together,'" 49).

31. For more information on matters of shame and blame, see U.S. Department of Justice, "Raising Awareness about Sexual Abuse: Facts and Statistics," and Rape,

Abuse & Incest National Network (RAINN), "Adult Survivors of Child Sexual Abuse." On children knowing their abusers or the relationship between perpetrators and survivors, see RAINN, as well as U.S. Department of Health & Human Services, "Child Maltreatment 2017," and Douglas and Finkelhor, "Childhood Sexual Abuse Fact Sheet."

32. Despite having no children with Bill Cosey, Heed also refers to Bill Cosey as "papa" in the narrative, which further illustrates the power dynamics in their relationship.

33. For more on how the neoliberal paradigm has affected protection services for children, see Parton, *Politics of Child Protection*.

34. Bennett and O'Donohue, "Construct of Grooming," 960.

35. Canadian Centre for Child Protection, *Child Sexual Abuse — It Is Your Business*, 6.

36. Bennett and O'Donohue, "Construct of Grooming," 962, 970.

37. Cosey also "took pains to teach her how to manicure, pedicure, keep all his nails in perfect shape. And how to shave him, too, with a straight razor and strop" (124).

38. Historian Danielle L. McGuire's *At the Dark End of the Street* discusses the reality that Black women and girls have been consistently vulnerable to sexual violations throughout history.

39. Serisier, "Sex Crimes," 11.

40. Morrison, *Love*, xi.

41. Serisier notes, "There are strong traditions of victim-blaming, with children frequently portrayed as participating in or even initiating sexual conduct with adults" ("Sex Crimes," 11). On the low arrest rates of perpetrators, see Morabito, Williams, and Pattavina, "Decision Making in Sexual Assault Cases," and RAINN, "The Criminal Justice System."

42. In describing Heed's background, the novel confirms this point, as she was a girl "who had never used two pieces of flatware to eat. Never knew food to be separated on special plates. Who slept on the floor and bathed on Saturday in a washtub full of the murky water left by her sisters" (75).

43. Herman Beavers describes it quite simply as "Cosey's illusion of generosity" (*Geography and the Political Imaginary*, 139).

44. Basile et al., "Sexual Violence," 232–33.

45. For information on sexual violence against men and women, see Smith et al., *The National Intimate Partner and Sexual Violence Survey*. Additionally, building on Nicola Gavey's *Just Sex? The Cultural Scaffolding of Rape*, Serisier explains, "Female perpetrators of sexual violence are also largely absent from media representations of sexual violence. Where they are reported, it is frequently as a 'novelty,' downplaying the seriousness of the harm involved. The primary context in which media coverage of female sex offenders occurs is cases of female adults and young males, most commonly teachers and students. Where these cases occur they tend to be presented in ways that minimize their seriousness and that over-write narratives of romance or sexual experimentation on the part of adolescent males" ("Sex Crimes," 10). For more on sexual offenders, see Center for Sex Offender Management, *Fact Sheet*.

46. Cocca, *Jailbait*, 130, 22.

47. A significant number of girls and women behind bars are survivors of various forms of abuse. See Saar et al., *The Sexual Abuse to Prison Pipeline*; McDaniels-Wilson and Belknap, "The Extensive Sexual Violation"; and Belknap, *The Invisible Woman*.

48. In "Signs of Social Class," psychologists Michael W. Kraus, Jun Won Park, and Jacinth J. X. Tan discuss social class signals, which are behaviors that indicate a person's class position (423).

49. Kraus, Park, and Tan, "Signs of Social Class," 432.

50. He quickly "comes under the sexual spell of June at the Coseys'" (Venkatesan and Neelakantan, "Family," 1).

51. Handeyside, Wickliffe, and Adams, *Striving for Justice*, 11.

52. For more information on Romeo and Juliet laws, see Dumond, "'Cast Me Not Away!'"

Chapter Three

1. For more on standardized testing within the Anglophone Caribbean, see Caribbean Examinations Council. Examples of secondary education placement exams include the Primary Exit Profile (PEP), which replaced the Grade Six Achievement Test (GSAT) in 2018 in Jamaica, and the Secondary Entrance Assessment (SEA), which replaced the Common Entrance Examination (CEE) in 2001 in Trinidad and Tobago.

2. Page citations for the novels will be made parenthetically in the text.

3. Senior, "Lessons from the Fruit Stand," 42.

4. Senior, "Poem as Gardening," 2.

5. Senior, "New Dance Steps," 68.

6. Hodge, "Challenges of the Struggle for Sovereignty," 206.

7. Hodge, "Challenges of the Struggle for Sovereignty," 202.

8. Hodge, "Responses to Questions," email interview by Robin Brooks, July 20, 2013.

9. Senior's poetry from *Gardening in the Tropics* and Hodge's *Crick Crack, Monkey* are featured. Additionally, Erna Brodber also claims literature can provide a social function, and she declares her fiction has "activist intentions" ("Scientific," 167, 164). Brodber, Hodge, and Senior suggest that insight from fiction, including *Crick Crack, Monkey* and *Dancing Lessons*, can contribute to the discussion on how to improve the educational systems so that disenfranchised working classes can have equal access to the resources of schools. See also Michael A. Bucknor, "'Grung'/Grounded Poetics," who mentions that Senior focuses on "those subjects marginalized by society" (85) in her work.

10. Christopher and Whitson, "Toward a Theory of Working-Class Literature," 72.

11. Campbell, *Young Colonials* and *Endless Education*; Cook and Jennings-Craig, "Perspectives of Jamaican Parents"; Chunnu, "Negotiating Worlds"; George and Lewis, "Exploring the Global/Local Boundary"; De Lisle, "Explaining Whole System Reform"; and Petgrave, "Equality in Education?"

12. For more on education as a path to upward class mobility, see Cook and Jennings-Craig, "Perspectives of Jamaican Parents," 97, Petgrave, "Equality in Education?," 24, and Chunnu, "Negotiating Worlds," 33–37.

13. Campbell, *Endless Education*, 9.

14. Petgrave, "Equality in Education?," 25.

15. Cook and Jennings-Craig, "Perspectives of Jamaican Parents," 97.

16. While the criticism on *Crick Crack, Monkey* and *Dancing Lessons* notes the theme of education, much is left to be desired regarding how the authors present the notion of being complicit with and then disrupting unjust systems for the greater good of the community. Concerning *Crick Crack, Monkey*, Tee's guardianship is a major point of interest in the scholarship. Critics vacillate on whether Tantie's or Aunt Beatrice's home environment is more suitable for Tee's success, which substantiates my point that both family units behave in ways that are counterproductive to their well-being, and they participate in reproducing relations of domination in their society. Ena V. Thomas is among the most straightforward about her beliefs concerning Tantie: "Tantie's world is a morally broken environment full of indecencies and obscenities. There is first the problem of Tantie's many lovers . . . and second there is the problem of physical and verbal violence that Tee has to endure" ("*Crick Crack, Monkey*," 212). In contrast, some critics praise the familial environment that Tantie offers because Tee appears happier with Tantie in the beginning of the novel. For instance, Marjorie Thorpe feels as inflamed about the nature of Beatrice's household as Thomas does about Tantie's household, criticizing Beatrice's parenting and her role as a wife: "Both as a mother and a wife, Aunt Beatrice is a failure" ("The Problem of Cultural Identification," 38). Though not much of the scholarship focuses on the larger social system in Trinidadian society, literary critic Joy Mahabir concentrates on the interrelations of class and education in the novel, writing that "education must be understood in a larger framework that is inevitably socio-economic rather than individual" (*Miraculous Weapons*, 104).

As the attention of critics continues to be on Senior's decades-long body of poetry, far less criticism exists on her debut novel, *Dancing Lessons*. In the existing criticism, the contrasting portrayals of the working-class and middle-class family units are not points of interest for critics unlike the family units portrayed in *Crick Crack, Monkey*. A review of the literary criticism on Senior's novel reveals that critics tend to focus mostly on the subjects of parent-child relationships and the significance of skin tone or color. For instance, Laura Tanna, in her brief article on the novel, includes excerpts from her interview with Senior discussing "the wider Jamaican phenomenon of children growing [up] with people who are not their parents" (*Dancing Lessons*), which is a Black feminist concept of "other mothering." The characters Celia and Mrs. Samphire both live with other guardians besides their parents at some point in the narrative. In "The Jamaican Dilemma," Donna Bailey Nurse similarly discusses children's distance from their parents and the meticulous physical descriptions Mrs. Samphire offers throughout the narrative, highlighting how Mrs. Samphire's features are a point of distress during childhood because they contrasted with the European-like features of her father's established family. In a review of the novel, Pat Watson expands on this latter topic, noting the character Mrs. Samphire "introduces every person in her life by skin tone, facial features, and hair texture—Senior's way of telegraphing the importance of these delineations to the spirit of the time the character came of age." Laura Giovannelli expounds on how ethnicity, skin tone, and social status have long gone hand in hand, including in the postcolonial period ("Olive Senior's *Dancing Les-*

sons," 152). On another note, Thomas offers reasoning for Tantie's behavior, stating that the society's inherent violent nature is to blame. These topics are all significant to the novels. My analysis of both novels delves further into the reality of child-shifting and the continuing connection between skin tone and class status via an expanded interrogation of the function of education in the novel. For more literary criticism on Hodge's novel, see Booker and Juraga, "Merle Hodge, *Crick Crack, Monkey*"; Balutansky, "We Are All Activists"; Gikandi, "Narration in the Post-Colonial Moment" and "Writing after Colonialism"; Japtok, "Two Postcolonial Childhoods"; Katrak, "'This Englishness Will Kill You'"; and Zodana, "'Tee,' 'Cyn-Cyn,' 'Cynthia,' 'Dou-Dou.'"

17. Parker, *How to Interpret Literature*, 224.

18. Mrs. Samphire best fits in the working class. Thus, this chapter identifies Mrs. Samphire as working class and the missionary couple, Ted and Phil Fraser, as (upper) middle class. Celia explains that the missionary couple who rear her throughout her adolescence were "considered rich" (120). Because the Frasers are white Americans, some would probably consider them upper class in this fictive Jamaican society. Also, I assert that Mrs. Samphire begins her life as a young child in a rural middle-class milieu living with her paternal grandmother and aunt, but she experiences a downward shift in her adult life. Several times throughout the novel she notes that she was "poor" or had fallen into "poverty" (100, 304, 335–36). Mrs. Samphire even says that a helper of hers (Millie) is now "way ahead of me" (305). I discuss these points later in this chapter. However, I want to note that Olive Senior sees a difference between urban and rural environments, and she does not believe "working class" describes those in rural environments like Mrs. Samphire. In my interview with Senior, she stated: "I wouldn't call her working class because working class, to me, is an urban phenomenon. She comes from a rural background where things work differently. So, within that rural milieu she comes from the "best family," although they rejected her. . . . So, in a way she sees herself as a cut above the ordinary people. Within the rural milieu, she'd be considered middle class, despite the fact that she's not very well off" (Senior, "New Dance Steps," 63). Based upon the descriptions Mrs. Samphire gives of herself in the novel, I (slightly) disagree. Additionally, there are multiple cross-class relationships in *Dancing Lessons*.

19. See Reddock, *Women and Family*, 17–28 for a discussion of kinship networks in which child shifting (children living with relatives other than their parents for various reasons) is practiced.

20. Louis Althusser writes, "All Ideological State Apparatuses, whatever they are, contribute to the same result: the reproduction of the relations of production, i.e. of capitalist relations of exploitation" ("Ideology and Ideological," 104. Subsequent page references to this work are given parenthetically in the text). See his "Ideology and Ideological" for a complete discussion of ISAs and how they work in tandem with the Repressive State Apparatus, which includes, for instance, the police, military, and prisons. Additionally, Patricia Hill Collins notes that Althusser's "thesis of the state ideological apparatus identified new avenues of investigation with increased emphasis on cultural analyses" (*Intersectionality as Critical Social Theory*, 299).

21. While Althusser's influential scholarship has many admirers, it also has its share of critics, including those who accuse him of oversimplification. See, for example,

Althusser, "Note on the ISAs" in *On the Reproduction of Capitalism*, as well as Giroux, *Theory and Resistance in Education*.

22. Cobham-Sander, "Revisioning Our Kumblas," 305–6.

23. Cobham-Sander, "Revisioning Our Kumblas," 305.

24. Senior, "New Dance," 64.

25. Discussing education and neoliberalism in the U.S. context, Darrick Hamilton cautions that "education is not the magic antidote for the enormous inherited disparities that result from laws, policies, and economic arrangements that facilitate the concentration of economic and political power" ("Neoliberalism and Race").

26. Senior, "New Dance," 63.

27. Cook and Jennings-Craig, "Perspectives of Jamaican Parents," 91.

28. Mrs. Samphire acknowledges her downward shift in class. In Senior's *Dancing Lessons*, readers become aware that the background in which she was reared was not working class. Her father's family, who raised her, was a respected family, who lived on a hill in the biggest house in the community. Later, Mrs. Samphire runs away and marries Mr. Samphire, whose family also was prominent in the community. Mr. Samphire was given four acres of family land when they married. However, when he left their marriage, he eventually stopped contributing to Mrs. Samphire's household so that her circumstances changed for the worse. Evidence of Mrs. Samphire's class status as an adult derives from her self-descriptions.

29. Cook and Jennings-Craig, "Perspectives of Jamaican Parents," 92.

30. Senior also subversively critiques the assumption that education staves off illegal and corrupt behaviors, as it is Junior's elite friend Pinto who has the best educational opportunities and will later influence Junior to become involved in the drug trade. Further, Senior dispels stereotypes about working-class people being the main ones in the drug trade or trying to circumvent the system by illegal methods. In the character of Pinto, she exposes the contribution of various classes to the state of the society.

31. Regarding "false consciousness," Robert Dale Parker notes it is "a way of thinking that is so interpellated into oppressive ideologies that it leads people to act against their own interest" (*How to Interpret Literature*, 228). Additionally, the Frasers and Celia are also reminiscent of the missionary couple and Bita Plant in Claude McKay's *Banana Bottom*.

32. Althusser, "Ideology and Ideological," 99; emphasis in original.

33. Althusser, "Ideology and Ideological," 102; emphasis in original.

34. Petgrave, "Equality in Education?," 25.

35. Petgrave, "Equality in Education?," 35.

36. Cook and Jennings-Craig, "Perspectives of Jamaican Parents," 92.

37. Althusser, "Ideology and Ideological," 99.

38. Manley wanted Jamaica to have a "social system in which upward and downward mobility are determined exclusively by individual merit" (quoted in Cook and Jennings-Craig, "Perspectives of Jamaican Parents," 92).

39. For more on organic intellectuals, see Gramsci and Buttigieg, *Prison Notebooks*.

40. A great deal of the media in Jamaica is heavily influenced by foreign nations. In particular, many of the television channels are from other countries, including the United States. Additionally, Caribbean education scholar Zellyne Jennings-Craig ob-

serves that "resource constraint is a major deterrent to the achievement of goals of reform in developing countries" ("Resource and Technology," 266).

41. Senior, "New Dance," 68.

42. See Senior's poetry collection *Gardening in the Tropic* and Senior's Philip Sherlock lecture, "The Poem as Gardening."

43. Brodber, "Juba's Head," 156–57.

44. Issues of class as well as a variety of other subjects, including vestiges of African culture, are under exploration in Marshall's *Praisesong for the Widow*; see Brooks, "Manifestations of Ogun Symbolism."

45. Brodber, "Juba's Head," 159.

46. See Jerome De Lisle, "Explaining Whole System Reform in Small States," for a discussion of the four education reforms Trinidad has had since independence and the importance of secondary education to the development of the nation.

47. Hodge, "Responses to Questions."

48. For instance, Winsome Chunnu writes, "The issues which the education system grappled with in the 1800s continued to challenge the system in the 1980s, and into the 21st Century: Inadequate facilities, overcrowded classrooms, low attendance, and inadequately trained teachers" ("Negotiating Worlds," 33).

49. De Lisle, "Explaining Whole System Reform," 65. Moreover, the Ministry of Education's "Draft Education Policy Paper 2017–2022" states that its three strategic goals include: "1. Effective governance and administration of the education system; 2. Access to educational opportunities by all learners; and 3. Quality education provided at all levels" (23).

50. Government of the Republic of Trinidad and Tobago, "Draft Education," 15.

51. Government of the Republic of Trinidad and Tobago, "Draft Education," 27.

52. George and Lewis, "Exploring the Global/Local Boundary," 730.

53. Hodge, "Language Use," 476.

54. Althusser, *On the Reproduction of Capitalism*, 235–36.

55. Cook and Jennings-Craig, "Perspectives of Jamaican Parents," 90.

56. Reddock, *Women, Labour and Politics*, 92. Reddock writes, "For blacks, coloureds and Indians the only possibility for social mobility was to become part of the middle strata of professionals (doctors, lawyers), civil servants or teachers. For these the main (and sometimes only) mechanism was education" (*Women, Labour and Politics*, 92).

57. For more about middle-class women's social mobility in this period, see Reddock, *Women, Labour and Politics*, 197, 202, 238, 253; see Reddock, *Women and Family*, 23.

58. Reddock, *Women and Family*, 19. Campbell adds that "scholastic and occupational success enabled men to marry upwards, often to women higher on the colour scale" (*Endless Education*, 11–12).

59. Chunnu, "Negotiating Worlds," 37.

60. For a discussion of skin tone being a form of capital, see Ulysse, *Downtown Ladies*, 19.

61. Senior, "New Dance," 65.

62. In her assessment of the character Tantie, Joy Mahabir proffers the argument that Tantie is an organic intellectual (*Miraculous Weapons*, chap. 4). In contrast, I argue that she has the potential to be one in the future.

63. In "The Education Challenges Facing Small Nation States," Mohammed Kazim Bacchus writes, "The provision of particular skills and knowledge should not be the only concern of local education institutions. Small states will only be able to survive economically and culturally if their populations receive an education that helps them to perceive new opportunities and provide them with the competencies and dispositions that would equip them to adapt readily to the changing social and economic world environment" (142).

64. Hodge, "Challenges of the Struggle for Sovereignty," 202.

65. Haynes, "Writing Is What I Do." Senior also observes in this Haynes's piece: "That's one duty of creative artists in general—to open the eyes of coming generations, showing them a variety of scenarios and possibilities beyond their everyday reality in the hope that some of them will be transformed enough by our work to spark new fires."

66. Chunnu writes, "Because education is inextricably linked to the development of any society (particularly a post-colonial society), understanding stratification and education is essential to developing a framework for addressing local, national, and regional challenges" ("Negotiating Worlds," 33).

Chapter Four

1. Page citations for the novel will be made parenthetically in the text.

2. The trope of the "two Jamaicas" has an extensive history with broad significance, and it has been used to mean divisions along racial as well as class axes. See Curtin's *Two Jamaicas*, for more on the subject. In this chapter, I use "two Jamaicas" to refer to the reality that the lived class experiences in the uptown and downtown areas are so different that it is as if these spaces are two different nations—hence, "two Jamaicas." McCaulay explains in an interview that she wanted to write about a collision between the two, although she is aware this is an oversimplification (McCaulay, "Uptown and Downtown," 95). See Ulysse, *Downtown Ladies*, 162–65, for more on socioeconomic uptown/downtown divisions in Kingston. Additionally, McCaulay uses the term "inner city" to describe those in downtown communities or members of the working classes (McCaulay, "Uptown and Downtown," 96); thus, I use that term throughout this chapter.

3. I use "neoliberal globalization" and "globalization" interchangeably throughout the chapter.

4. The cross-class relationship trope is distinct from the narrative structure, although it is related to McCaulay's narrative structure in this particular novel, as *Dog-Heart* alternates between the two protagonists who are from different class backgrounds.

5. For more on the welfare state, see Mounk, *The Age of Responsibility*.

6. The literary criticism on the novel (which exists overwhelmingly in the form of book reviews) is united in pointing out that the central issue in the novel is class, but the scholarship is limited and does not present substantive analyses of class or its interconnections with other issues such as the larger framework of globalization and human rights. Perhaps one of the most thorough reviewers, Lorna Down, suggests

that McCaulay's greatest achievement in the novel "is that she helps us see that there are no easy answers to questions of class structures and class relations, to poverty and violence" (108). However, presumably because of the restricted format of the book review, Down does not detail specifics concerning the difficulties between classes. In her review of *Dog-Heart*, Lisa Allen-Agostini also points out the serious issues raised by the novel concerning education for inner-city children. While in attendance at the uptown schools, Dexter experiences prejudice from school officials and other students, which hinders his educational success. Moreover, the novel's low sales immediately after its publication may be one reason for the lack of scholarship. While the novel gained favorable interest among locals, it did not sell many copies initially, and its popularity did not translate internationally (Scafe, "Re-Placing Wealth," 217).

7. Brysk, "Introduction," 1.

8. F. Harrison, "Introduction," 11.

9. Brysk, "Introduction," 1.

10. F. Harrison notes, "Many advocates and researchers argue that human rights appear to be in increased jeopardy under the conditions of globalization, especially the neoliberal form dominant today" ("Introduction," 11). In discussing the effects of globalization, Brysk asserts that "different elements and levels of globalization may produce distinct elements of empowerment, exploitation, and evolution" ("Introduction," 7).

11. F. Harrison writes: "Jamaica has a human rights crisis, according to reports from international human rights organizations (e.g., Amnesty International, Human Rights Watch)" ("Everyday Neoliberalism," 7).

12. Scholte, *Globalization*, 323. See also DuRand, "Neoliberal Globalization"; C. Thompson, *Reflections on Leadership*.

13. For more on this topic, see Thomas-Brown, "Coping with Neoliberalism," 7.

14. This novel also fits within Harrison's claim about African American writer Alice Walker's fiction, specifically that the "interrelationship between the use of historical and anthropological literatures as sources for facts and ideas, and the writing of culture in fictive rhetoric, is salient in Walker's work" and that ethnographic writers should recognize its value for their work (*Outsider Within*, 124).

15. Sophia A. McClennen and Alexandra Schultheis Moore discuss "the centrality of literary expression as a key part of human rights advocacy" ("Mapping the Landscape," 10). They also note that "starting in the 1970s, there was clear and direct attention to the connections among human rights, literature, and personal stories, as well as to the ways in which these connections emerge out of geopolitical contexts. Following that, . . . by the 1990s, the production of life narratives—especially memoirs—had become a central, if not ubiquitous, feature of human rights campaigns" (10). McClennen and Moore also assert that "the use of literature as a vehicle for human rights advocacy is at once a way to illuminate the humanity of the speaking subject as it is a mode of reflecting a true 'story' that has been erased [or ignored and undervalued] by official 'history'" (12). Hence, a reading that places McCaulay's fictional representation of Jamaica in the context of human rights discourse helps exemplify how novels can be a crucial site of inquiry in human rights studies. Moreover, studying the problems of classism, globalization, and human rights abuses in

contemporary Jamaica is not a new undertaking, as many scholars of the Caribbean, including Stephen Vasciannie, "The Inter-American Commission On Human Rights"; Tracy Robinson, "Legalising Norms Related to Sexual, Gender and Bodily Diversity"; Verene Shepherd, *Engendering Caribbean History*; and Rhon Reynolds, "Not Safe at Home," have written on these topics. Still, *Dog-Heart* participates in these discourses by sketching them in fictive form, thus offering another perspective and potentially raising these issues with audiences who may not be privy to this information when presented in modes such as case studies in history or the social sciences. The novel presents an alternative to such studies and is a "representation of truth-telling" (McClennen and Moore, "Mapping the Landscape," 14). McCaulay's novel aligns with Evelyn O'Callaghan's description of the ways that "imaginative writing challenges, reframes and fills in the gaps in narrative accounts of these statistical and 'fact' based disciplines" ("Imagined Nations," 1). Similarly reinforcing the primacy of fiction, Harrison writes, "*Fiction encodes truth claims—and alternative modes of theorizing—*in a rhetoric of imagination that accommodates and entertains the imaginable" (*Outsider Within*, 121; emphasis in original). Fiction, in short, can operate similarly to social-science discourses by revealing another way of theorizing real life. Harrison further declares that ethnic/minority fiction "represents a rich mode of *writing the cultures, cultural politics, and history* of our multicultural world structured in relations of dominance" (*Outsider Within*, 119–20; emphasis in original). Alison Donnell additionally notes how "literature in the Caribbean has been a vital mode of re-describing received reality" ("The Lives of Others," 422), while Glyne Griffith discusses literature and its possibilities for changing the world ("Reading Class," 290–91). Ultimately, thinking of literature as making a critical intervention in contemporary injustices and imbalances can work well, both to advance thinking around socioeconomic abuses and to strengthen the analysis of literary texts.

16. See Posner, *The Twilight of Human Rights Law*; Hathaway, "Do Human Rights Treaties Make a Difference?"; and Hill, "Estimating the Effects of Human Rights."

17. Unless otherwise noted, the ICESCR is the covenant being referenced in this chapter.

18. Harrison, "Global Apartheid," 53.

19. Jasper Krommendijk notes that despite the process of state reporting being "one of the most important international mechanisms to monitor the implementation of UN human rights," there are only a few studies that examine its effectiveness ("The Domestic Effectiveness of International Human Rights Monitoring," 490).

20. Other scholars have examined class within Caribbean societies, including Gordon K. Lewis in *Gordon K. Lewis on Race*. Like many working-class studies scholars, he notes that members of the working classes are often unemployed.

21. Goldberg, "Gendering Human Rights," 61.

22. D. Thomas, *Modern Blackness*, 10.

23. McCaulay, "Uptown and Downtown," 96.

24. Mohammed, "Towards Indigenous Feminist Theorizing," 26–27.

25. UNCESCR, "Right to Adequate Housing," para. 7. The General Comments by the CESCR are documents that expound on and clarify parts of the International Covenant of Economic, Social and Cultural Rights.

26. For more on this topic, see Posner, *The Twilight of Human Rights Law*.

27. Harrison asserts that "while the International Covenant on Economic, Social and Cultural Rights may lend legitimacy to those rights . . . in reality socioeconomic rights are being repudiated within the 'New World Order'" ("Expanding the Concept," 6). Although the rights are outlined, in other words, they are often not being protected.

28. UNCESCR, "Concluding Observations," para. 25.

29. See Thomas-Brown, "Coping with Neoliberalism," 15.

30. See Abramovitz, "Economic Crises," where she cites scholars who offer these elements as making up a social-democratic welfare state.

31. UNCESCR, "Concluding Observations," para 25.

32. UNCESCR, "The Right to Adequate Housing," para. 7.

33. A Jamaica Public Service (JPS) news article, "JPS Reduces Service to Communities with High Levels of Theft, Says It Has Tried Everything," published on May 12, 2014, states: "In 2013, JPS removed over 197,000 illegal lines, carried out more than 113,000 account audits and meter investigations, and facilitated the arrest of more than 1200 persons for theft of electricity." JPS has implemented several initiatives to halt electricity theft.

34. There are other shame-inducing circumstances in Dexter's home situation; for instance, they have to defecate and urinate in a bucket out back. Since they do not have running water in their house, Dexter and Marlon also have to go every morning, like so many other children, to a water stop in the neighborhood to retrieve water. This is no small task, but Dexter is relieved that "at least where [he] live[s] is close to standpipe" (24). Still, the safety and cleanliness of the water are uncertain. McCaulay illustrates here that one of their human rights is compromised, as the "human right to water entitles everyone to sufficient, safe, acceptable, physically accessible and affordable water for personal and domestic uses" (UNCESCR, "Human Right to Water," para. 2). Again, this human right is on the books, but is it really effective in the lives of those like Dexter and his family?

35. UNCESCR, "Right to Adequate Food," Article 11.1, 11.2.

36. They added this comment because "only a few States parties have provided information sufficient and precise enough to enable the Committee to determine the prevailing situation in the countries concerned with respect to this right and to identify the obstacles to its realization" (UNCESCR, "Right to Adequate Food," para. 2).

37. According to Sahara, who chastises him, Carl is seemingly ungrateful for the things in his life. She admits that Carl is taking his circumstances for granted when she thinks about the day she met Dexter: "Carl probably ate more than [Dexter] does in a week" (22).

38. UNCESCR, "Concluding Observations," para 26.

39. UNCESCR, "Right to Adequate Food," para. 6.

40. UNCESCR, "Right to Adequate Food," para. 8.

41. Thomas-Brown, "Coping with Neoliberalism," 8.

42. Munroe and Blake, "Governance and Disorder," 588.

43. Goldberg, "Gendering Human Rights," 63.

44. United Nations General Assembly, "International Covenant on Economic, Social and Cultural Rights," Articles 7(a), 6.1.

45. Figueroa, "In Search of Compassion," n.p.; Figueroa writes, "Materially the two protagonists and their families are worlds apart, but experientially there are many parallels and it is these parallels that illuminate the injustices in the society where colour and class provide separate outcomes for the same predicaments."

46. McCaulay, "Uptown and Downtown," 96.

47. Ulysse, *Downtown Ladies*, 13.

48. Ulysse, *Downtown Ladies*, 19. In recent times, Jamaica has experienced an increase in darker-skinned citizens bleaching their skin, and the government is trying to stop the sale of illegal bleaching products, according to the Ministry of Health. Some believe that lighter skin—gained by artificial products lightening (and, unfortunately, damaging) their skin—will provide access to things they feel are closed to them as dark-skinned people, including employment. However, there are not always easy class/color distinctions in the novel or in real life. Sahara's successful friend Lydia, the restaurant owner, is black, and so is the principal of Dexter's school. Dexter explains, "Uptown people can be black, brown, white, chiney, coolie or [s]yrian" (14). A considerable body of Caribbean scholarship theorizes class and color in Jamaica (e.g., see Ulysse, *Downtown Ladies*).

49. Harrison, *Outsider Within*, 185–86.

50. In a compassionate description of his mother, Dexter recounts the type of work she does to help him and his siblings: "Sometime I feel sorry for Mumma, like today. I know she do her best to look after the three a we. Mumma sew 'til her finger cramp and her eye run water" (63).

51. See Caribbean scholarship that includes women's history and gender studies such as Barriteau, "The Relevance of Black Feminist Scholarship," and Verene Shepherd, *Engendering Caribbean History*.

52. McCaulay, "Uptown and Downtown," 9.

53. Many families are female-headed in Jamaica, so McCaulay does not stereotype inner-city people as being abnormal concerning that family structure. That Arleen has three different fathers for her children, however, is a point of difference. Rawwida Baksh-Soodeen notes that the lower-class family is "always discussed in terms of the female-headed household" ("Issues of Difference," 79). Jessica Byron and Diana Thorburn note that nearly half of the homes are female-headed in some Caribbean societies ("Gender and International Relations," 217). More recent scholarship discusses these matters as well.

54. Some scholars also reveal that young girls become pregnant sometimes as a way to escape their family of origin. The fathers of their children are sometimes viewed as a means to enact a financial transaction, a way to secure money. Unfortunately, this motivation does not always turn out well, as many scholars reveal that there is often little financial support for the children. McCaulay says in an interview: "That often, fathering in Jamaica is seen as a transaction—they provide school fees, money for bus fare. And that's Arleen's motivation. She figures if she has children for different men, they will support those children" ("Uptown and Downtown," 10). For more on fatherhood and class in Jamaica, see Patricia Anderson and Camille Daley, "Parenting across Social Classes."

55. West, *Race Matters*, 12.

56. McCaulay, "Uptown and Downtown," 97.

57. UNCESCR, "Concluding Observations," para 13.

58. Building on the work of A. Lynn Bolles, Harrison explains that "those bearing the heaviest burden in coping with the social and economic austerity are women, a large proportion of whom have the responsibility—whether they are formally employed or not—to support households and family networks" (*Outsider Within*, 186).

59. Maria Thorin, in her research on gender and globalization, illuminates these larger factors when she asserts that "after the positive impacts have been balanced against the negative impacts in the various dimensions of the globalization process, women's material well-being is generally found to have deteriorated and gender inequality to have increased as a consequence of globalization, thereby intensifying the marginalization of women and the 'feminization of poverty'" (*Gender Dimension*, 13). Thorin describes a troubling and unhealthy cycle that is becoming all too familiar in contemporary Jamaican society.

60. Michaeline A. Crichlow discusses Project Land Lease in *Negotiating Caribbean Freedom*.

61. Harrison asserts that "postcolonial Jamaica, like many other Third World and Southern Hemisphere countries, is beset by a serious case of debt bondage" (*Outsider Within*, 185).

62. Posner emphasizes that there is little evidence that human rights treaties have improved people's well-being, and he notes that some nations are "not wealthy enough or well organized enough to comply with the treaty obligations" (*Twilight*, 7, 32).

63. Scholte, *Globalization*, 324.

64. Scholte, *Globalization*, 324.

65. Harrison, "Introduction," 14.

66. Documentaries such as Stephanie Black's *Life and Debt* and Esther Figueroa's *Jamaica for Sale* highlight the predicament. Ian G. Strachan's documentary, *I's Man: Manhood in the Bahamas*, explores manhood and crime in the contemporary period. Additionally, Harrison explains that "these policies are responsible for the slashing of social provisioning and for eliminating the public sector jobs that poor people once had access to through political patronage. The denationalization and privatization thrust so central to current policies of economic restructuring eliminated that category of work, leaving many even more dependent on the informal and often the illegal economy" ("Everyday Neoliberalism," 7). Scholte further explains that globalization has caused changes in already existing inequalities in nations around the world (*Globalization*, 322–23), while Thorin also claims that the IMF, WB, and WTO ignore preexisting inequalities (*Gender Dimension*, 14).

67. United Nations General Assembly, "International Covenant on Economic, Social and Cultural Rights," Article 13.

68. For more on the history of dons operating in this capacity, see Munroe and Blake, "Governance and Disorder," 584.

69. Bucknor, "On Caribbean Masculinities," 1. Strachan's documentary, *I's Man: Manhood in the Bahamas*, explores manhood and crime in the contemporary period.

70. McCaulay, "Uptown and Downtown," 98.

71. This leads to a discussion of another human rights issue emerging during the contemporary era of globalization: police violence. Dexter's community is overrun by crime (committed by dons and police), and he describes often having to hide under the bed to escape stray bullets. This issue is addressed by the International Covenant on Civil and Political Rights, which outlines the obligation of law enforcement officials to respect the human rights of all people (United Nations General Assembly, "International Covenant on Civil and Political Rights").

72. Christopher "Dudus" Coke is an example of a don (now imprisoned in the United States for various criminal activities involving drugs) who was revered and hated in Jamaican communities because he allegedly both helped and harmed many people.

73. Figueroa also comments, "In answering, I want to be your son, Dexter is saying, I would like a life of comfort, where I am fed, clothed, housed, treated with love and affection and not beaten, and where I am not damned before I have even started" ("The Future Unimaginable," 6).

74. For more on Bourdieu's concept of habitus and how people's class backgrounds influence their worldview, see his *Reproduction* and *Outline of a Theory of Practice*.

75. Figueroa, "In Search of Compassion."

76. Lydia says that "his mother probably has a violent criminal for a baby father and [Sahara will] be the next one found in a gully with [her] throat cut" (22). Having never met Arleen or Dexter, Lydia is comfortable making such a crude statement because of "the categorical, stereotypic and uncritical association of poor urban people with crime" (Harrison, "Everyday Neoliberalism," 3). To be fair, a history of violence does exist in many inner-city neighborhoods, so Lydia's being (overly) cautious is not surprising. Caribbean feminist scholars Jessica Byron and Diana Thorburn elaborate on this history and discuss the increase in drug trafficking over the last few years in Caribbean nations, including Jamaica, and how it leads to additional crime, especially in inner-city areas. They explain that "the root causes [of violence] identified range from tradition, culture, substance abuse and the media to economic structures, male marginalization and aggression and women's intensifying quest for economic survival" ("Gender and International Relations," 218). The don system in Kingston inner-city communities has made world news headlines. For instance, Christopher "Dudus" Coke shined a light on the violent drug culture present in some places. Lisa Allen-Agostini also mentions that the themes of the novel are tied "to a national history of violence, violation, and willful neglect" ("Suffer the Children"). It appears that she is referring to colonial history in Jamaica. Likewise, Gina Ulysse mentions violence in downtown Kingston (*Downtown Ladies*, 74). For more information on drug politics in Jamaica, see Harrison, "Jamaica and the International Drug Economy."

77. Some may wonder why Sahara is now trying to help people. Her son Carl is getting older and will soon leave home; she seems to be scrutinizing her priorities.

78. Later in the novel, Dexter reveals that some of the uptown students' parents have been complaining to school officials about "ghetto children" being allowed to attend the school (108). Additionally, in the educational history of Jamaica, some inner-city students have received scholarships to attend schools in uptown commu-

nities. See Jennings-Craig, "Resource and Technology"; Campbell, *Endless Education* and *The Young Colonials*; and Petgrave, "Equality in Education?"

79. Kimberlé Crenshaw, "Demarginalizing the Intersection of Race and Sex," and Patricia Hill Collins, *Black Feminist Thought*, point to the importance of considering multiple relations of oppression such as race, gender, and class that Black women encounter. Additionally, Carl struggles with his identity or the reality that his mother is half Black. At one point, Carl wants to change his last name to his English father's last name, displaying further identity struggles.

80. McCaulay, "Uptown and Downtown," 13.

81. Down, "Review of *Dog-Heart*," 109.

82. Senior, *Working Miracles*. A number of scholars observe that working classes in Jamaica tend to emphasize education so that their children can experience upward mobility. Toward the end of the narrative, when Arleen and Sahara are going to St. Stephen's because Dexter burned down one of the school bathrooms, Sahara observes Arleen who walks behind Sahara to the principal's office: "She acted like a slave, head bowed, afraid of authority, childlike" (187).

83. Also, see Harrison, "Everyday Neoliberalism," 6. Though published nearly fifteen years ago, Harrison makes a point about conditions in Jamaica with which many people still agree. Harrison makes, perhaps, one of the most chilling statements concerning the conditions in contemporary Jamaica when she writes, "Jamaica's debt crisis, the IMF's imposition of a structural adjustment policy climate, and export driven pattern of economic development have produced conditions of economic austerity that have resulted in a quality of life that may be worse than what enslaved people faced two hundred years ago" (6). In essence, neoliberalism is turning back the hands of time, specifically as it concerns the material conditions of marginalized people's lives. It is troubling, to say the least, that contemporary conditions could rival those under slavery.

Epilogue

1. The use of the terms "romance," "romantic," "liaison," and "intimate" in this chapter is meant to connote relationships in which characters are sexually involved. It does not necessarily mean that the characters are "in love" or bonded by an emotional tie of love. Moreover, this chapter is not focused on Romanticism that was popular in Europe and the United States from the late eighteenth century to the mid-nineteenth century, although Stephen Sharot reveals that novels dating as far back as the eighteenth century featured cross-class romances ("Wealth and/or Love," 89). This chapter also does not concentrate on the contemporary romance fiction genre that includes a number of Black romance novels by writers such as Brenda Jackson, Donna Hill, Rochelle Alers, Carl Weber, E. Lynn Harris, and Eric Jerome Dickey. This chapter centers on romantic relationships in the works of African American and Caribbean writers that generally are not classified as part of the romance genre.

2. For more on cross-class romances, see Sharot, *Love and Marriage* as well as "Wealth and/or Love"; Shary, "Buying Me Love"; Launius, "The Three Rs"; and Fox, "The 'Revolt of the Gentle.'" Sharot writes in "Wealth and/or Love" that "films with the

theme of cross-class romance, most with virtuous heroines, have been made throughout almost the entire history of the cinema" (89).

3. Page citations for the novels will be made parenthetically in the text.

4. For more on slavery's legacies in the twenty-first century, see Diggs Colbert, Patterson, and Levy-Hussen, *The Psychic Hold of Slavery*.

5. See Scholte, *Globalization*, 323, and Howe, *Empire*, for more on this topic. While the literary criticism concerning both novels has been wide-ranging, I want to focus on critics' attention to the romantic relationships. Kempadoo's *Tide Running* has received much less attention than has Morrison's *Tar Baby*, but I particularly want to highlight the assessments of Paula E. Morgan and Jennifer Rahim on Kempadoo's novel. My analysis builds on their work, though with attention to the final scene in the novel and key factors that lead to it. To express the power dynamics at play in the relationship, Rahim describes Peter rather clearly: "He is the liberal 'white man' consorting freely with locals. Yet, he re-enacts the 'master' discourse that hyper-sexualizes and eroticizes blackness" ("Electronic Fictions," 13). Rahim additionally describes what many call "cultural imperialism" in her discussion of U.S.-based media representations, especially television, that influence Cliff: "The new global culture also has its apparatuses of dissemination and control" ("Electronic Fictions," 6). *Tide Running* displays that Cliff is enamored by the images of American people that he sees on TV, and he erroneously believes that he can imitate what he sees on TV when he connects with Bella and Peter. With a similar focus on power relations in the novel, Morgan comments on the history of the global sex trade: "Its ingredients included, on the one hand, a master race with economic prowess and political ascendancy and, on the other, a servant race which was economically and politically subordinate" ("Meet Me in the Islands," 3). She further explains motivations for participation in the trade from both sides, noting that there existed a desire "to exoticize and denigrate, as well as to consume the vitality and sexual energies of the racialized Other" at the same time that "there was both resistance to possession and an established practice of using interracial sexual liaisons for intergenerational skin lightening and upward social mobility" ("Meet Me in the Islands," 3). In essence, both parties had their respective reasons for partaking in the sexual relations, perceiving benefits they could gain. Ultimately, Rahim and Morgan attend to the unequal power dynamics of the relationship between Peter, Bella, and Cliff.

Much interest in Jade and Son's relationship appears in the scholarship on *Tar Baby* as well. Patricia Magness underscores parallels between *Tar Baby* and *Lancelot* (*Le Chevalier de la Charrette*), noting that Morrison mimics "the structure of courtly love" ("The Knight and the Princess," 96) that is present in the Arthurian legend. Other scholars such as Doreatha D. Mbalia suggest that Jadine, imitating the Streets, has middle-class values and that she esteems their culture more than her own African American culture, which proves problematic in her relationship with Son (*Developing Class*). In relation to this point, Valerie Smith discusses how the novel deals with the "residual impact of slavery" on later African American generations (*Toni Morrison*, 53). Scholars such as Marilyn Mobley claim that the romance between the two dwindles because they have opposing worldviews that lead them to stereotype and attempt to rescue one another ("Telling Stories"). In further discussion of the hierarchy of the

Streets' house, Ann Jurecic and Arnold Rampersad assert that Jadine and Son complicate the structure, instead of placing Jadine and Son within the hierarchy ("Teaching *Tar Baby*," 148). Without a doubt, Morrison's portrayal of Jade and Son's relationship and its demise is of great interest in the criticism on *Tar Baby*.

6. In recent decades, more scholars have been boldly associating the United States with imperialism. To be sure, in "'Left Alone with America'" Amy Kaplan discusses "the absence of empire from the study of American culture; and the absence of the United States from the postcolonial study of imperialism" (11). See also Ballantyne and Burton, *Bodies in Contact*, and Kaplan, "Romancing the Empire." For a longer discussion of imperialism in relation to literary culture, see Said, *Culture and Imperialism*.

7. Julian Go asserts, "Postcolonial thought is primarily an anti-imperial discourse that critiques empire and its persistent legacies" (*Postcolonial Thought*, 1).

8. Boyce-Davies and Jardine, "Imperial Geographies," 161. Boyce-Davies also examines discourses of empire in *Black Women, Writing and Identity*, chap. 4. Trinidadian literary scholar Jennifer Rahim similarly describes the relationship between the United States and other nations as akin to a "global dictatorship" ("Electronic Fictions," 3).

9. Go, *Patterns of Empire*, 7. Go's scholarship provides a detailed examination of different forms of imperialism. Additionally, Stephen Howe explains that U.S. imperialism shares similarities with formal colonialism of previous centuries, and it "indeed may share the same essential, exploitative aims—although it now operates mostly not through direct colonial rule, so much as through local client regimes, and through less formalized, less obvious economic, diplomatic, cultural, and other means of control" (*Empire*, 25). Elucidating the contested terms of imperialism and empire, Howe also writes: "The terms 'empire' and 'imperialism,' at their most general, have been used to refer to any and every type of relation between a more powerful state or society and a less powerful one" (13). Furthermore, *Class Interruptions* does not treat "colonialism" and "imperialism" as synonyms, as some scholars do.

10. Forms of U.S. imperialism or hegemony are also obvious within the United States through the oppression of marginalized populations, and the novels demonstrate this reality. In the past, especially during the Black power movement, scholars used the term "internal colonialism" to describe the position of African Americans within the United States. Robert L. Allen says this term was widely used during the Black power movement of the 1960s to describe predicaments of Blacks in urban ghettoes and the U.S. South ("Reassessing the Internal"). Regarding the contemporary period of neoliberal globalization, scholars such as Ramon Grosfoguel prefer the term "coloniality of power" (*Colonial Subjects*). Additionally, when analyzing *Tar Baby*, scholars tend to focus on Valerian, the representative colonialist/capitalist, which places the focus on what I call the imperialist (i.e., Valerian). For examples of analyses on *Tar Baby*, see V. Smith, *Toni Morrison*; Mobley, "Telling Stories"; and Jurecic and Rampersad, "Teaching *Tar Baby*." In contrast, I focus on those being marginalized. I also see Valerian and his wife as being representative of the continued imperialist leanings of superpower countries like the United States.

11. In *Agent of Empire*, Brady Harrison notes that many critics examine how literary forms "play key roles in the fostering of empires" and how writers can "disseminate imperialist attitudes" (84). Harrison provides examples of several creative works that

celebrate the feats of William Walker, a representative figure of American imperialism. One example is Bret Harte's romance novel *The Crusade of the Excelsior* (1887), which chronicles the imperial projects of Walker. Harte's novel is a mercenary romance novel, which is a subgenre of the historical romance novel.

12. For Morrison's discussion of American romanticism, see *Playing in the Dark*, chap. 2. In her essay "Home," Morrison says she "was interested in the impact of race on the romance of community and individuality" (9) in *Tar Baby*. Additionally, Elizabeth Ann Beaulieu, in *The Toni Morrison Encyclopedia*, discusses the romantic tradition in Morrison's novels and how scholars often compare Morrison's works with those by American romance writers such as Nathaniel Hawthorne (294–97).

13. Terms such as "imperialism," "colonialism," and "hegemony" are often used interchangeably; see Howe, *Empire*. Also, Morrison highlights French and American imperialism in *Tar Baby*. For a discussion of imperialism and its effects on the British West Indies from the 1880s to the 1920s, see Rosenberg, *Nationalism and the Formation of Caribbean Literature*.

14. Rahim describes Bella as "a type who signifies the multicultural/creolized possibility transcending racial tensions in a world that is becoming more cosmopolitan" ("Electronic Fictions," 13).

15. For more on forts in Trinidad and Tobago, see Cameron, *Trinidad & Tobago*. Cameron explains, "By some reckonings Tobago changed hands as many as 29 times and for this reason there are a large number of forts" (89).

16. See, for example, Petra, *US Imperialism: The Changing Dynamics of Global Power*, 156. Additionally, Harvey R. Neptune argues in *Caliban and the Yankees* that "resituating Trinidad squarely within the realm of the U.S. empire" is instructive on many levels, as it opens further insight into the region (13). For more on this topic in general, see Nixon, *Resisting Paradise*; Chapman, *Bananas*; Grosfoguel, Maldonado-Torres, and Saldivar, *Latino/as in the World-System*; and Go, *Patterns of Empire*.

17. Important to note here is that the period under examination in *Class Interruptions* is one when the United States dominates the Caribbean region. In the 1980s, the United States launched the Caribbean Basin Initiative, and the United States continues to extend its power through loan policies and through security arrangements, for example. Also, as M. Keith Booker and Dubravka Juraga observe, "The cultural, economic, and social fabric of the island was powerfully altered by the presence of large numbers of American troops on bases established on the island by the United States" ("Merle Hodge," 62).

18. For more on sex tourism in the Caribbean, see K. Kempadoo, *Sun, Sex, and Gold*. Additionally, Rahim asserts, "Kempadoo treats the affair with Bella and Peter as a kind of benign or masked sex tourism. Sexual experimentation as the leisure afforded the wealthy, rather than overt solicitation for sex, seems the motivation behind the couple's seduction of Cliff" ("Electronic Fictions," 10).

19. For more on tourism and sexual identity, see Nixon, *Resisting Paradise*.

20. Kempadoo, Interview by Harald Leusmann. Rahim also mentions "Tobago's resistance to Trinidadinization" and "the subtext of Tobago's tense relations with Trinidad, resulting from the island's disadvantaged political and economic position in the twin-island Republic of Trinidad and Tobago" ("Electronic Fictions," 3, 4).

21. See B. Williams, *The Pursuit of Happiness*, for additional discussion of romance tourism.

22. Morgan makes an astute point about the effect of their TV-watching: "Arguably its most penetrating message—significance exists in another place not here—alienates the impoverished islander from immediate conditions of meanness, squalor and meaninglessness, in the interest of a fantasized luxury, wealth, order and beauty" ("Meet Me in the Islands," 15–16).

23. Despite their precarious circumstances and having no jobs, Cliff and Ossi (Cliff's brother) have some name-brand clothes and shoes, such as Filas and Nikes. They are mimicking what they see on American TV shows. Having these things makes them happy when they visit the couple's home, as they feel as though they are in a movie. See Evelyn O'Callaghan, "Women Writing" for more on the obsession with consumerism in the novel.

24. Valerian's wife, Margaret Street, is from a white working-class background as well. Though Morrison provides some information about Margaret's background, she focuses more on the Caribbean and African American working classes in the novel. Additionally, I believe Valerian and Margaret are in positions equivalent to imperialists or modern-day enslavers, while Sydney and Ondine are analogous to "house slaves," and the local residents who work for the Streets (Gideon, Marie Therese, and Alma Estee) are in the position of "field slaves."

25. Malin Pereira observes that colonization is the major concern in *Tar Baby* ("Periodizing Toni Morrison's Work," 72).

26. For instance, Margot Gayle Backus suggests that Valerian represents a capitalist patriarch while the others are his workers ("'Looking for That Dead Girl,'" 425).

27. Toward the beginning of the novel, Therese senses that someone is "starving to death" (105) right before they become aware of Son lurking on the premises. Gideon tells her that he (Gideon) is starving. It is not clear if he is joking, as Therese dismisses him and says, "No, not you. A really starving somebody" (105). They begin to leave food for the starving stranger who they later learn is Son.

28. Howe, in his discussion on relationships based on imperialism, writes that "some analysts also use terms like dependency—closely associated with economic underdevelopment—to describe these relationships" (*Empire*, 30).

29. It is important to remember that it was Haitian laborers who cleared the land and built the Streets' house (8), so the Streets' house itself "represents the history and legacy of European colonialists" (Gillespie, *Critical Companion*, 215).

30. See Jurecic and Rampersad, "Teaching *Tar Baby*," 151–52, for a discussion of the role of the tar baby tale in the story. They mention different versions of the tale.

31. See Waligora-Davis, *Sanctuary*. Her chapter on the U.S. occupation of Haiti (chap. 5) and her chapter on Du Bois (chap. 2) discuss similarities between segregation and colonialism. Howe further notes that for a number of scholars in the contemporary period, the term "'imperialism' is effectively a simple synonym for American foreign policy" (*Empire*, 25).

32. Magness describes a hierarchy of Blacks with Ondine and Sydney at the top, Son in the middle, and the local population at the bottom. She also notes: "Scorn for

others is also a trait of a third class of blacks, the island people, Gideon, Marie-Therese, and Alma Estee" ("The Knight," 95).

33. See Bhaba, "Of Mimicry and Man," who further explains that the colonized often mimic those in power.

34. For more on the breakdown of Caribbean populations in the United States, see Anderson, "Statistical Portrait of the U.S. Black Immigrant Population," and Zong and Batalova, "Caribbean Immigrants in the United States."

35. Brown, "Jamaica Prime Minister Holness Congratulates 46th U.S. President-Elect Joe Biden"; "PM Rowley Extends Congratulations to Biden, Harris."

36. hooks, *Where We Stand*, 9.

37. Mehrsa Baradaran, among others such as Darrick Hamilton, offers bold ideas for government policy changes that can be implemented immediately. See Baradaran, *The Color of Money*, and "The Neoliberal Looting of America."

38. Noni Limar, "10 Reasons Why Art + Culture Is Imperative," n.p.

39. In the introduction to *Occupying Political Science*, Matthew Bolton et al. write that the Occupy Movement "has heightened the urgency and visibility of the issue of economic inequality. Ninety-nine percent is not only a number now, it is a symbol, a discourse, an idea" (13). Additionally, stratification economist Darrick Hamilton proposes several ideas that can have structural impacts (some of which have been adopted by political leaders) such as a federal job guarantee, baby bonds, postal banking, and reparations. See his "Neoliberalism and Race," as well as his scholarship with colleagues, including Collins et al., "Ten Solutions to Bridge the Racial Wealth Divide"; Paul, Darity, and Hamilton, "The Federal Job Guarantee—A Policy to Achieve Permanent Full Employment"; and Darity et al., "What We Get Wrong about Closing the Racial Wealth Gap."

Bibliography

Abramovitz, Mimi. "Economic Crises, Neoliberalism, and the US Welfare State: Trends, Outcomes and Political Struggle." In *Global Social Work: Crossing Borders, Blurring Boundaries*, edited by Carolyn Noble, Helle Strauss, and Brian Littlechild, 225–40. Sydney, New South Wales: Sydney University Press, 2014.

Adair, Vivyan C. "Class Absences: Cutting Class in Feminist Studies." *Feminist Studies* 31, no. 3 (2005): 575–603.

Aidoo, Lamonte. *Slavery Unseen: Sex, Power, and Violence in Brazilian History.* Durham, NC: Duke University Press, 2018.

Allen, Robert L. "Reassessing the Internal (Neo) Colonialism Theory." *Black Scholar* 35, no. 1 (2005): 2–11.

Allen-Agostini, Lisa. "Suffer the Children." Review of *Dog-Heart*, by Diana McCaulay. *Caribbean Review of Books*, November 24, 2010. caribbeanreviewofbooks.com/crb -archive/24-november-2010/suffer-thechildren/.

Althusser, Louis. "Ideology and Ideological State Apparatuses (Notes towards an Investigation)." In *Lenin and Philosophy and Other Essays*, translated by Ben Brewster, 85–126. New York: Monthly Review Press, 1971.

———. *On the Reproduction of Capitalism: Ideology and Ideological State Apparatuses.* Translated by G. M. Goshgarian. London: Verso, 2014.

Anderson, Monica. "Chapter 1: Statistical Portrait of the U.S. Black Immigrant Population." In *A Rising Share of the U.S. Black Population Is Foreign Born*, 11–21. Pew Research Center, 2015. https://www.pewresearch.org/social-trends/2015/04 /09/chapter-1-statistical-portrait-of-the-u-s-black-immigrant-population/.

Anderson, Patricia, and Camille Daley. "Parenting across Social Classes: Perspectives on Jamaican Fathers." In *Parenting across Cultures: Childrearing, Motherhood and Fatherhood in Non-Western Cultures*, edited by Helaine Selin, 335–48. New York: Springer, 2014.

Andrews, William L. *Slavery and Class in the American South: A Generation of Slave Narrative Testimony, 1840–1865.* New York: Oxford University Press, 2019.

Arnold, Albert James, Julio Rodríguez-Luis, and J. Michael Dash, eds. *A History of Literature in the Caribbean, Volume Two: English- and Dutch-Speaking Regions.* Amsterdam: John Benjamins Publishing, 2001.

Assari, Shervin, and Rohan D. Jeremiah. "Intimate Partner Violence May Be One Mechanism by Which Male Partner Socioeconomic Status and Substance Use Affect Female Partner Health." *Frontiers in Psychiatry* 9, no. 160 (May 8, 2018). doi:10.3389/fpsyt.2018.00160.

Bacchus, Mohammed Kazim. "The Education Challenges Facing Small Nation States in the Increasingly Competitive Global Economy of the Twenty-First Century." *Comparative Education* 44, no. 2 (2008): 127–45.

Backus, Margot Gayle. "'Looking for That Dead Girl': Incest, Pornography, and the Capitalist Family Romance in *Nightwood*, *The Years*, and *Tar Baby*." *American Imago* 51, no. 4 (1994): 421–45.

Baksh-Soodeen, Rawwida. "Issues of Difference in Contemporary Caribbean Feminism." *Feminist Review* 59, no. 1 (1998): 74–85.

Ballantyne, Tony, and Antoinette Burton. *Bodies in Contact: Rethinking Colonial Encounters in World History*. Durham, NC: Duke University Press, 2005.

Balthaser, Benjamin. "The Race of Class: The Role of Racial Identity Production in the Long History of U.S. Working-Class Writing." In *Working-Class Literature(s): Historical and International Perspectives*, edited by John Lennon and Magnus Nilsson, 31–64. Stockholm: Stockholm University Press, 2017.

Balutansky, Kathleen. "We Are All Activists: An Interview with Merle Hodge." *Callaloo* 12, no. 4 (1989): 651–62.

Baradaran, Mehrsa. *The Color of Money: Black Banks and the Racial Wealth Gap*. Cambridge, MA: Belknap Press of Harvard University Press, 2019.

———."The Neoliberal Looting of America." *New York Times*, July 2, 2020. https://www.nytimes.com/2020/07/02/opinion/private-equity-inequality.html.

Barriteau, Violet Eudine. *Love and Power: Caribbean Discourses on Gender*. Kingston, Jamaica: University of the West Indies Press, 2012.

———. "The Relevance of Black Feminist Scholarship: A Caribbean Perspective." *Feminist Africa*, no. 7 (2006): 9–31.

Basile, Kathleen C., Sharon G. Smith, Dawnovise N. Fowler, Mikel L. Walters, and Merle E. Hamburger. "Sexual Violence Victimization and Associations with Health in a Community Sample of African American Women." *Journal of Aggression, Maltreatment & Trauma* 25, no. 3 (2016): 231–53.

Bass, Margaret. "Race, Class, and Gender in Four West Indian Novels: *Pitch Lake, Corentyne Thunder, The Hills Were Joyful Together, Wide Sargasso*." In *Imagination, Emblems, and Expressions: Essays on Latin American, Caribbean, and Continental Culture and Identity*, edited by Helen Ryan-Ranson, 127–37. Bowling Green, OH: Bowling Green State University Popular Press, 1993.

Baugh, Edward. "A History of Poetry." In *A History of Literature in the Caribbean, Volume Two: English- and Dutch-Speaking Regions*, edited by James Arnold, 227–82. Amsterdam: John Benjamins Publishing, 2001.

Beale, Frances. "Double Jeopardy: To Be Black and Female." In *Words of Fire: An Anthology of African American Feminist Thought*, edited by Beverly Guy-Sheftall, 146–56. New York: New Press, 1995.

Beaulieu, Elizabeth Ann, ed. *The Toni Morrison Encyclopedia*. Westport, CT: Greenwood Publishing, 2003.

Beavers, Herman. *Geography and the Political Imaginary in the Novels of Toni Morrison*. New York: Palgrave Macmillan, 2018.

Belknap, Joanne. *The Invisible Woman: Gender, Crime, and Justice*, 4th ed. Independence, KY: Cengage Learning, 2014.

Benedict, Helen. *Virgin or Vamp: How the Press Covers Sex Crimes*. New York: Oxford University Press, 1992.

Bennett, Natalie, and William O'Donohue. "The Construct of Grooming in Child Sexual Abuse: Conceptual and Measurement Issues." *Journal of Child Sexual Abuse* 23, no. 8 (2014): 957–76.

Bhaba, Homi. "Of Mimicry and Man: The Ambivalence of Colonial Discourse." *The Location of Culture*. New York: Routledge, 2004.

Black, Stephanie, dir. *Life and Debt*. Kingston, Jamaica: Tuff Gong Pictures, 2001.

Block, Sharon. *Rape and Sexual Power in Early America*. Chapel Hill: Omohundro Institute and University of North Carolina Press, 2006.

Bolton, Matthew, Emily Welty, Meghana Nayak, and Christopher Malone. "We Had a Front Row Seat to a Downtown Revolution." In *Occupying Political Science: The Occupy Wall Street Movement from New York to the World*, edited by Emily Welty, Matthew Bolton, Meghana Nayak, and Christopher Malone, 1–24. New York: Palgrave Macmillan, 2013.

Bonetti, Kay. "An Interview with Gloria Naylor." In *Conversations with Gloria Naylor*, edited by Maxine L. Montgomery, 39–64. Jackson: University Press of Mississippi, 2004.

Booker, M. Keith, and Dubravka Juraga. "Merle Hodge, *Crick Crack, Monkey* (Trinidad, 1970)." In *The Caribbean Novel in English: An Introduction*, 50–63. Portsmouth, NH: Heinemann, 2001.

Bourdieu, Pierre. *Distinction: A Social Critique of the Judgment of Taste*. Translated by Richard Nice. Cambridge, MA: Harvard University Press, 1984 (1979).

———. *Outline of a Theory of Practice*. Translated by Richard Nice. Cambridge: Cambridge University Press, 1977.

———. *Reproduction: In Education, Society and Culture*. Translated by Richard Nice. Thousand Oaks, CA: Sage Publications, 1977.

Bouson, J. Brooks. "Uncovering 'The Beloved' in the Warring and Lawless Women in Toni Morrison's *Love*." *Midwest Quarterly* 49, no. 4 (2008): 358–73.

Bouvier, Luke. "Reading in Black and White: Space and Race in *Linden Hills*." In *Gloria Naylor: Critical Perspectives Past and Present*, edited by Henry Louis Gates Jr. and K. A. Appiah, 140–52. New York: Amistad Press, 1993.

Boyce-Davies, Carole. *Black Women, Writing and Identity: Migrations of the Subject*. New York: Routledge, 1994.

———. *Left of Karl Marx: The Political Life of Black Communist Claudia Jones*. Durham, NC: Duke University Press, 2008.

Boyce-Davies, Carole, and Monica Jardine. "Imperial Geographies and Caribbean Nationalism at the Border between 'A Dying Colonialism' and U.S. Hegemony." *CR: The New Centennial Review* 3, no. 3 (2003): 151–74.

Bracks, Lean'tin. "Dawn Turner." In *Contemporary African American Novelists: A Bio-Bibliographical Critical Sourcebook*, edited by Emmanuel S. Nelson, 454–57. Westport, CT: Greenwood Press, 1999.

Brathwaite, Kamau. "The Caribbean Artists Movement," *Caribbean Quarterly* 14, no. 1/2 (March–June 1968): 57–59.

———. *History of the Voice: The Development of Nation Language in Anglophone Caribbean Poetry*. London: New Beacon Books, 1984.

Brodber, Erna. "From Juba's Head." In *The Continent of Black Consciousness: On the History of the African Diaspora from Slavery to the Present Day*, 139–59. London: New Beacon Books Ltd., 2003.

Brooks, Robin. "Looking to Foremothers for Strength: A Brief Biography of the Colored Woman's League." *Women's Studies: An Interdisciplinary Journal* 47, no. 6 (2018): 609–16.

———. "Manifestations of Ogun Symbolism in Paule Marshall's *Praisesong for the Widow*." *Journal of Africana Religions* 2, no. 2 (2014): 161–83.

Brown, Adrienne R. *The Black Skyscraper: Architecture and the Perception of Race*. Baltimore, MD: Johns Hopkins University Press, 2017.

Brown, Oswald. "Jamaica Prime Minister Holness Congratulates 46th U.S. President-Elect Joe Biden." *Bahamas Chronicle*, November 8, 2020. https://bahamaschronicle.com/jamaica-prime-minister-holness-congratulates-46th-u-s-president-elect-joe-biden/.

Brown, Wendy. *Undoing the Demos: Neoliberalism's Stealth Revolution*. Princeton, NJ: Zone Books, 2015.

Brysk, Alison. "Introduction." In *Globalization and Human Rights*, edited by Alison Brysk, 1–17. Oakland: University of California Press, 2002.

Bucknor, Michael A. "'Grung'/Ground(ed) Poetics: 'The Voice from the Bottom of the Well.'" In *The Routledge Companion to Anglophone Caribbean Literature*, edited by Michael A. Bucknor and Alison Donnell, 85–92. New York: Routledge, 2011.

———. "On Caribbean Masculinities." *Anthurium: A Caribbean Studies Journal* 10, no. 2 (2013): 1–4. scholarlyrepository.miami.edu/cgi/viewcontent.cgi?article=1299&context=anthurium.

Bucknor, Michael A., and Alison Donnell, eds. *The Routledge Companion to Anglophone Caribbean Literature*. New York: Routledge, 2011.

Bulson, Eric. *Novels, Maps, Modernity: The Spatial Imagination, 1850–2000*. New York: Routledge, 2007.

Burke, Tarana. "Me Too Is a Movement, Not a Moment." TED, November 2018. www.ted.com/talks/tarana_burke_me_too_is_a_movement_not_a_moment.

Byron, Jessica, and Diana Thorburn. "Gender and International Relations: A Global Perspective and Issues for the Caribbean." *Feminist Review* 59, no. 1 (1998): 211–32.

Cameron, Sarah. *Trinidad & Tobago: Footprint Focus Guide*. Bath, UK: Footprint Handbooks, 2014.

Campbell, Carl C. *Endless Education: Main Currents in the Education System of Modern Trinidad and Tobago, 1939–1986*. Mona, Jamaica: University of the West Indies Press, 1997.

———. *The Young Colonials: A Social History of Education in Trinidad and Tobago, 1834–1939*. Mona, Jamaica: University of the West Indies Press, 1996.

Canadian Centre for Child Protection. *Child Sexual Abuse — It Is Your Business*. 2014. cybertip.ca/pdfs/C3P_ChildSexualAbuse_ItIsYourBusiness_en.pdf.

Carden, Mary Paniccia. "'Trying to Find a Place When the Streets Don't Go There': Fatherhood, Family, and American Racial Politics in Toni Morrison's *Love*." *African American Review* 44, no. 1/2 (2011): 131–47.

Caribbean Examinations Council (CXC). https://www.cxc.org/.

Center for Sex Offender Management. *Fact Sheet: What You Need to Know About Sex Offenders*. Washington, DC: US Department of Justice, Office of Justice Programs, 2008. https://cecom/wp-content/uploads/2020/01/1-Fact-Sheet-.pdf.

Chapman, Peter. *Bananas: How the United Fruit Company Shaped the World*. Edinburgh, Scotland: Canongate, 2009.

Chicago Housing Authority. "History." https://www.thecha.org/about. Accessed September 15, 2018.

Christian, Barbara. "Gloria Naylor's Geography: Community, Class, and Patriarchy in *The Women of Brewster Place* and *Linden Hills*." In *Reading Black, Reading Feminist: A Critical Anthology*, edited by Henry Louis Gates Jr., 348–73. New York: Meridian, 1990.

Christopher, Renny, and Carolyn Whitson. "Toward a Theory of Working-Class Literature." *NEA Higher Education Journal* 15, no. 1 (1999): 71–81.

Chunnu, Winsome. "Negotiating Worlds (Yards, Shantytowns, Ghettos, Garrisons): Inequality Maintained and the Epistemologies of Social Factors Influencing Stratification and Education in Jamaica." *International Journal of Educational Research* 78 (2016): 32–40.

Class Action. "About Class." June 9, 2014. https://classism.org/about-class/.

Cobham-Sander, Rhonda. "Revisioning Our Kumblas: Transforming Feminist and Nationalist Agendas in Three Caribbean Women's Texts." In *Postcolonial Theory and the United States: Race, Ethnicity, and Literature*, edited by Amritjit Singh and Peter Schmidt, 300–319. Jackson: University of Mississippi Press, 2000.

Cocca, Carolyn E. *Jailbait: The Politics of Statutory Rape Laws in the United States*. Albany: State University of New York Press, 2004.

Cohen, Cathy. *The Boundaries of Blackness: AIDS and the Breakdown of Black Politics*. Chicago: University of Chicago Press, 1999.

Cole, Elizabeth R., and Safiya R. Omari. "Race, Class and the Dilemmas of Upward Mobility for African Americans." *Journal of Social Issues* 59, no. 4 (2003): 785–802.

Coles, Nicholas, and Janet Zandy. *American Working-Class Literature: An Anthology*. New York: Oxford University Press, 2007.

Collins, Chuck, Darrick Hamilton, Dedrick Asante-Muhammad, and Josh Hoxie. "Ten Solutions to Bridge the Racial Wealth Divide." https://ips-dc.org/report-racial-wealth-divide-solutions. Accessed November 2, 2020.

Collins, Grace E. "Narrative Structure in *Linden Hills*." *College Language Association* 34, no. 3 (1991): 290–300.

Collins, Patricia Hill. *Black Feminist Thought: Knowledge, Consciousness, and the Politics of Empowerment*. New York: Routledge, 2000.

———. *Intersectionality as Critical Social Theory*. Durham, NC: Duke University Press, 2019.

Connolly, Nathan D. B. "This, Our Second Nadir." *Boston Review: A Political and Literary Forum*, February 2018. http://bostonreview.net/forum/remake-world-slavery-racial-capitalism-and-justice/n-d-b-connolly-our-second-nadir.

Cook, Loraine D., and Zellynne Jennings-Craig. "Perspectives of Jamaican Parents and Their Secondary School Children on the Value of Education: Effects of

Selected Variables on Parents' Perspectives." *International Journal of Educational Development* 50 (2016): 90–99.

Crawford, Margo Natalie. *Black Post-Blackness: The Black Arts Movement and Twenty-First-Century Aesthetics*. Champaign: University of Illinois Press, 2017.

Crenshaw, Kimberlé. "Demarginalizing the Intersection of Race and Sex: A Black Feminist Critique of Antidiscrimination Doctrine, Feminist Theory and Antiracist Politics." *University of Chicago Legal Forum* 1989, no. 1 (1989): 139–67.

———. "Mapping the Margins: Intersectionality, Identity Politics, and Violence against Women of Color." *Stanford Law Review* 43, no. 6 (1991): 1241–99.

Crichlow, Michaeline A. *Negotiating Caribbean Freedom: Peasants and the State in Development*. Lanham, MD: Lexington, 2005.

Curtin, Philip. *Two Jamaicas: The Role of Ideas in a Tropical Colony, 1830–1865*. Cambridge, MA: Harvard University Press, 1955.

Darity, William, Jr., Darrick Hamilton, Mark Paul, Alan Aja, Anne Price, Antonio Moore, and Caterina Chiopris. "What We Get Wrong about Closing the Racial Wealth Gap." Samuel DuBois Cook Center on Social Equity and Insight Center for Community Economic Development, April 2018. https://socialequity.duke.edu/sites /socialequity.duke.edu/files/siteimages/FINAL%20COMPLETE%20REPORT_.pdf.

David, Marlo. *Mama's Gun: Black Maternal Figures and the Politics of Transgression*. Columbus: Ohio State University Press, 2016.

Davis, Angela Y. *Blues Legacies and Black Feminism: Gertrude "Ma" Rainey, Bessie Smith, and Billie Holiday*. New York: Vintage, 1998.

De Lisle, Jerome. "Explaining Whole System Reform in Small States: The Case of Trinidad and Tobago Secondary Education Modernization Program." *Current Issues in Comparative Education* 15, no. 1 (2012): 64–82.

Denard, Carolyn. "'Some to Hold, Some to Tell': Secrets and the Trope of Silence in *Love*." In *Toni Morrison: Paradise, Love, A Mercy*, edited by Lucille P. Fultz, 77–91. New York: Bloomsbury, 2013.

Desmond, Matthew. *Evicted: Poverty and Profit in the American City*. New York: Penguin Random House, 2016.

———. "Questions & Answers about Eviction." The Eviction Lab, Princeton University. https://evictionlab.org/why-eviction-matters/#understanding -eviction. Accessed September 15, 2018.

Diggs Colbert, Soyica, Robert J. Patterson, and Aida Levy-Hussen. *The Psychic Hold of Slavery: Legacies in American Expressive Culture*. New Brunswick, NJ: Rutgers University Press, 2016.

Donington, Katie. "Eric Williams' Foundational Work on Slavery, Industry, and Wealth." September 2020. https://www.aaihs.org/eric-williams-foundational -work-on-slavery-industry-and-wealth/.

Donnell, Alison. "The Lives of Others: Happenings, Histories and Literary Healing." In *The Routledge Companion to Anglophone Caribbean Literature*, edited by Michael A. Bucknor and Alison Donnell, 422–31. New York: Routledge, 2011.

Douglas, Emily M., and David Finkelhor. "Childhood Sexual Abuse Fact Sheet." Crimes against Children Research Center, 2005. http://www.unh.edu/ccrc /factsheet/pdf/ childhoodSexualAbuseFactSheet.pdf.

Dow, William. *Narrating Class in American Fiction*. New York: Palgrave Macmillan, 2008.

Down, Lorna. Review of *Dog-Heart*, by Diana McCaulay. *Jamaica Journal* 33, nos. 1–2 (2010): 108–9.

Dubey, Madhu. *Black Women Novelists and the Nationalist Aesthetic*. Indianapolis: Indiana University Press, 1994.

———. *Signs and Cities: Black Literary Postmodernism*. Chicago: University of Chicago Press, 2003.

Duboin, Corinne. "A New Voice in African American Literature: An Interview with Dawn Turner." *Sources: Revue d'études Anglophones* 11 (2001): 115–27.

———. "Writing the Fragmented City: Black Neighborhoods in Dawn Turner's *Only Twice I've Wished for Heaven*." *Alizés* 22 (2002): 55–76.

Dumond, Kelsey. "'Cast Me Not Away!': The Plight of Modern Day Romeo and Juliet." *Quinnipiac Law Review* 36, no. 3 (2018): 455–87.

DuRand, Cliff. "Neoliberal Globalization and the Crisis of Liberal Democracy." *Socialism and Democracy* 33, no. 3 (2019): 107–24. https://doi.org/10.1080/08854300.2019.1705648

Durante, Federica, and Susan T. Fiske. "How Social-Class Stereotypes Maintain Inequality." *Current Opinion in Psychology* 18 (2017): 43–48.

Edwards, Norval. "Sylvia Wynter: Insurgent Criticism and a Poetics of Disenchantment." In *The Routledge Companion to Anglophone Caribbean Literature*, edited by Michael A. Bucknor and Alison Donnell, 91–108. New York: Routledge, 2011.

Engles, Tim. "African American Whiteness in Gloria Naylor's *Linden Hills*." *African American Review* 43, no. 4 (2009): 661–79.

Epstein, Rebecca, Jamilia J. Blake, and Thalia Gonzalez. *Girlhood Interrupted: The Erasure of Black Girls' Childhood*. Washington, DC: Center on Poverty and Inequality, Georgetown University Law Center, 2017. https://genderjustice andopportunity.georgetown.edu/wp-content/uploads/2020/06/girlhood -interrupted.pdf.

Felski, Rita. "Nothing to Declare: Identity, Shame, and the Lower Middle Class." *PMLA* 115, no. 1 (2000): 33–45.

Feng, Pin-chia. "'We Was Girls Together': The Double Female Bildungsroman in Toni Morrison's *Love*." *Feminist Studies in English Literature* 15, no. 2 (2007): 37–63.

Ferguson, Roderick. *The Reorder of Things: The University and Its Pedagogies of Minority Difference*. Minneapolis: University of Minnesota Press, 2012.

Fields, Barbara J., and Karen Elise Fields. *Racecraft: The Soul of Inequality in American Life*. Brooklyn: Verso, 2014.

Figueroa, Esther. "The Future Unimaginable, the Past So Impossible! Historical Trauma and Generational Damage in Diana McCaulay's *Dog-Heart* and Jamaica Kincaid's *Mr. Potter*." Challenges of the Independence Experience in Small Developing Countries, Sir Arthur Lewis Institute of Social & Economic Studies Conference, University of the West Indies at Mona, Kingston, Jamaica, March 23, 2011.

———, dir. *Jamaica for Sale*. Kingston, Jamaica: Vagabond Media & Jamaica Environment Trust, 2008.

———. "In Search of Compassion—Diana McCaulay's Novel "Dog-Heart." *Caribbean Writer* (unpublished conference paper).

Ford-Smith, Honor. *Ring Ding in a Tight Corner: A Case Study of Funding and Organizational Democracy in Sistren, 1977–1988*. Toronto: Women's Program, International Council for Adult Education, 1989.

Foster, Thomas A. "The Sexual Abuse of Black Men under American Slavery." *Journal of the History of Sexuality* 20, no. 3 (2011): 445–64.

Fox, Pamela. "The 'Revolt of the Gentle': Romance and the Politics of Resistance in Working-Class Women's Writing." *Novel: A Forum on Fiction* 27, no. 2 (1994): 140–60.

Franklin, John H., and Alfred A. Moss. *From Slavery to Freedom: A History of African Americans*. New York City: Knopf, 2000.

Franko, William, and Christopher Witko. *The New Economic Populism: How States Respond to Economic Inequality*. New York: Oxford University Press, 2017.

Freedman, Estelle. *Redefining Rape: Sexual Violence in the Era of Suffrage and Segregation*. Cambridge, MA: Harvard University Press, 2015.

Fultz, Lucille P. "Love: An Elegy for the African American Community, or the Unintended Consequences of Desegregation/Integration." In *Toni Morrison: Memory and Meaning*, edited by Adrienne L. Seward and Justine Tally, 93–104. Jackson: University of Mississippi Press, 2014.

Gallego, Mar. "Love and the Survival of the Black Community." In *The Cambridge Companion to Toni Morrison*, edited by Justine Tally, 92–100. New York: Cambridge University Press, 2007.

García, Ivis. "Historically Illustrating the Shift to Neoliberalism in the U.S. Home Mortgage Market." *Societies* 9, no. 6 (2019): 1–16. https://doi.org/10.3390 /soc9010006.

George, June, and Theodore Lewis. "Exploring the Global/Local Boundary in Education in Developing Countries: The Case of the Caribbean." *Compare* 41, no. 6 (2011): 721–34.

Gest, Justin. *The New Minority: White Working-Class Politics in an Age of Immigration and Inequality*. New York: Oxford University Press, 2016.

Gikandi, Simon. "Narration in the Post-Colonial Moment: Merle Hodge's *Crick Crack, Monkey*." In *Past the Last Post: Theorizing Post-Colonialism and Post-Modernism*, edited by Ian Adam and Helen Tiffin, 13–22. Calgary, Canada: University of Calgary Press, 1990.

———. "Writing after Colonialism: *Crick Crack, Monkey* and *Beka Lamb*." In *Writing in Limbo: Modernism and Caribbean Literature*, 197–230. Ithaca, NY: Cornell University Press, 1992.

Gillespie, Carmen. *A Critical Companion to Toni Morrison*. New York: Infobase Publishing, 2009.

Gilmore, Ruth Wilson. "Abolition Geography and the Problem of Innocence." In *Futures of Black Radicalism*, edited by Gaye Theresa Johnson and Alex Lubin, 225–40. London: Verso, 2017.

Giovannelli, Laura. "Olive Senior's *Dancing Lessons*: On the Rhythm and Flow of Life." In *Interconnecting Music and the Literary Word*, edited by Fausto Ciompi,

Laura Giovannelli, and Roberta Ferrari, 151–70. Newcastle upon Tyne, UK: Cambridge Scholars Publishing, 2018.

Giroux, Henry. *Theory and Resistance in Education: Towards a Pedagogy for the Opposition*. Westport, CT: Praeger, 2001.

Go, Julian. *Patterns of Empire: The British and American Empires, 1688 to the Present*. New York: Cambridge University Press, 2011.

———. *Postcolonial Thought and Social Theory*. New York: Oxford University Press, 2016.

Goldberg, Elizabeth Swanson. "Gendering Human Rights and Their Violation: A Reading of Chris Cleave's Little Bee." In *The Routledge Companion to Literature and Human Rights*, edited by Sophia A. McClennen and Alexandra Schultheis Moore, 60–68. New York: Routledge, 2016.

Government of the Republic of Trinidad and Tobago, Ministry of Education. "Draft Education Policy Paper 2017–2022." 2017. https://www.moe.gov.tt/education-policy-paper-2017-2022/.

Graham, Lawrence Otis. *Our Kind of People: Inside America's Black Upper Class*. New York: HarperCollins, 2009.

Gramsci, Antonio, and Joseph A. Buttigieg. *Prison Notebooks*. New York: Columbia University Press, 1992.

Green, Sharon L. "On a Knife Edge: Sistren Theatre Collective, Grassroots Theatre, and Globalization." *Small Axe: A Caribbean Journal of Criticism* 11, no. 1 (2006): 111–24.

———. "Sistren Theatre Collective: Struggling to Remain Radical in an Era of Globalization." *Theatre Topics* 14, no. 2 (2004): 473–95.

Greenfield-Sanders, Timothy, dir. *Toni Morrison: The Pieces I Am*. New York: Magnolia Pictures, 2019.

Griffin, Farah J. "Key Texts in African American Literary Criticism." In *Cultural Life*, edited by Colin A. Palmer and Howard Dodson, 65–122. East Lansing: Michigan State University Press, 2007.

Griffith, Glyne. "Reading Class in Anglophone Caribbean Literature." In *The Routledge Companion to Anglophone Caribbean Literature*, edited by Michael A. Bucknor and Alison Donnell, 285–94. New York: Routledge, 2011.

Grosfoguel, Ramon. *Colonial Subjects: Puerto Ricans in a Global Perspective*. Oakland: University of California Press, 2003.

Grosfoguel, Ramon, Nelson Maldonado-Torres, and Jose David Saldivar, eds. *Latino/as in the World-System: Decolonization Struggles in the 21st Century U.S. Empire*. New York: Routledge, 2015.

Hakutani, Yoshinobu, and Robert Butler, eds. *The City in African-American Literature*. Teaneck, NJ: Fairleigh Dickinson University Press, 1995.

Hall, Stuart. "Pluralism, Race and Class in Caribbean Society." In *Race and Class in Post-Colonial Society: A Study of Ethnic Group Relations in the English-Speaking Caribbean, Bolivia, Chile and Mexico*. Paris: UNESCO, 1978.

———. "Race, Articulation and Societies Structured in Dominance." In *Sociological Theories: Race and Colonialism*. Paris: UNESCO, 1980.

Hamilton, Darrick. "Neoliberalism and Race." *Democracy* 53 (Summer 2019). https://democracyjournal.org/magazine/53/neoliberalism-and-race/.

Hamilton, Darrick, William Darity Jr., Anne E. Price, Vishnu Sridharan, and Rebecca Tippett. *Umbrellas Don't Make It Rain: Why Studying and Working Hard Isn't Enough for Black Americans*, Durham, NC: Duke University, Research Network on Racial and Ethnic Inequality, 2015. doi:10.13140/RG.2.1.2081.5128.

Handeyside, Anne K., Samara L. Wickliffe, and Jennifer Adams. *Striving for Justice: A Toolkit for Judicial Resolution Officers on College Campuses — Responding to Sexual Assault and Dating and Domestic Violence*. East Lansing: University of Michigan Press, 2007. https://sapac.umich.edu/files/sapac/StrivingForJustice.pdf.

Hanna, Mary. Review of *Dog-Heart* by Diana McCaulay. *Jamaican Literature*, January 21, 2011.

Harack, Katrina. "'Not Even in the Language They Had Invented for Secrets': Trauma, Memory, and Re-Witnessing in Toni Morrison's *Love*." *Mississippi Quarterly: The Journal of Southern Cultures* 66, no. 2 (2013): 255–78.

Harper, Philip B. *Abstractionist Aesthetics: Artistic Form and Social Critique in African American Culture*. New York: New York University Press, 2015.

Harrison, Brady. *Agent of Empire: William Walker and the Imperial Self in American Literature*. Athens: University of Georgia Press, 2004.

Harrison, Faye V. "Anthropology Interrogating Power and Politics." In *UNESCO-Encyclopedia of Life Support Systems (EOLSS). Ethnography, Ethnology, & Cultural Anthropology*. Paris: UNESCO, 2016.

———. "Everyday Neoliberalism, Diminishing Subsistence Security, and the Criminalization of Survival: Gendered Urban Poverty in Three African Diaspora Contexts." International Union of Anthropological and Ethnological Sciences Inter Congress on Mega Urbanization, Multi-Ethnic Society, Human Rights, and Development. Kolkata, India, December 12–15, 2004. www.researchgate.net /publication/256442077_ Everyday_Neoliberalism_Diminishing_Subsistence _Security_and_the_Criminalization_of_ Survival_Gendered_Urban_Poverty_in _Three_African_Diaspora_Contexts.

———. "Expanding the Concept of Human Rights: Social and Economic Rights in the Era of Global Restructuring." Paper presented at the 15th International Conference on Anthropological and Ethnological Sciences, Pre-Congress Program, "Individual Liberties/Collective Liberties on the 300th Birth Anniversary of Tommaso Crudeli," Poppi, Italy, July 7, 2003.

———. "Global Apartheid, Foreign Policy, and Human Rights." *Souls: A Critical Journal of Black Politics, Culture, and Society* 4, no. 3 (2002): 48–68. doi.org/10.1080 /10999940290105309.

———. "Introduction: Global Perspective on Human Rights and Interlocking Inequalities of Race, Gender, and Related Dimensions of Power." In *Resisting Racism and Xenophobia: Global Perspectives on Race, Gender, and Human Rights*, edited by Faye Harrison, 1–31. Lanham, MD: AltaMira Press, 2005.

———. "Jamaica and the International Drug Economy." *Transafrica Forum* 7, no. 3 (1990): 49–57.

———. *Outsider Within: Reworking Anthropology in the Global Age*. Champaign: University of Illinois Press, 2008.

Hartman, Saidiya. *Wayward Lives, Beautiful Experiments: Intimate Histories of Social Upheaval*. New York: W. W. Norton, 2019.

Harvey, David. *A Brief History of Neoliberalism*. New York: Oxford University Press, 2007.

———. "Neoliberalism Is a Political Project." Interview with David Harvey by Bjarke Skærlund Risager. *Jacobin Magazine*, 2016. https://www.jacobinmag.com /2016/07/david-harvey-neoliberalism-capitalism-labor-crisis-resistance/.

———. *Social Justice and the City*, rev. ed. Athens: University of Georgia Press, 2009 (1973).

Hathaway, Oona A. "Do Human Rights Treaties Make a Difference?" *Yale Law Journal* 111, no. 8 (2002): 1935–2042. doi:10.2307/797642.

Haynes, Leanne. "'Writing Is What I Do; It Keeps Me Sane': Olive Senior on Writing." *ARC Magazine*, 2014. http://arcthemagazine.com/arc/2014/02/writing-is -what-i-do-it-keeps-me-sane-olive-senior-on-writing/.

Henderson, Aneeka A. *Veil and Vow: Marriage Matters in Contemporary African American Culture*. Chapel Hill: University of North Carolina Press, 2020.

Hill, Daniel. "Estimating the Effects of Human Rights Treaties on State Behavior." *Journal of Politics* 72, no. 4 (2010): 1161–74.

Hine, Darlene Clark. *Hine Sight: Black Women and the Re-Construction of American History*. Indianapolis: Indiana University Press, 1997.

Hine, Darlene Clark, and Earnestine Jenkins. "Black Men's History: Toward a Gendered Perspective." In *A Question of Manhood: A Reader in U.S. Black Men's History and Masculinity*, edited by Darlene C. Hine and Earnestine Jenkins, 1:1–58. Indianapolis: Indiana University Press, 1999.

"History & Vision." Me Too Movement, 2018. metoomvmt.org/about/.

"History of Racial Injustice: Sexual Exploitation of Black Women." Equal Justice Initiative, eji.org/history-racial-injustice-sexual-exploitation-black-women, August 8, 2016. Accessed February 3, 2019.

Hodge, Merle. "Challenges of the Struggle for Sovereignty: Changing the World versus Writing Stories." In *Caribbean Women Writers: Essays from the First International Conference*, edited by Selwyn R. Cudjoe, 202–8. Wellesley, MA: Calaloux, 1990.

———. *Crick Crack, Monkey*. Portsmouth, NH: Heinemann, 2000.

———. "Language Use and West Indian Literary Criticism." In *The Routledge Companion to Anglophone Caribbean Literature*, edited by Michael A. Bucknor and Alison Donnell, 470–79. New York: Routledge, 2011.

Hong, Grace. *Death beyond Disavowal: The Impossible Politics of Difference*. Minneapolis: University of Minnesota Press, 2015.

hooks, bell. *Killing Rage: Ending Racism*. New York: H. Holt, 1995.

———. *Where We Stand: Class Matters*. New York: Routledge, 2000.

Howe, Stephen. *Empire: A Very Short Introduction*. New York: Oxford University Press, 2002.

Hudson, Peter J. "Racial Capitalism and the Dark Proletariat." *Boston Review: A Political and Literary Forum*, February 2018. http://bostonreview.net/forum

/remake-world-slavery-racial-capitalism-and-justice/peter-james-hudson-racial
-capitalism-and.

Humann, Heather Duerre. *Domestic Abuse in the Novels of African American Women: A Critical Study*. Jefferson, NC: McFarland, 2014.

Isenberg, Nancy. *White Trash: The 400-Year Untold History of Class in America*. New York: Penguin, 2017.

Iton, Richard. *In Search of the Black Fantastic: Politics and Popular Culture in the Post–Civil Rights Era*. New York: Oxford University Press, 2010.

James, Stanlie M., Frances S. Foster, and Beverly Guy-Sheftall. *Still Brave: The Evolution of Black Women's Studies*. New York: Feminist Press, 2009.

Japtok, Martin. "Two Postcolonial Childhoods: Merle Hodge's *Crick Crack, Monkey* and Simi Bedford's *Yoruba Girl Dancing*." *Jouvert* 6, no. 1–2 (2001): 27 paragraphs.

Jarrett, Gene A. *Representing the Race: A New Political History of African American Literature*. New York: New York University Press, 2011.

Jenkins, Candice M. *Black Bourgeois: Class and Sex in the Flesh*. Minneapolis: University of Minnesota Press, 2019.

Jennings-Craig, Zellynne. "Resource and Technology: A Beacon for Change in the Reform of Jamaica's Secondary Education System—or a 'Pipedream'?" *International Review of Education* 58, no. 2 (2012): 247–69.

Johnson, Walter. "To Remake the World: Slavery, Racial Capitalism, and Justice." *Boston Review: A Political and Literary Forum*, February 2018. http://bostonreview.net/forum/walter-johnson-to-remake-the-world.

Jones, Shevrin. "Florida's Failed Pandemic Response Is Gutting the Black Community." *Sun Sentinel*, August 25, 2020. https://www.sun-sentinel.com/opinion/commentary/fl-op-com-florida-pandemic-response-black-community-20200825-4g5zfw4hnvamhpjjelwl6jz2vy-story.html.

Jones-Rogers, Stephanie E. *They Were Her Property: White Women as Slave Owners in the American South*. New Haven, CT: Yale University Press, 2019.

"JPS Reduces Service to Communities with High Levels of Theft, Says It Has Tried Everything." *Jamaica Gleaner*, May 12, 2014. jamaica-gleaner.com/power/52828.

Jurecic, Ann, and Arnold Rampersad. "Teaching *Tar Baby*." In *Approaches to Teaching the Novels of Toni Morrison*, edited by Nellie Y. McKay and Kathryn Earle, 147–53. New York: Modern Language Association, 1997.

Kaplan, Amy. "'Left Alone with America': The Absence of Empire in the Study of American Culture." In *Cultures of United States Imperialism*, edited by Amy Kaplan and Donald E. Pease, 3–21. Durham, NC: Duke University Press, 1993.

———. "Romancing the Empire: The Embodiment of American Masculinity in the Popular Historical Novel of the 1890s." *American Literary History* 2, no. 4 (1990): 659–90.

Katrak, Ketu. "'This Englishness Will Kill You': Colonial[ist] Education and Female Socialization in Merle Hodge's *Crick Crack, Monkey* and Bessie Head's 'Maru.'" *College Literature* 22, no. 1 (1995): 62–77.

Keizer, Arlene R. *Black Subjects: Identity Formation in the Contemporary Narrative of Slavery*. Ithaca, NY: Cornell University Press, 2004.

Kelley, Robin D. G. *Race Rebels: Culture, Politics, and the Black Working Class*. New York: Free Press, 1994.

———. "We Hold the Future." Foreword to *America at War with Itself* by Henry A. Giroux. San Francisco: City Lights Publishers, 2016.

———. *Yo' Mama's Disfunktional!: Fighting the Culture Wars in Urban America*. Boston: Beacon Press, 1997.

Kempadoo, Kamala, ed. *Sun, Sex, and Gold: Tourism and Sex Work in the Caribbean*. Washington, DC: Rowman & Littlefield Publishers, 1999.

Kempadoo, Oonya. Interview by Harald Leusmann. 2001. *World Literature Written in English* 39, no. 1 (2001): 107–15.

———. *Tide Running*. Boston: Beacon Press, 2001.

King, Deborah. "Multiple Jeopardy, Multiple Consciousness: The Context of Black Feminist Ideology." *Signs* 14, no. 1 (1988): 42–72.

King, Wilma. "'Prematurely Knowing of Evil Things': The Sexual Abuse of African American Girls and Young Women in Slavery and Freedom." *Journal of African American History* 99, no. 3 (2014): 173–96. doi:10.5323/jafriamerhist.99.3.0173.

Kraus, Michael W., Jun Won Park, and Jacinth J. X. Tan. "Signs of Social Class: The Experience of Economic Inequality in Everyday Life." *Perspectives on Psychological Science* 12, no. 3 (2017): 422–35.

Krommendijk, Jasper. "The Domestic Effectiveness of International Human Rights Monitoring in Established Democracies. The Case of the UN Human Rights Treaty Bodies." *Review of International Organizations* 10, no. 4 (2015): 489–512.

Kuhn, Thomas. *The Structure of Scientific Revolutions*. Chicago: University of Chicago Press, 1996.

Lacy, Karyn. *Blue-Chip Black: Race, Class, and Status in the New Black Middle Class*. Oakland: University of California Press, 2007.

La Guerre, J. G. "A Review of Race and Class in the Caribbean." In *Race, Class & Gender in the Future of the Caribbean*, edited by J. E. Greene, 15–41. Mona, Kingston, Jamaica: Institute of Social & Economic Research, University of the West Indies, 1993.

Lamming, George. "The Occasion for Speaking." In *The Pleasures of Exile*, 23–50. East Lansing: University of Michigan Press, 1992.

Lang, Clarence. *Black America in the Shadow of the Sixties: Notes on the Civil Rights Movement, Neoliberalism, and Politics*. East Lansing: University of Michigan Press, 2015.

Launius, Christie. "The Three Rs: Reading, (W)riting, and Romance in Class Mobility Narratives by Yezierska, Smedley and Saxton." *College Literature* 34, no. 4 (2007): 125–47.

Lauter, Paul. "Under Construction: Working-Class Writing." In *New Working-Class Studies*, edited by John Russo and Sherry L. Linkon, 63–77. Ithaca, NY: Industrial and Labor Relations Press, 2005.

Lauter, Paul, and Ann Fitzgerald. *Literature, Class and Culture: An Anthology*. New York: Longman, 2000.

Lawson, Andrew. *Class and the Making of American Literature: Created Unequal*. New York: Taylor & Francis Group, 2013.

————. *Downwardly Mobile: The Changing Fortunes of American Realism*. New York: Oxford University Press, 2012.

Leondar-Wright, Betsy. *Class Matters: Cross-Class Alliance Building for Middle-Class Activists*. Gabriola Island, BC, Canada: New Society Publishers, 2005.

Lewis, Gordon K. *Gordon K. Lewis on Race, Class, and Ideology in the Caribbean*. Edited by Anthony P. Maingot. Kingston, Jamaica: Ian Randle, 2010.

Limar, Noni. "10 Reasons Why Art + Culture Is Imperative for Our Movement." In *Celebrating Four Years of Organizing to Protect Black Lives*, prepared by Shanelle Matthews and Miski Noor, 2017. https://blacklivesmatter.com/arts-culture/. Accessed February 2, 2020.

Lombardi, Thomas F. *Wallace Stevens and the Pennsylvania Keystone*. Plainsboro, NJ: Associated University Press, 1996.

Lubrano, Alfred. *Limbo: Blue-Collar Roots, White-Collar Dreams*. Hoboken, NJ: Wiley, 2005.

Lynch, Michael. "The Wall and the Mirror in the Promised Land: The City in the Novels of Gloria Naylor." In *The City in African American Literature*, edited by Yoshinobu Hakutani and Robert Butler, 181–95. Teaneck, NJ: Fairleigh Dickinson University Press, 1995.

"Lynching in America: Confronting the Legacy of Racial Terror." Equal Justice Initiative. https://eji.org/reports/lynching-in-america. Accessed February 3, 2019.

Maes-Jelinek, Hena, and Bénédicte Ledent. "The Caribbean Novel from 1970 to 1995." In *A History of Literature in the Caribbean, Volume Two: English- and Dutch-Speaking Regions*, edited by A. James Arnold, 149–98. Amsterdam: John Benjamins Publishing, 2001.

Magness, Patricia. "The Knight and the Princess: The Structure of Courtly Love in Toni Morrison's *Tar Baby*." *South Atlantic Review* 54, no. 4 (1989): 85–100.

Mahabir, Joy A. I. *Miraculous Weapons: Revolutionary Ideology in Caribbean Culture*. New York: Peter Lang International Academic Publishers, 2003.

Markus, Hazel, and Nicole M. Stephens. "Editorial Overview: Inequality and Social Class: The Psychological and Behavioral Consequences of Inequality and Social Class: A Theoretical Integration." *Current Opinion in Psychology* 18 (2017): iv–xii.

Marsh, John. *Hog Butchers, Beggars, and Busboys: Poverty, Labor, and the Making of Modern American Poetry*. East Lansing: University of Michigan Press, 2011.

Marshall, Paule. *The Fisher King*. New York: Scribner, 2001.

Martin, Emmie. "70% of Americans Consider Themselves Middle Class—but Only 50% Are." Editorial, CNBC, June 30, 2017. https://www.cnbc.com/2017/06/30/70 -percent-of-americans-consider-themselves-middle-class-but-only-50-percent -are.html.

Mayberry, Susan Neal. "Laying Down the Law of the Father: Men in *Love*." *Can't I Love What I Criticize? The Masculine and Morrison*, 261–92. Athens: University of Georgia Press, 2007.

Mbalia, Doreatha D. *Toni Morrison's Developing Class Consciousness*. Cranbury, NJ: Associated University Press, 1991.

Mbembe, Achille. *Necropolitics*. Durham, NC: Duke University Press, 2019.

McBride, Dwight A. *Why I Hate Abercrombie & Fitch: Essays on Race and Sexuality*. New York: New York University Press, 2005.

McCaulay, Diana. *Dog-Heart*. Leeds, UK: Peepal Tree Press, 2010.

———. "Uptown and Downtown: A Conversation on Class Stratification with Diana McCaulay." Interview by Robin Brooks. *Jamaica Journal* 35, nos. 1–2 (2014): 94–99.

McClennen, Sophia A., and Alexandra Schultheis Moore. "Mapping the Landscape of Literary Approaches to Human Rights Research." In *The Routledge Companion to Literature and Human Rights*, edited McClennen and Moore, 1–26. New York: Routledge, 2016.

McCormick, Stacie. *Staging Black Fugitivity*. Columbus: Ohio State University Press, 2019.

McDaniels-Wilson, Cathy, and Joanne Belknap. "The Extensive Sexual Violation and Sexual Abuse Histories of Incarcerated Women." *Violence against Women* 14, no. 10 (2008): 1090–127.

McDowell, Deborah E. *"The Changing Same": Black Women's Literature, Criticism, and Theory*. Indianapolis: Indiana University Press, 1995.

McGuire, Danielle L. *At the Dark End of the Street: Black Women, Rape, and Resistance—A New History of the Civil Rights Movement from Rosa Parks to the Rise of Black Power*. New York: Vintage, 2011.

McKittrick, Katherine. *Demonic Grounds: Black Women and the Cartographies of Struggle*. Minneapolis: University of Minnesota Press, 2006.

McMillan Cottom, Tressie. *Lower Ed: The Troubling Rise of For-Profit Colleges in the New Economy*. New York: New Press, 2017.

Melamed, Jodi. *Represent and Destroy: Rationalizing Violence in the New Racial Capitalism*: Minneapolis: University of Minnesota Press, 2011.

Melancon, Trimiko. *Unbought and Unbossed: Transgressive Black Women, Sexuality, and Representation*. Philadelphia: Temple University Press, 2014.

Merish, Lori. *Archives of Labor: Working-Class Women and Literary Culture in the Antebellum United States*. Durham, NC: Duke University Press, 2017.

Mitchell, Angelyn. *Within the Circle: An Anthology of African American Literary Criticism from the Harlem Renaissance to the Present*. Durham, NC: Duke University Press, 1994.

Mitchell, Koritha. *Living with Lynching: African American Lynching Plays, Performance, & Citizenship, 1890–1930*. Champaign: University of Illinois Press, 2011.

Mobley, Marilyn. "Telling Stories: A Cultural Studies Approach to *Tar Baby*." In *Approaches to Teaching the Novels of Toni Morrison*, edited by Nellie Y. McKay and Kathryn Earle, 141–46. New York: Modern Language Association, 1997.

Mohammed, Patricia. *Gendered Realities: Essays in Caribbean Feminist Thought*. Mona, Jamaica: University of the West Indies Press, 2012.

———. "Towards Indigenous Feminist Theorizing in the Caribbean." *Feminist Review* 59, no. 1 (1998): 6–33.

Montgomery, Maxine. *The Fiction of Gloria Naylor: Houses and Spaces of Resistance*. Knoxville: University of Tennessee Press, 2010.

Moore, Marlon R. *In the Life and in the Spirit: Homoerotic Spirituality in African American Literature*. Albany: State University of New York Press, 2014.

Morabito, Melissa S., Linda M. Williams, and April Pattavina. "Decision-Making in Sexual Assault Cases: Replication Research on Sexual Violence Case Attrition in the U.S." National Institute of Justice, Office of Justice Programs, U.S. Department of Justice, University of Massachusetts, Lowell, 2019. https://www.ncjrs.gov/pdffiles1/nij/grants/252689.pdf.

Morgan, Paula E. "Meet Me in the Islands: Sun Sand and Transactional Sex in Caribbean Discourse." *Anthurium: A Caribbean Studies Journal* 10, no. 1 (2013): article 5.

Morrison, Toni. "Home" (1997). In *The House That Race Built: Original Essays by Toni Morrison, Angela Y. Davis, Cornel West, and Others on Black Americans and Politics in America Today*, edited by Wahneema Lubiano, 3–12. New York: Vintage, 1998.

———. *Lecture and Speech of Acceptance, upon the Award of the Nobel Prize for Literature, Delivered in Stockholm on the Seventh of December, Nineteen Hundred and Ninety Three*. New York: Alfred A. Knopf, 1995.

———. *Love*. New York: Vintage, 2005.

———. *Playing in the Dark*. Cambridge, MA: Harvard University Press, 1992.

———. *Tar Baby*. New York: Plume/Penguin, 1982.

Mounk, Yascha. *The Age of Responsibility: Luck, Choice, and the Welfare State*. Cambridge, MA: Harvard University Press, 2017.

Mullen, Bill V. "Breaking the Signifying Chain: A New Blueprint for African-American Literary Studies." *Modern Fiction Studies* 47, no. 1 (2001): 145–63.

Mullen, Bill, and James Smethurst, eds. *Left of the Color Line: Race, Radicalism, and Twentieth-Century Literature of the United States*. Chapel Hill: University of North Carolina Press, 2003.

Mullings, Leith. *On Our Own Terms: Race, Class and Gender in the Lives of African American Women*. New York: Routledge, 1997.

Munroe, Michelle A., and Damion K. Blake. "Governance and Disorder: Neoliberalism and Violent Change in Jamaica." *Third World Quarterly* 38, no. 3 (2017): 580–603. doi:10.1080/01436597.2016.1188660.

Murray, Rolland. "The Time of Breach: Class Division and the Contemporary African American Novel." *Novel* 43, no. 1 (2010): 11–17.

Naylor, Gloria. *Linden Hills*. New York: Penguin, 1986.

Neptune, Harvey R. *Caliban and the Yankees: Trinidad and the United States Occupation*. Chapel Hill: University of North Carolina Press, 2007.

Nixon, Angelique V. *Resisting Paradise: Tourism, Diaspora, and Sexuality in Caribbean Culture*. Jackson: University Press of Mississippi, 2017.

Nurse, Donna Bailey. "The Jamaican Dilemma: Slavery's Legacy Plays Out in a Story of Absent Mothers and Distant Fathers." Review of *Dancing Lessons* by Olive Senior. *Literary Review of Canada* 20, no. 3 (April 2012). https://reviewcanada.ca/magazine/2012/04/the-jamaican-dilemma/.

O'Callaghan, Evelyn. "Imagined Nations, 50 Years Later." *Anthurium: A Caribbean Studies Journal* 10, no. 2 (2013): 1–5. scholarlyrepository.miami.edu/cgi/viewcontent. cgi?article=1262&context=anthurium.

———. "Women Writing Male Marginalization? Oonya Kempadoo's *Tide Running*." *La torre/Tercera época* 11, nos. 41–42 (2006): 329–44.

Ongiri, Amy. *Spectacular Blackness: The Cultural Politics of the Black Power Movement and the Search for a Black Aesthetic*. Charlottesville: University of Virginia Press, 2010.

Orr, Lisa. *Transforming American Realism: Working-Class Women Writers of the Twentieth Century*. Lanham, MD: University Press of America, 2007.

Ortner, Sherry. "Bourdieu and 'History.'" Review of *Bourdieu and Historical Analysis*, edited by Philip S. Gorski. *Anthropology of this Century* 8 (October 2013). http://aotcpress.com/articles/bourdieu-history/.

Parker, Robert D. *How to Interpret Literature: Critical Theory for Literary and Cultural Studies*. New York: Oxford University Press, 2011.

Parton, Nigel. *The Politics of Child Protection: Contemporary Developments and Future Directions*. New York: Palgrave Macmillan, 2014.

Patterson, Robert J. "Introduction: Dreams Reimagined: Political Possibilities and the Black Cultural Imagination." In *Black Cultural Production after Civil Rights*, edited by Robert J. Patterson, 1–28. Champaign: University of Illinois Press, 2019.

Pattillo, Mary. "Black Middle-Class Neighborhoods." *Annual Review of Sociology* 31 (2005): 305–29.

———. *Black on the Block: The Politics of Race and Class in the City*. Chicago: University of Chicago Press, 2007.

———. *Black Picket Fences: Privilege and Peril among the Black Middle Class*, 2nd ed. Chicago: University of Chicago Press, 1999.

———. "Investing in Poor Black Neighborhoods 'As Is.'" In *Public Housing and the Legacy of Segregation*, edited by Margery Austin Turner, Susan J. Popkin, and Lynette A. Rawlings, 31–46. Washington, DC: Urban Institute Press, 2009.

Paul, Mark, William Darity Jr., and Darrick Hamilton. "The Federal Job Guarantee — A Policy to Achieve Permanent Full Employment." Center on Budget and Policy Priorities, March 9, 2018. https://www.cborg/research/full-employment/the-federal-job-guarantee-a-policy-to-achievepermanent-full-employment.

Pearce, Diana. "The Feminization of Ghetto Poverty." *Society* 21, no. 1 (1983): 70–74.

———. "The Feminization of Poverty: Women, Work, and Welfare." *Urban & Social Change Review* 11, nos. 1–2 (1978): 28–36.

Pearlman, Mickey, and Katherine Usher Henderson. "Gloria Naylor." In *Conversations with Gloria Naylor*, edited by Maxine Montgomery, 71–75. Jackson: University of Mississippi Press, 2004.

Pereira, Malin. "Periodizing Toni Morrison's Work from *The Bluest Eye* to *Jazz*: The Importance of *Tar Baby*." *MELUS* 22, no. 3 (1997): 71–82.

Perera, Sonali. *No Country: Working-Class Writing in the Age of Globalization*. New York: Columbia University Press, 2014.

Petgrave, Khitanya. "Equality in Education? A Study of Jamaican Schools under Michael Manley, 1972–80." *Caribbean Quarterly* 57, no. 2 (2011): 24–50.

Petras, James F. *US Imperialism: The Changing Dynamics of Global Power*. New York: Routledge, 2020.

Philp, Geoffrey. "Review of McCaulay's *Dog-Heart*." Blog. May 2010. https://geoffreyphilp.blogspot.com/2010/05/book-review-dog-heart-by-diana-mccaulay.html.

Pirtle, Whitney. "Racial Capitalism: A Fundamental Cause of Novel Coronavirus (COVID-19) Pandemic Inequities in the United States." *Health Education & Behavior* 47, no. 4 (2020): 504–8. doi:10.1177/1090198120922942.

"PM Rowley Extends Congratulations to Biden, Harris." *Loop News—Trinidad and Tobago*, November 7, 2020. https://www.looptt.com/content/pm-rowley-extends -congratulations-biden-harris.

Posner, Eric. *The Twilight of Human Rights Law*. New York: Oxford University Press, 2014.

Prince, Sabiyha. *African Americans and Gentrification in Washington, D.C.: Race, Class and Social Justice in the Nation's Capital*. New York: Routledge, 2014.

Rahim, Jennifer. "Electronic Fictions and Tourist Currents: Constructing the Island-Body in Kempadoo's *Tide Running*." *Anthurium: A Caribbean Studies Journal* 2, no. 2 (2004): article 4.

Rape, Abuse & Incest National Network (RAINN). "Adult Survivors of Child Sexual Abuse." https://www.rainn.org/articles/adult-survivors-child-sexual-abuse. Accessed March 20, 2019.

———. "The Criminal Justice System: Statistics." https://www.rainn.org/statistics /criminal-justice-system. Accessed March 20, 2019.

Reddock, Rhoda. *Women and Family in the Caribbean: Historical and Contemporary Considerations*. Guyana: CARICOM Secretariat, 1999.

———. *Women, Labour and Politics in Trinidad and Tobago: A History*. London: Zed Books, 1994.

Reynolds, Rhon. *Not Safe at Home: Violence and Discrimination against LGBT People in Jamaica*. Human Rights Watch, October 21, 2014. https://www.hrw.org/report /2014/10/21/not-safe-home/violence-and-discrimination-against-lgbt-people -jamaica.

Roberts, Dorothy. *Killing the Black Body: Race, Reproduction, and the Meaning of Liberty*. New York: Pantheon, 1997.

Robinson, Cedric. *Black Marxism: The Making of the Black Radical Tradition*. Chapel Hill: University of North Carolina Press, 2000.

Robinson, Michelle M. *Dreams for Dead Bodies: Blackness, Labor, and the Corpus of American Detective Fiction*. East Lansing: University of Michigan Press, 2016.

Robinson, Tracy. "Legalising Norms Related to Sexual, Gender and Bodily Diversity in the Inter-American Human Rights System." Latin American Seminar on Constitutional and Political Theory (SELA), Quito, Ecuador, June 8, 2017.

Rodney, Walter. *The Groundings with My Brothers*. London: Bogle-L'Ouverture Publications, 1969.

———. *How Europe Underdeveloped Africa*. Brooklyn: Verso, 2018.

Rody, Caroline. *The Daughter's Return: African-American and Caribbean Women's Fictions of History*. New York: Oxford University Press, 2001.

Rosenberg, Leah. *Nationalism and the Formation of Caribbean Literature*. New York: Palgrave Macmillan, 2007.

Rothstein, Richard. *The Color of Law: A Forgotten History of How Our Government Segregated America*. New York: Liveright, 2017.

Roynon, Tessa. "Sabotaging the Language of Pride: Toni Morrison's Representations of Rape." In *Feminism, Literature and Rape Narratives: Violence and Violation*, edited by Sorcha Gunne and Zoe Brigley Thompson, 38–53. New York: Routledge, 2010.

Russo, John, and Sherry L. Linkon, eds. "Introduction: What's New about New Working-Class Studies?" In *New Working-Class Studies*, edited by John Russo and Sherry L. Linkon, 1–18. Ithaca, NY: Industrial and Labor Relations Press, 2005.

Saar, Malika Saada, Rebecca Epstein, Lindsay Rosenthal, and Yasmin Vafa. *The Sexual Abuse to Prison Pipeline: The Girls' Story*. Washington, DC: Center for Poverty and Inequality, Georgetown University Law Center, 2015. https://www.law.georgetown.edu/poverty-inequality-center/wp-content/uploads/sites/14/2019/02/The-Sexual-Abuse-To-Prison-Pipeline-The-Girls%E2%80%99-Story.pdf.

Said, Edward. *Culture and Imperialism*. New York: Vintage, 1994.

———. *Orientalism*. New York: Vintage, 1979.

Scafe, Suzanne. "Re-Placing Wealth, Re-Mapping Social Division: Kingston in the Fiction of Brian Meeks and Diana McCaulay." *Zeitschrift für Anglistik und Amerikanistik* 63, no. 2 (2015): 215–27. doi:10.1515/zaa-2015-0019.

Scholte, Jan Aart. *Globalization: A Critical Introduction*. New York: St. Martin's Press, 2000.

Schreiber, Evelyn Jaffe. "Power and Betrayal: Social Hierarchies and the Trauma of Loss in Love." In *Toni Morrison: Paradise, Love, A Mercy*, edited by Lucille P. Fultz, 92–106. New York: Bloomsbury, 2013.

Senior, Olive. *Dancing Lessons*. Toronto: Cormorant Books, 2011.

———. *Gardening in the Tropics*. Toronto: McClelland & Stewart, 1994.

———. "Lessons from the Fruit Stand: Or, Writing for the Listener." *Journal of Modern Literature* 20, no. 1 (1996): 39–44.

———. "New Dance Steps to a Jamaican Beat: A Conversation with Olive Senior." In "Caribbean Women: Riding the Waves of Resistance." Special issue, *ProudFlesh: New Afrikan Journal of Culture, Politics & Consciousness* 8 (2013): 61–68.

———. "Poem as Gardening, the Story as Su-Su: Finding a Literary Voice." *Journal of West Indian Literature* 14, no. 1–2 (2005): 35–50.

———. *Working Miracles: Women's Lives in the English-speaking Caribbean*. Indianapolis: Indiana University Press, 1992.

Serisier, Tanya. "Sex Crimes and the Media." In *Oxford Research Encyclopedia of Criminology and Criminal Justice*, 2017. doi:10.1093/acrefore/9780190264079.013.118.

Sharot, Stephen. *Love and Marriage across Social Classes in American Cinema*. New York: Palgrave Macmillan, 2016.

———. "Wealth and/or Love: Class and Gender in the Cross-Class Romance Films of the Great Depression." *Journal of American Studies* 47, no. 1 (2013): 89–108.

Shary, Timothy. "Buying Me Love: 1980s Class-Clash Teen Romances—2011." *Journal of Popular Culture* 44, no. 3 (2011): 563–82.

Shepherd, Verene, ed. *Engendering Caribbean History, Cross-Cultural Perspectives*. Kingston, Jamaica: Ian Randle Publishers, 2011.

Sidanius, Jim, and Felicia Pratto. *Social Dominance: An Intergroup Theory of Social Hierarchy and Oppression*. New York: Cambridge University Press, 1999.

Sistren, with Honor Ford-Smith. *Lionheart Gal: Life Stories of Jamaican Women*. Mona, Jamaica: University of the West Indies Press, 2005.

Smallwood, Stephanie. "What Slavery Tells Us about Marx." *Boston Review: A Political and Literary Forum*, February 2018. http://bostonreview.net/forum/remake-world -slavery-racial-capitalism-and-justice/stephanie-smallwood-what-slavery-tells -us#:~:text=Elsewhere%20in%20his%20discussion%20of,understood%20as%20 having%20only%20recently.

Smethurst, James E. *Black Arts Movement: Literary Nationalism in the 1960s and 1970s*. Chapel Hill: University of North Carolina Press, 2005.

Smiles, Robin V. "Popular Black Women's Fiction and the Novels of Terry McMillan." In *A Companion to African American Literature*, edited by Gene Andrew Jarrett, 347–59. Hoboken, NJ: Wiley-Blackwell, 2010.

Smith, Sharon G., Xinjian Zhang, Kathleen C. Basile, Melissa T. Merrick, Jing Wang, Marcie-jo Kresnow, and Jieru Chen. *The National Intimate Partner and Sexual Violence Survey (NISVS): 2015 Data Brief—Updated Release*. National Center for Injury Prevention and Control, Centers for Disease Control and Prevention, 2018. https://www.cdc.gov/violenceprevention/pdf/2015data-brief508.pdf. Accessed March 3, 2019.

Smith, Valerie. *Not Just Race, Not Just Gender: Black Feminist Readings*. New York: Routledge, 1998.

———. *Toni Morrison: Writing the Moral Imagination*. Hoboken, NJ: Wiley-Blackwell, 2012.

Spillers, Hortense. "Mama's Baby, Papa's Maybe: An American Grammar Book." In *Black, White, and in Color: Essays on American Literature and Culture*, 203–29. Chicago: University of Chicago Press, 2003.

Stiglitz, Joseph E. *The Price of Inequality: How Today's Divided Society Endangers Our Future*. New York: W. W. Norton, 2012.

Strachan, Ian G., dir. *I's Man: Manhood in the Bahamas*. Nassau, Bahamas: Marble Head Films, 2013.

Strong, Narender. "Interview with Darrick Hamilton." *Public Seminar*, April 20, 2017. https://publicseminar.org/2017/04/interview-with-darrick-hamilton/.

Summers, Brandi Thompson. *Black in Place: The Spatial Aesthetics of Race in a Post-Chocolate City*. Chapel Hill: University of North Carolina Press, 2019.

Tanna, Laura. "*Dancing Lessons* with Olive Senior." Review of *Dancing Lessons* by Olive Senior. *Jamaica Gleaner*, December 18, 2011. http://jamaica-gleaner.com/ gleaner/20111218/ arts/ arts3.html.

Taylor, Keeanga-Yamahtta. *Race for Profit: How Banks and the Real Estate Industry Undermined Black Homeownership*. Chapel Hill: University of North Carolina Press, 2019.

Thomas, Deborah. *Modern Blackness: Nationalism, Globalization, and the Politics of Culture in Jamaica*. Durham, NC: Duke University Press, 2004.

Thomas, Ena V. "*Crick Crack, Monkey*: A Picaresque Perspective." In *Caribbean Women Writers: Essays from the First International Conference*, edited by Selwyn R. Cudjoe, 209–14. Wellesley, MA: Calaloux, 1990.

Thomas-Brown, Karen. "Coping with Neoliberalism in Jamaican Towns and Cities: How Poor Jamaicans Use Informal Employments as a Means of Survival." *Caribbean Geography* 18 (August 2013): 6–20.

Thompson, Canute S. *Reflections on Leadership and Governance in Jamaica: Towards a Better Society.* Kingston, Jamaica: Arawak Publications, 2018.

Thompson, Lisa B. *Beyond the Black Lady: Sexuality and the New African American Middle Class.* Champaign: University of Illinois Press, 2012.

Thorin, Maria. *The Gender Dimension of Globalization: A Survey of the Literature with a Focus on Latin America and the Caribbean.* Santiago, Chile: United Nations Publications, 2001.

Thorpe, Marjorie. "The Problem of Cultural Identification in *Crick Crack, Monkey.*" *Savacou* 13 (1977): 31–38.

Tokarczyk, Michelle. *Class Definitions: On the Lives and Writings of Maxine Hong Kingston, Sandra Cisneros, and Dorothy Allison.* Selinsgrove, PA: Susquehanna University Press, 2008.

———. *Critical Approaches to American Working-Class Literature.* New York: Routledge, 2011.

Turner, Dawn. *Only Twice I've Wished for Heaven.* New York: Doubleday, 1996.

Ulysse, Gina. *Downtown Ladies: Informal Commercial Importers, a Haitian Anthropologist and Self-Making in Jamaica.* Chicago: University of Chicago Press, 2007.

United Nations Committee on Economic, Social and Cultural Rights (UNCESCR). "Concluding Observations on the Combined Third and Fourth Periodic Reports of Jamaica, Adopted by the Committee at Its 50th Session, 29 April–17 May 2013." E/C.12/JAM/CO/3-4, June 10, 2013. https://www.refworld.org/docid/52d54a854.html.

———. "The Right to Adequate Food (Art. 11): 5/12/1999. CESCR General Comment 12. General Comments." The Office of the United Nations High Commissioner for Human Rights, 1999. tbinternet.ohchr.org/_layouts/treatybodyexternal/TBSearch. aspx?Lang=en&TreatyID=9&DocTypeID=11.

———. "The Right to Adequate Housing (Art.11 (1)): 12/13/1991. CESCR General Comment 4. General Comments." The Office of the United Nations High Commissioner for Human Rights, 1991. tbinternet.ohchr.org/_layouts/treatybodyexternal/Download.aspx?symbolno=INT/CESCR/ GEC/4759&Lang=en.

———. "The Right to Adequate Water (Arts. 11 and 12): 1/20/2003. CESCR General Comment 15. General Comments." The Office of the United Nations High Commissioner for Human Rights, 2003. www2.ohchr.org/english/issues/water/docs/CESCR_GC_15.pdf.

United Nations General Assembly. "International Covenant on Civil and Political Rights." Adopted by the General Assembly of the United Nations on 16 December 1966. *United Nations Treaty Series* 999, no. 14668 (1976): 171–348.

———. "International Covenant on Economic, Social and Cultural Rights. Adopted by the General Assembly of the United Nations on 16 December 1966." Articles 7(a), 6.1, *United Nations Treaty Series* 993, no. 14531 (1976): 6–8.

———. "International Covenant on Economic, Social and Cultural Rights. Adopted by the General Assembly of the United Nations on 16 December 1966." Article 13, *United Nations Treaty Series* 993, no. 14531 (1976): 8.

U.S. Census Bureau. QuickFacts. Miami-Dade County, Florida. https://www.census .gov/quickfacts/fact/table/miamidadecountyflorida/POP060210. Accessed September 13, 2020.

U.S. Constitution. Amendment XIV, Section 1. July 9, 1868.

U.S. Department of Health & Human Services, Administration for Children and Families, Administration on Children, Youth and Families, Children's Bureau. "Child Maltreatment 2017." 2019. https://www.acf.hhs.gov/cb/research-data -technology/statistics-research/child-maltreatment.

U.S. Department of Health & Human Services, Office on Women's Health. "Sexual Assault." www.womenshealth.gov/relationships-and-safety/sexual-assault-and -rape/sexual-assault. Accessed February 3, 2019.

U.S. Department of Justice. "Raising Awareness about Sexual Abuse: Facts and Statistics." Dru Sjodin National Sex Offender Public Website. www.nsopw.gov /en US/Education/FactsStatistics?AspxAutoDetectCookieSupport=1. Accessed February 3, 2019.

Vasciannie, Stephen. "The Inter-American Commission on Human Rights: Reform and the Question of University." *International Law Students Association (ILSA) Journal of International & Comparative Law* 21, no. 2 (2014): 409–23.

Venkatesan, Sathyaraj, and Gurumurthy Neelakantan. "Family and Parenting in Toni Morrison's Love." *Notes on Contemporary Literature* 36, no. 4 (2006): 9–10.

Viglucci, Andres, C. Isaiah Smalls II, Rob Wile, and Yadira Lopez. "'A History of Broken Promises': Miami Remains Separate and Unequal for Black Residents." *Miami Herald*, August 20, 2020. https://www.miamiherald.com/news/local /community/miami-dade/article244524772.html.

Waligora-Davis, Nicole A. *Sanctuary: African Americans and Empire*. New York: Oxford University Press, 2011.

Walmsley, Anne. *The Caribbean Artists Movement, 1966–1972: A Literary and Cultural History*. London: New Beacon Books, 1992.

Ward, Earlise, Jacqueline C. Wiltshire, Michelle A. Detry, and Roger L. Brown. "African American Men and Women's Attitude toward Mental Illness, Perceptions of Stigma, and Preferred Coping Behaviors." *Nursing Research* 62, no. 3 (2013): 185–94.

Washington, Mary Helen. "Alice Childress, Lorraine Hansberry, and Claudia Jones: Black Women Write the Popular Front." In *Left of the Color Line: Race, Radicalism, and Twentieth-Century Literature of the United States*, edited by Bill V. Mullen and James Smethurst, 183–204. Chapel Hill: University of North Carolina Press, 2003.

Watson, Pat. Review of *Dancing Lessons* by Olive Senior. *Quill & Quire*, 2011. https://quillandquire.com/review/dancing-lessons/.

West, Cornel. *Race Matters*. Boston: Beacon Press, 2001.

White, Deborah Gray. *Too Heavy a Load: Black Women in Defense of Themselves, 1894–1994*. New York: W. W. Norton, 1999.

Williams, Andreá N. *Dividing Lines: Class Anxiety and Postbellum Black Fiction*. East Lansing: University of Michigan Press, 2013.

Williams, Bianca C. *The Pursuit of Happiness: Black Women, Diasporic Dreams, and the Politics of Emotional Transnationalism*. Durham, NC: Duke University Press, 2018.

Williams, Raymond. *The Country and the City*. New York: Oxford University Press, 1975.

Williamson, Terrion L. *Scandalize My Name: Black Feminist Practice and the Making of Black Social Life*. New York: Fordham University Press, 2017.

Wilson, William Julius. *More Than Just Race: Being Black and Poor in the Inner City*. New York: W. W. Norton, 2009.

Wolff, Edward N. *A Century of Wealth in America*. Cambridge, MA: Belknap Press of Harvard University Press, 2017.

Woods, Clyde, and Katherine McKittrick, eds. *Black Geographies and the Politics of Place*. Boston: South End Press, 2007.

Wright, Erik O. *Class Counts: Comparative Studies in Class Analysis*. New York: Cambridge University Press, 1997.

Wright, Michelle M. *Physics of Blackness: Beyond the Middle Passage Epistemology*. Minneapolis: University of Minnesota Press, 2015.

Wright, Nazera. *Black Girlhood in the Nineteenth Century*. Champaign: University of Illinois Press, 2016.

Young, Harvey. *Embodying Black Experience: Stillness, Critical Memory, and the Black Body*. East Lansing: University of Michigan Press, 2010.

Zandy, Janet. *Calling Home: An Anthology of Working-Class Women's Writing*. New Brunswick, NJ: Rutgers University Press, 1990.

———. *Hands: Physical Labor, Class, and Cultural Work*. New Brunswick, NJ: Rutgers University Press, 2004.

Zodana, Joyce. "'Tee,' 'Cyn-Cyn,' 'Cynthia,' 'Dou-Dou': Remembering and Forgetting the 'True-True Name' in Merle Hodge's *Crick Crack, Monkey*." In *Middle Passages and the Healing Place of History: Migration and Identity in Black Women's Literature*, edited by Elizabeth Brown-Guillory, 139–54. Columbus: Ohio State University Press, 2006.

Zong, Jie, and Jeanne Batalova. "Caribbean Immigrants in the United States." Migration Policy Institute, 2019. https://www.migrationpolicy.org/article /caribbean-immigrants-united-states-2017#:~:text=As%20of%202013%2D17%2C %20the,in%20these%20two%20metro%20areas.

Zweig, Michael. *What's Class Got to Do with It? American Society in the Twenty-First Century*. Ithaca, NY: Cornell University Press, 2004.

———. *The Working Class Majority: America's Best Kept Secret*, 2nd ed. Ithaca, NY: Cornell University Press, 2011.

Index

Page numbers in *italics* refer to illustrations.

independence for, 24; international debt burden of, 124; underground economy in, 124, *125*

James, C. L. R., 6

James, Marlon, 111

Jardine, Monica, 135

Jarrett, Gene A., 15

Jaruga, Dubravka, 176–77n16, 190n17

Jazz (Morrison), 38

Jenkins, Candice M., 8, 158n22

Jenkins, Earnestine, 173n23

Jennings-Craig, Zellynne, 102, 178–79n38, 178–79n40, 186–87n78

"The Johnson Girls" (Bambara), 161–62n68

Jones, Claudia, 135, 163–64n83

Jones, Gayl, 67

Jordan, June, 8

Jubilee (Walker), 158–59n28

Jumping the Broom (film), 132, *133*

Jurecic, Ann, 188–89n5, 189n10, 191n30

Kaplan, Amy, 189n6

Keizer, Arlene, 18, 162n70

Kelley, Robin D. G., 6, 7, 15, 56

Kempadoo, Oonya, 2; *Tide Running* (Kempadoo), 21, 25, 29, 111, 133–40, 144, 145; cross-class romance in works of, 29

Kenan, Randall, 161–62n68

Killing Rage (hooks), 156–57n18

Kincaid, Jamaica, 17, 86, 161–62n68

King, Deborah, 13–14

Krommendijk, Jasper, 182n19

Kuhn, Thomas, 7

labor: under neoliberalism, 7, 12, 25; organized, 14–15; racial discrimination and, 25; sexual, 137; under slavery, 5, 19, 146

Lacy, Karyn, 10, 156–57n18

Lamming, George, 27, 86, 156–57n18

Lang, Clarence, 9

language: Hodge's use of, 102; Kempadoo's use of, 138; McCaulay's use of, 115; Morrison's views and use of, 8, 65–66; Senior's views and use of, 84, 91, 98

LaRose, John, 8, 156–57n18

Larsen, Nella, 23

Lauter, Paul, 11, 13, 155n8, 162n74

Ledent, Bénédicte, 156n17, 158–59n28

Lee, Andrea, 161–62n68

Leondar-Wright, Betsy, 44–45

"The Lesson" (Bambara), 161–62n68

Lesson before Dying, A (Gaines), 161–62n68

Lewis, Theodore, 101

Like One of the Family (Childress), 158–59n28

Linden Hills (Naylor), 25, 33–60, 73, 110, 114, 120–21; cross-class relationship trope in, 33–36, 44, 47, 56–58, 60, 88; greed and inequality in, 53–54; housing discrimination in, 37–39; physical barriers in, 45–46, 47, 60; poverty and precarity in, 39–43; power and capital in, 48–49; stereotypes and myths deflated in, 44, 47–48, 50–53, 55–57, 60

Linkon, Sherry Lee, 85, 159n30, 160n39, 160n41, 161n53

Living Is Easy, The (West), 10

Lombardi, Thomas F., 53

Lopez, Jennifer, 132

Love (Morrison), 62–79; amorality in, 72–73; cross-class relationship trope in, 62, 63–64, 67–70, 72, 74, 78–79; language of, 65–66; marriage in, 69–71, 73; patriarchy in, 64; Romeo and Juliet invoked in, 76–77; sexual abuse in, 28, 62, 64–75, 76, 78

Lubrano, Alfred, 27

Lynch, Michael, 171n71

lynching, 67–68

Maes-Jelinek, Hena, 156n17, 158–59n28

Magness, Patricia, 188–89n5, 191–92n32

Mahabir, Joy, 176–77n16, 179n62

Maid in Manhattan (film), 132

respectability, 55, 64, 72, 84, 85, 102

Roberts, Dorothy, 173n21

Roberts, Julia, 132

Robinson, Cedric, 5–6, 156–57n18, 163n83

Rodney, Walter, 6, 156–57n18

Roosevelt, Franklin D., 39

Rosenberg, Leah, 27, 156–57n18, 162n69, 190n13

Rothstein, Richard, 56, 165n1

Rowley, Keith, 146

Roynon, Tessa, 171–72n5

Rucker, Walter, 6,

Russo, John, 159n30, 160n39, 160n41, 161n53

Said, Edward, 36, 189n6

Salkey, Andrew, 8

Sanchez, Sonia, 8

Sapphire, 17, 38, 61

Sarah Phillips (Lee), 161–62n68

Scholte, Jan Aart, 124, 181n12, 185n66, 188n5

Schreiber, Evelyn Jaffe, 171–72n5

Senior, Olive, 2, 28–29; as activist, 84–85; colorism viewed by, 104; language and, 84, 98; writing's power viewed by, 106

—*Dancing Lessons*: 20, 25, 83–99, 105, 106–7, 111; complicity and resistance in, 87, 90, 97, 99; education and mobility linked in, 86, 87, 91, 100

Serisier, Tanya, 64, 71, 172n7, 174n41, 174n45

sexual abuse, sexual violence, 16; of Black females, 68, 73, 75; of children, 58, 71; by family members and acquaintances, 69; "grooming" victims of, 70–71; male victims of, 61, 67; in Morrison's *Love*, 28, 62, 64–74, 76, 78; pipeline to prison from, 75; resistance to, 17, 79; under slavery, 17, 20, 64–67, 75

sex trafficking, sex tourism, 17, 61, 137

Shange, Ntozake, 17

Sharot, Stephen, 187nn1–2

Shields, Tanya L., 14

Sidanius, Jim, 168n31

Sister Souljah, 61

slavery, 18, 115, 130; abolition of, 38; biblical justifications for, 75; Black poverty stereotypes linked to, 11–12; economics of, 61; legacy of, 96, 134, 137; Marx's inattention to, 6; mulattoes under, 156–57n18; racial capitalism linked to, 19; sexual violence linked to, 17, 20, 64–67, 70, 75; as shared experiences, 19–20

Smallwood, Stephanie, 6, 155n10

Smith, Valerie, 188–89n5, 189n10

standardized testing, 16, 83, 85

standard of living, 20, 47, 51, 76, 112, 115–16, 134; of Black middle class, 39; of working class, 50

statutory rape, 17, 61, 73, 77

stereotypes, 10, 25, 67; alliances hampered by, 49–51, 60, 72, 127; in *Dog-Heart*, 127, 128, 129, 130; in *Linden Hills*, 38, 44, 47–48, 50–53, 55–57, 60; in *Only Twice I've Wished for Heaven*, 43–44, 48, 49–51, 54–56, 58–60; slavery and, 11–12

Stevens, Wallace, 53

Stevenson, Bryan, 68

"The Story of a Scar" (McPherson), 161–62n68

Street, The (Petry), 162n69

Structural Adjustment Programs (SAPs), 9, 111, 115, 119

subprime mortgage crisis, 16–17, 33

Sula (Morrison), 46

Tar Baby (Morrison), 24, 25, 29, 88, 133–36, 140–44

Their Eyes Were Watching God (Hurston), 158–59n28

Thomas, Deborah, 112, 182n22

Thompson, Lisa B., 8

Thorburn, Diana, 184n53, 186n76

Thorin, Maria, 158n26, 185n59, 185n66

Tide Running (Kempadoo), 21, 25, 29, 111, 133–40, 144, 145

CPSIA information can be obtained
at www.ICGtesting.com
Printed in the USA
LVHW091619181221
706581LV00008B/406